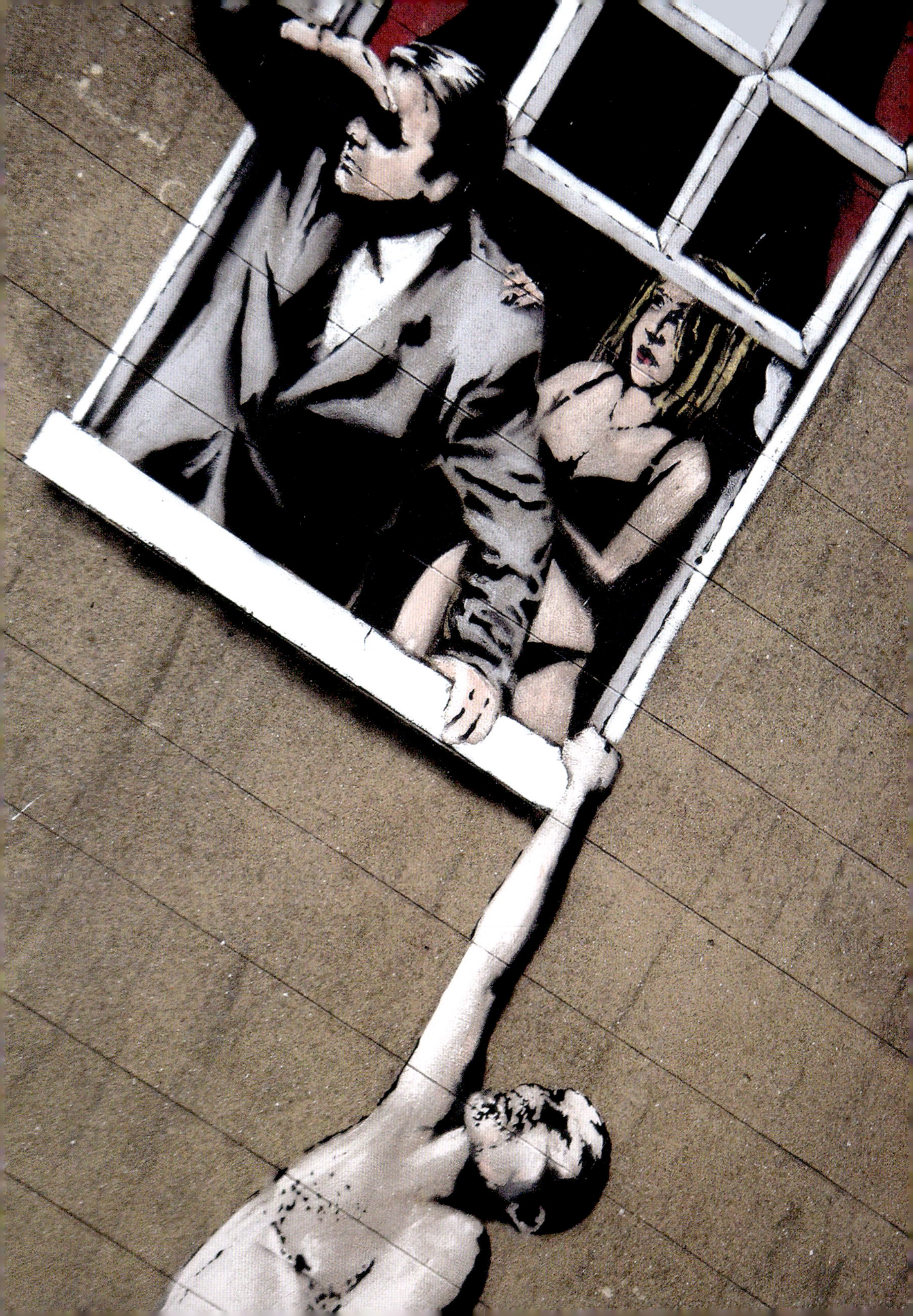

A catalogue record for this book is available from the British Library.

ISBN. 978-1-908211-88-0

First edtion.
First published in Great Britain in 2021 under the imprint of Carpet Bombing Culture
Email: books@carpetbombingculture.com
© Pro-Actif Communications

Words by: Patrick Potter
Compiled and Edited by: Gary Shove

Printed on natural recyclable products (ie paper).

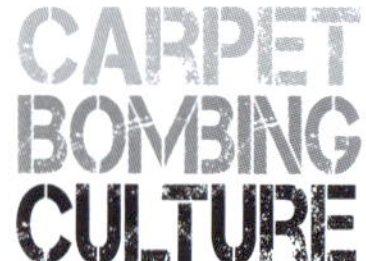

www.carpetbombingculture.com

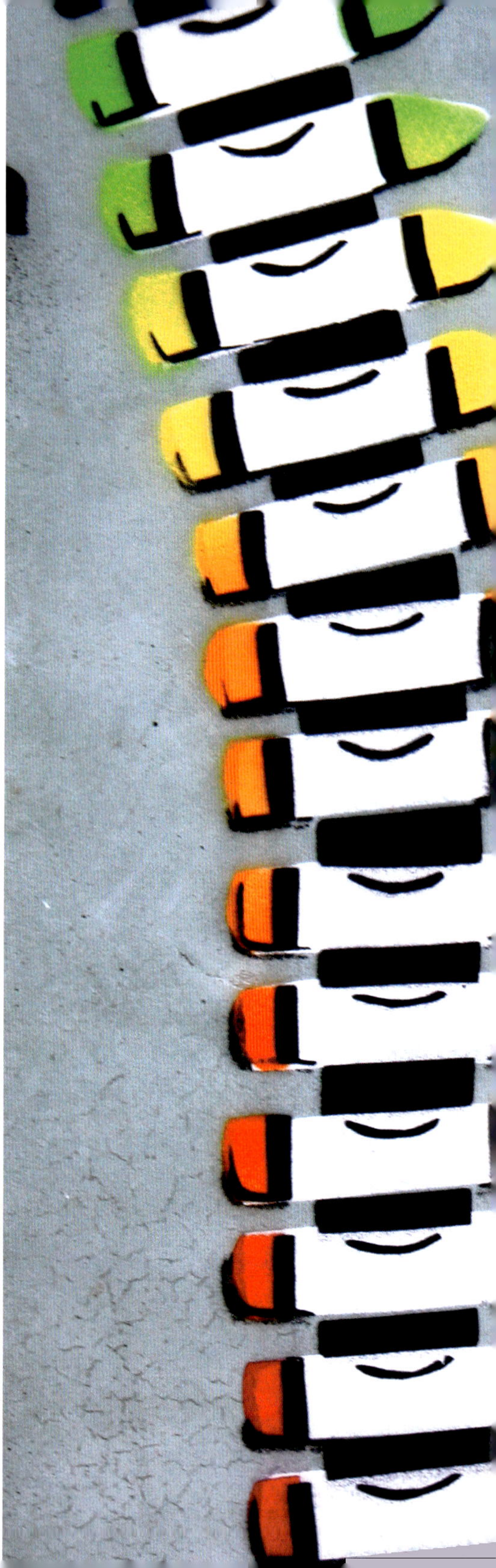

BANKSY ISMS

THE WIT WISDOM AND INSPIRATION OF AN ART OUTLAW

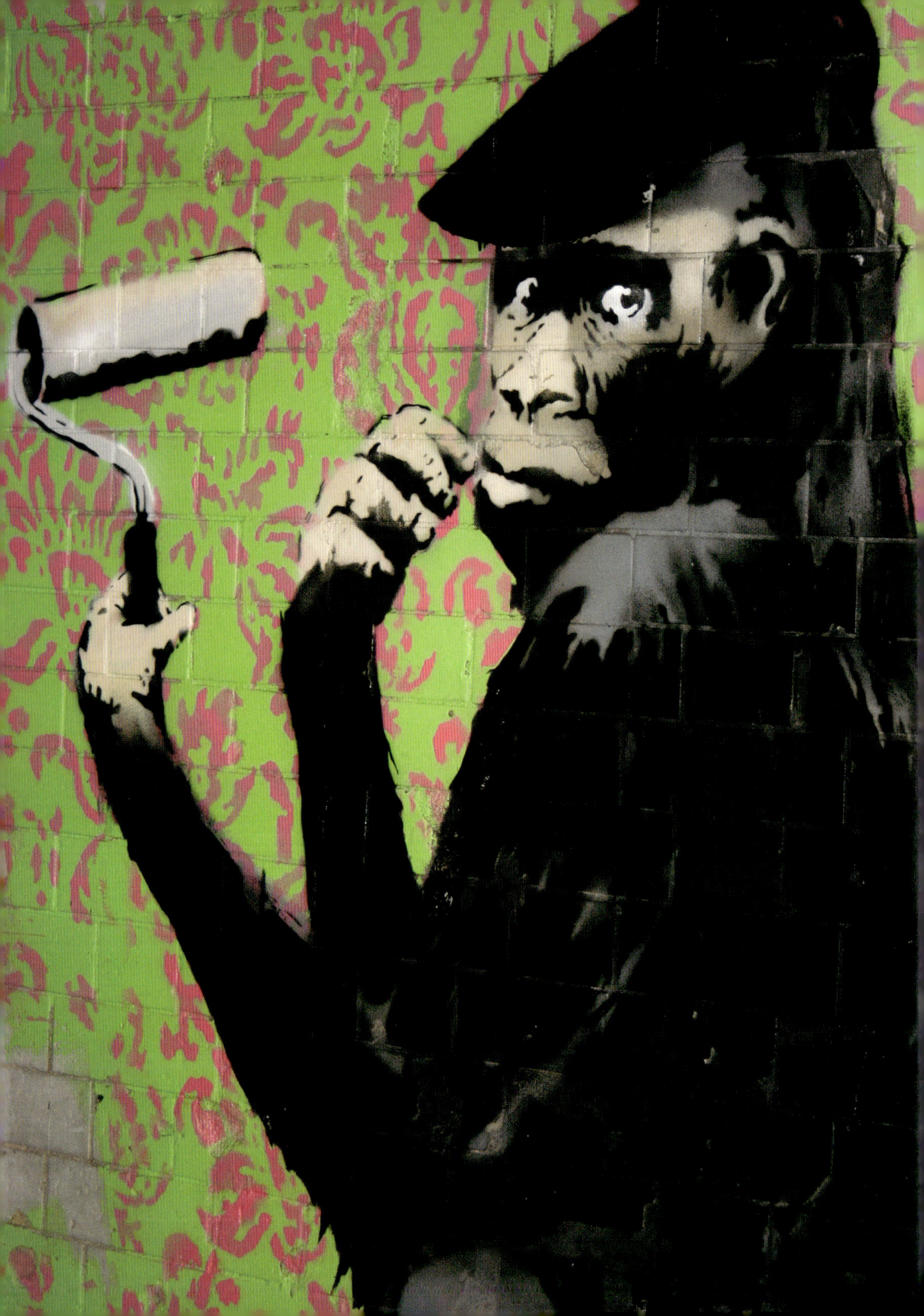

BANKSYISMS

The Wisdom of Banksy

From self-help to help-yourself all the way to just plain old, help! If you've been crying yourself to sleep over your failings as a rat athlete in the rat olympics of late-capitalist life then take comfort, because...

"People who get up early in the morning cause war, death and famine."

- Banksy, Banging Your Head Against a Brick Wall

Sick of the power of positive thinking? Let the power of Banksy into your life instead. The musings of the ornery old street urchin with a spray can from Bristol can transform your miserable quest for an Instagram lifestyle into something more like Edward Norton riding a tricycle round a squat in Fight Club.

(There is no guarantee that this will actually happen.)

Fungus grows on your collected Self-Help books - discover the wisdom of Banksy. You might love it.

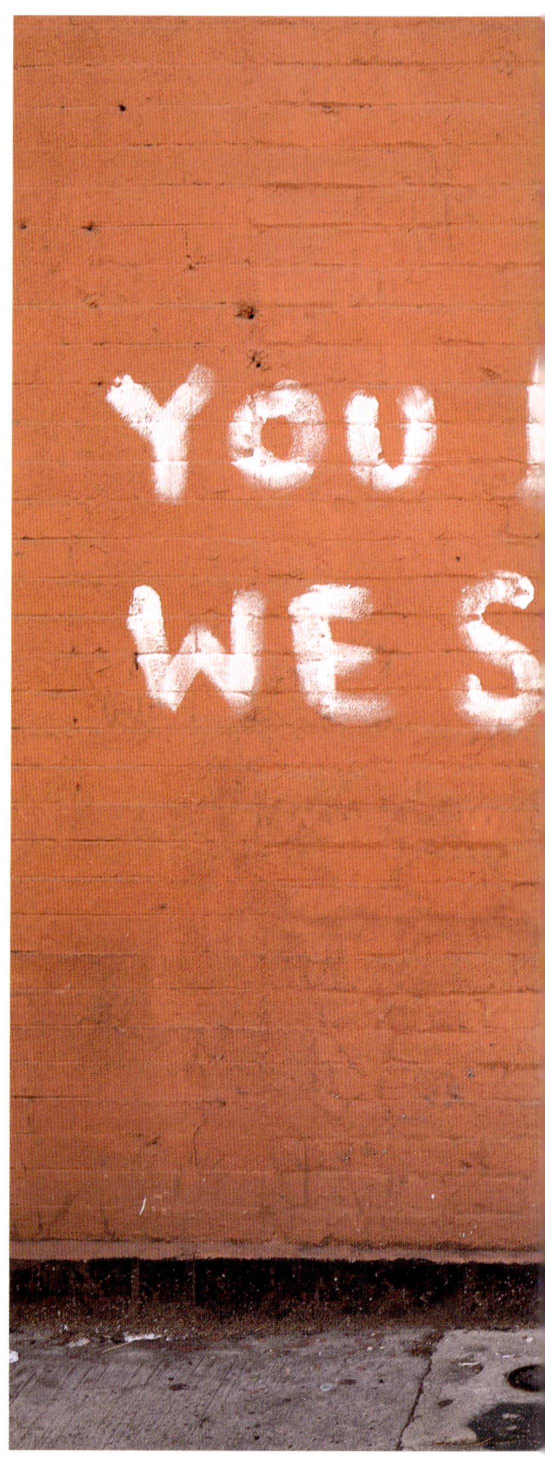

Banksy's return to New York.
Painted on the side of a 110th Street
bodega, March 2018.

The work appeared alongside others at
16th and 6th, Midwood Brooklyn and Coney
Island Avenue. The Zehra Dogan mural at
the corner of Houston and Bowery was
painted at the same time.

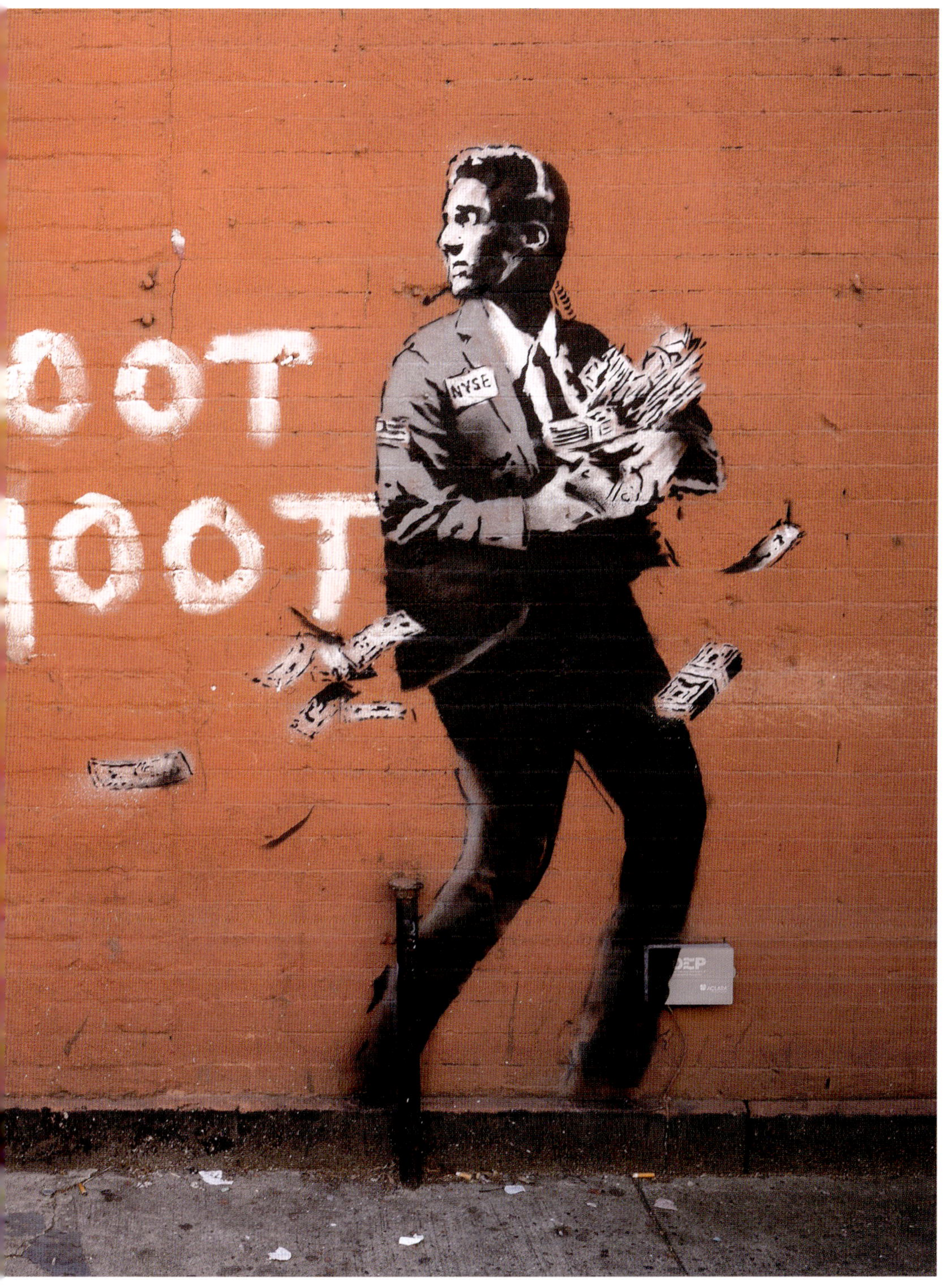
OOT
OOT
NYSE

REVENGE OF THE MODERN

Modernism: Another world is possible.

Postmodernism: Oh no it isn't.

So is there anything to say about Banksy that has not already been said?

My **generation**. Children in the 80's, youths in the 90's, hustling in the naughties, struggling parents in the 20s, is Banksy's generation.

When we arrived at that moment in life when the call to adventure came, we discovered we had been born into a world where the 'risk of dying of hunger had been replaced by the risk of dying of boredom'.

And because 'boredom is political' our political awakenings mostly came through attempts to 'escape from the 20th century' meaning that the search for excitement 'real life erupting within the spectacle' pre-dated any Politics with a capital P - just like Banksy, who indeed has never moved on to the capital P, still taking the P thirty years later.

We experienced the end of history as some kind of lithium daze, (every day is like the next), we railed against the political apathy of our peers and we retreated to a holy and pure stance of irony. Everything ironic, all of the time. Banksy's twin and contradictory move was to embrace action (just do it) and use irony (as if it were a subversive tool, not an escape from commitment).

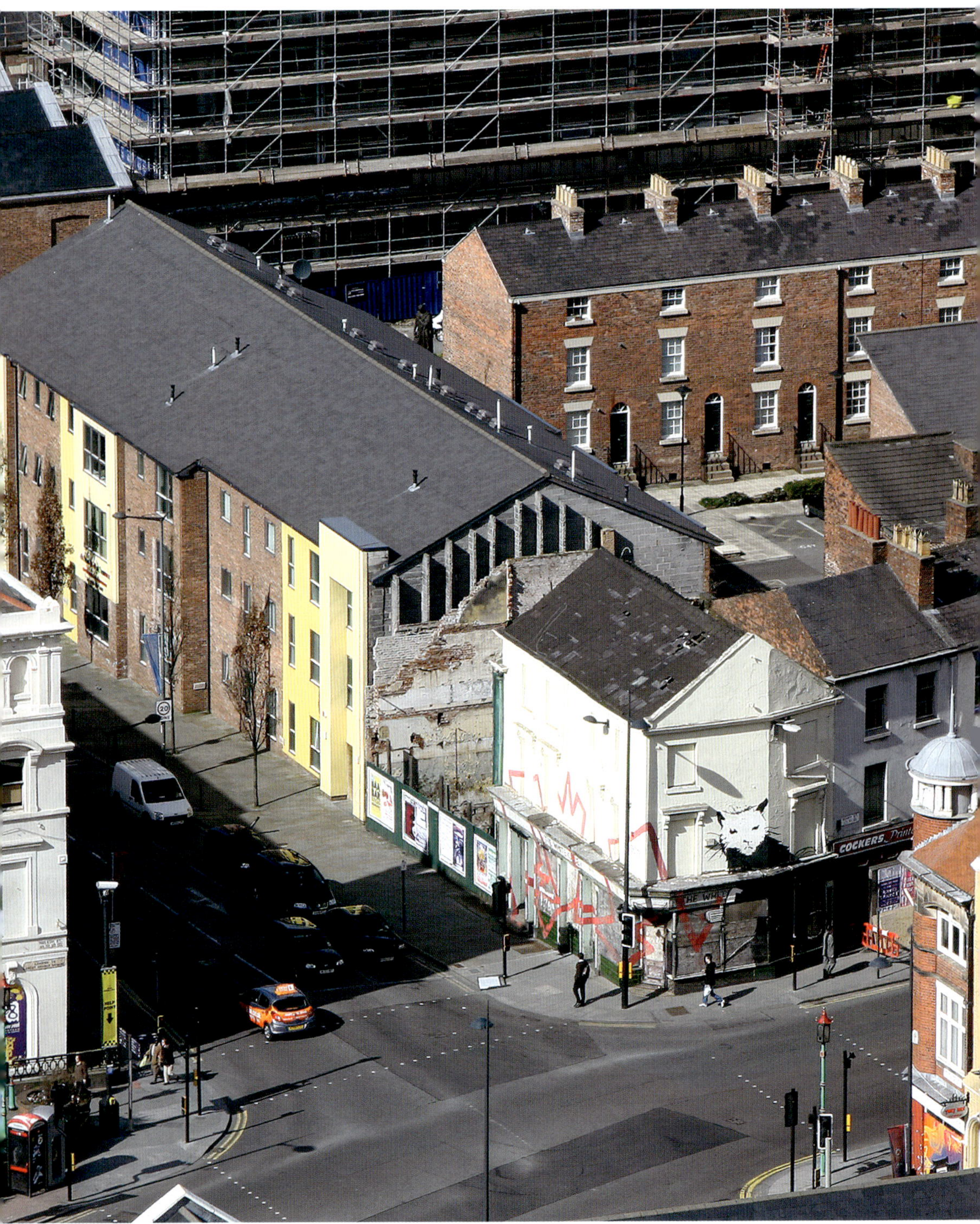

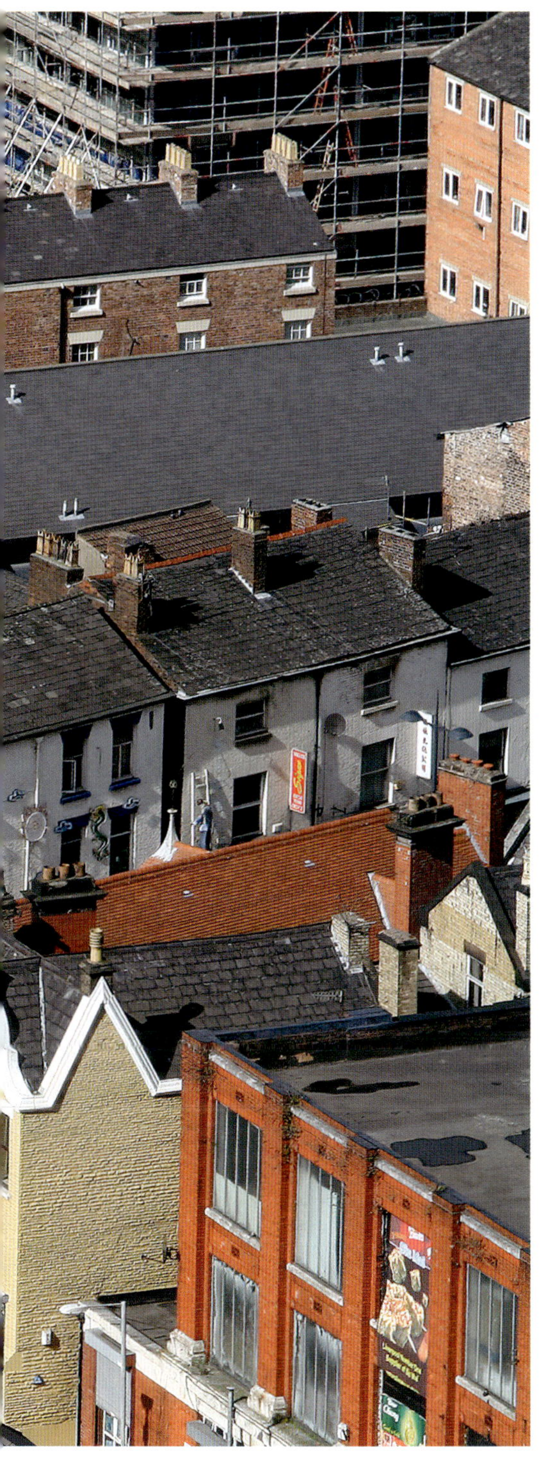

Banksy's irony was irony with purpose. His belief in the power of his work was never ironic.

We were told that it was too late for everything, after the horrors of 20th century ideology - ideas were no longer viable, projects of social change were always doomed, even the belief in progress was a sham lie. The postmodernists had debunked everything. Now who among us still believes in choice?

Banksy's response to this was refusal. And he wasn't the only one. His insistence that 'another world is possible' is, I'm arguing, clearly implied in his whole body of work. And it is this sentiment that is at least an attempted, **revenge of the modern.** The modern being a fundamental belief in, at least the possibility of, progress towards a better world.

His cohort, on the other side of the fence, avowed postmodernists all, the YBAs (Young British Artists) shared his aggressive self-promotion, his natural talent for branding and his 'revolutionary mystique'. But will Damien Hirst be a famous name to the man in the street in fifty years time? Banksy will. I'll put money on it. Their work does not 'say things'. Banksy's work always says something. And you can often write it down on the back of a fag packet.

Speaking of writing, is Banksy a writer who makes images?

Early graffiti artists called themselves writers. And when Banksy started playing the game, he was playing precisely the same rules as the New York originals in the 1970's. Get up, everywhere. Position is everything. When your name is everywhere - you win.

Exactly the same game that Nike were playing at exactly the same time.

And Banksy spotted the irony of that early. Coining the term 'brandalism' he put out little zines promoting his vision of fighting the corporates for control of public space, advocating others to follow his lead - making public space into an arena of public communication, a vision of the city dripping with art on every visible surface.

Again, this was part of a milieu - the counterculture of the time was in love with the work of Hakim Bey, who suggested that it was possible to create Temporary Autonomous Zones where post-revolutionary life could be lived for a moment. Young progressives were reading Adbusters and talking about culture jamming. Subvertising was a thing, Banksy did not invent it. He was good at it though, and really bloody committed.

Banksy's dream of a graffiti city was drowned in a flood of CCTV cameras as Britain went from being a society of shopkeepers to a society of content creators.

But Banksy just kept going. Contending that the guy who is supposed to be watching the CCTV footage is too busy watching porn, and apparently he was right, as he remains uncaught.

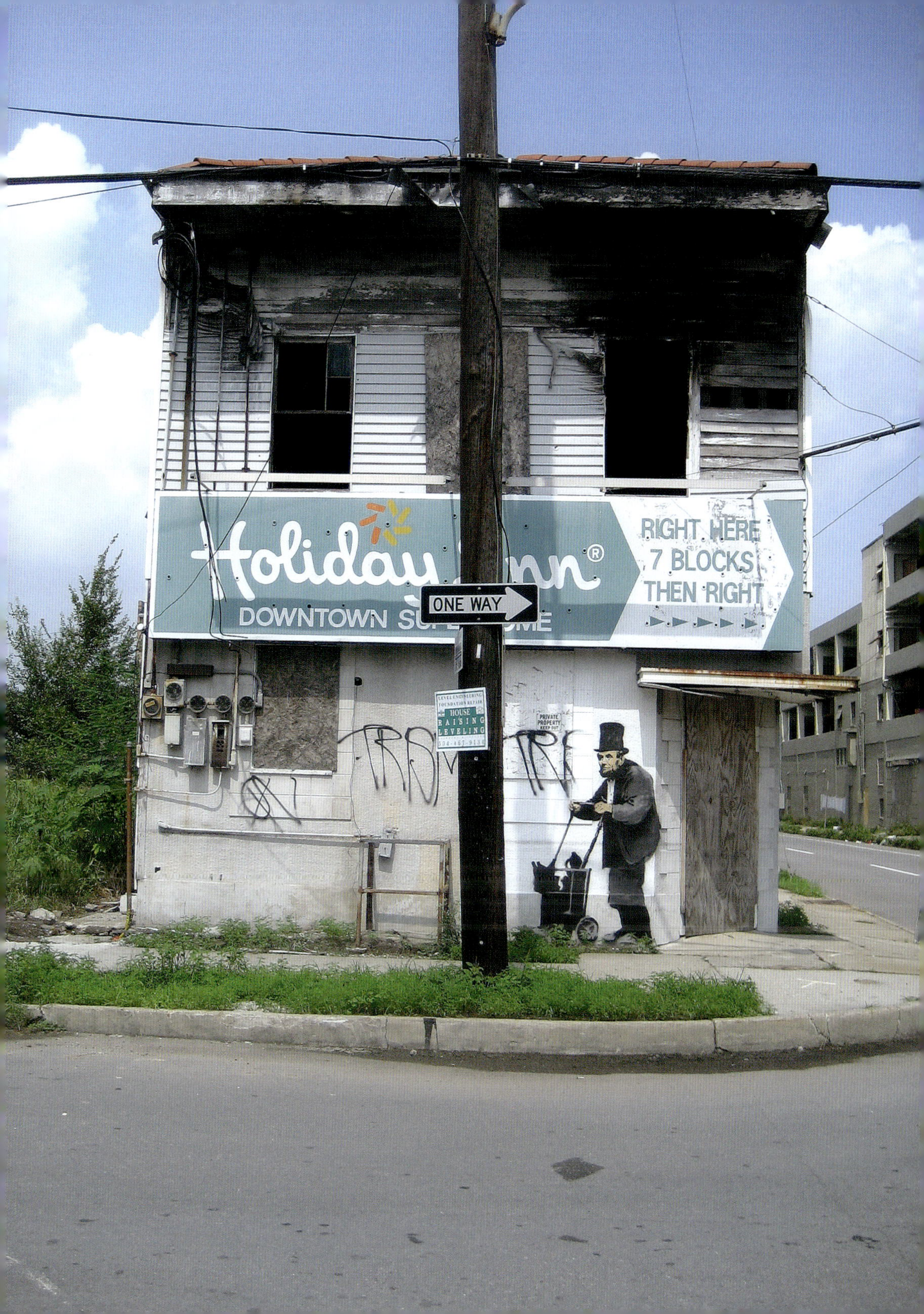
Holiday Inn®
DOWNTOWN SUPERDOME
RIGHT HERE
7 BLOCKS
THEN RIGHT
ONE WAY
PRIVATE
PROPERTY
KEEP OUT
LEVEL ENGINEERING
FOUNDATION REPAIR
HOUSE
RAISING
LEVELING

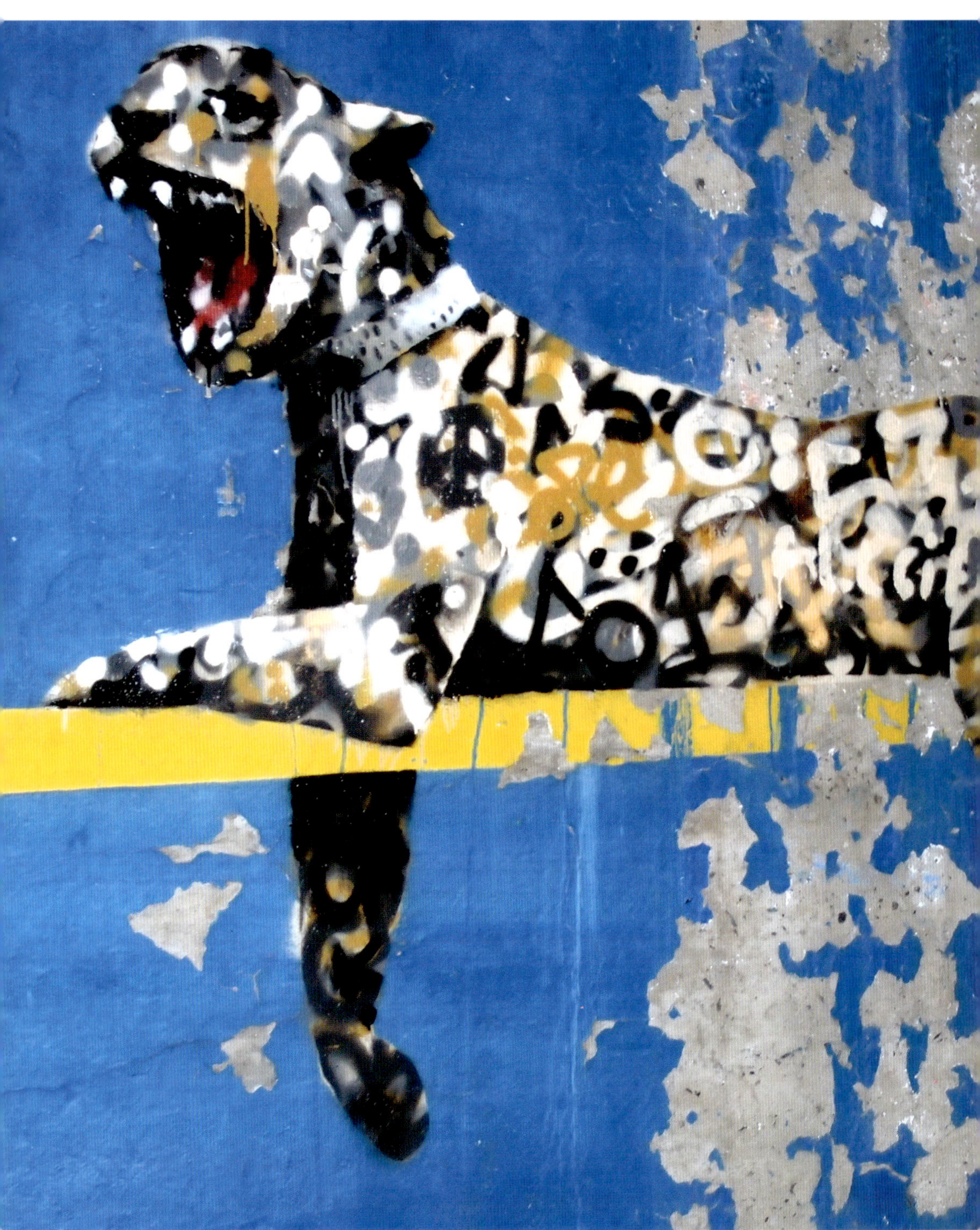

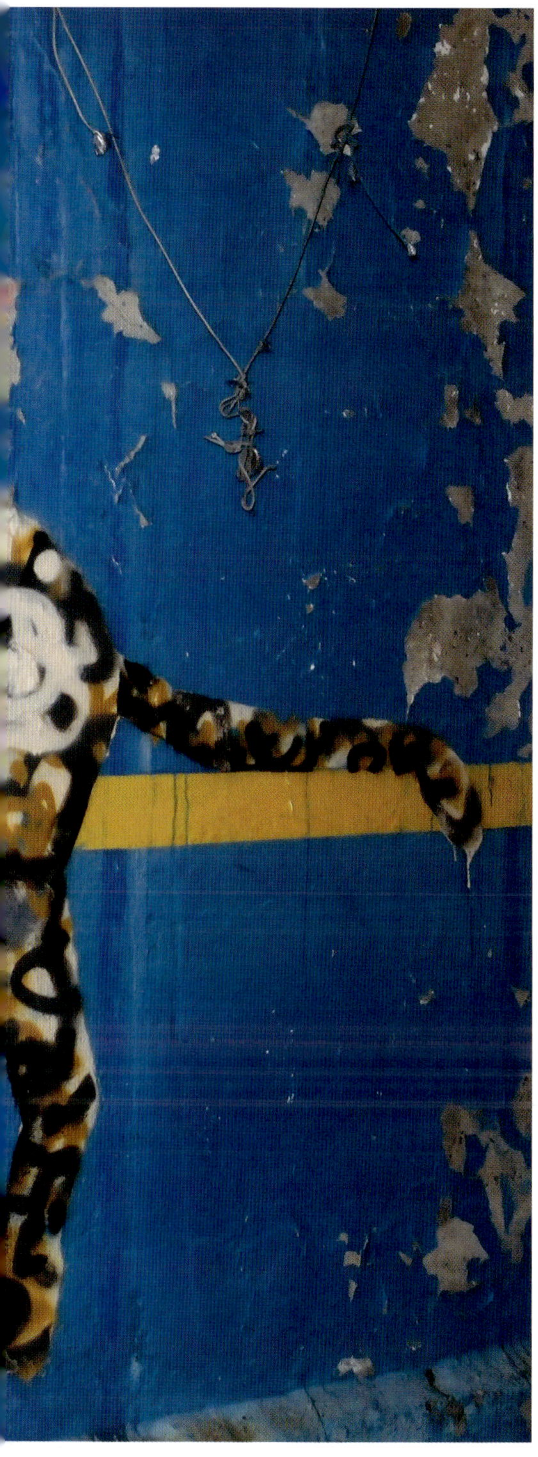

Sometime around the millennium, Banksy stopped putting his name up.

Now the artist formerly known as Banksy deliberately creates confusion around his own authorship, waiting days to claim or not claim a piece. What does this mean? I think probably he is still struggling against the commodification of his work, because he still wants it to mean something more than just another commodity for the marketplace, still a very **modernist** fight to fight. And this struggle takes place against the uncomfortable backdrop of trying to assert ownership of his images (and failing) to defend himself against companies selling 'Girl with Balloon' birthday cards.

Banksy's irony evaporates when he is advocating for those people forced to attempt crossing the unforgiving waters for a new life in Europe or Britain. His Croydon shop played this contradictory role of advocating his own intellectual property rights at the same time as advocating the human rights of migrants.

And it is this awkward, painful twisting and turning in a web of contradictions that is so familiar to all of us, but especially those of the same generation. Always aware that our material need to interact with capitalism makes a mockery of our attempts to act in accordance with our chosen values.

Banksy once created an image of a big cat as part of his month long residency in New York 'Better Out Than In.' Lounging on a branch, idly baring its teeth but no real threat, it wears a studded collar, a pet for some rich asshole. Banksy always knew that graffiti culture and street art had that weakness, of becoming yet another toy for the rich. Watch out for corporate sponsored rebellions.

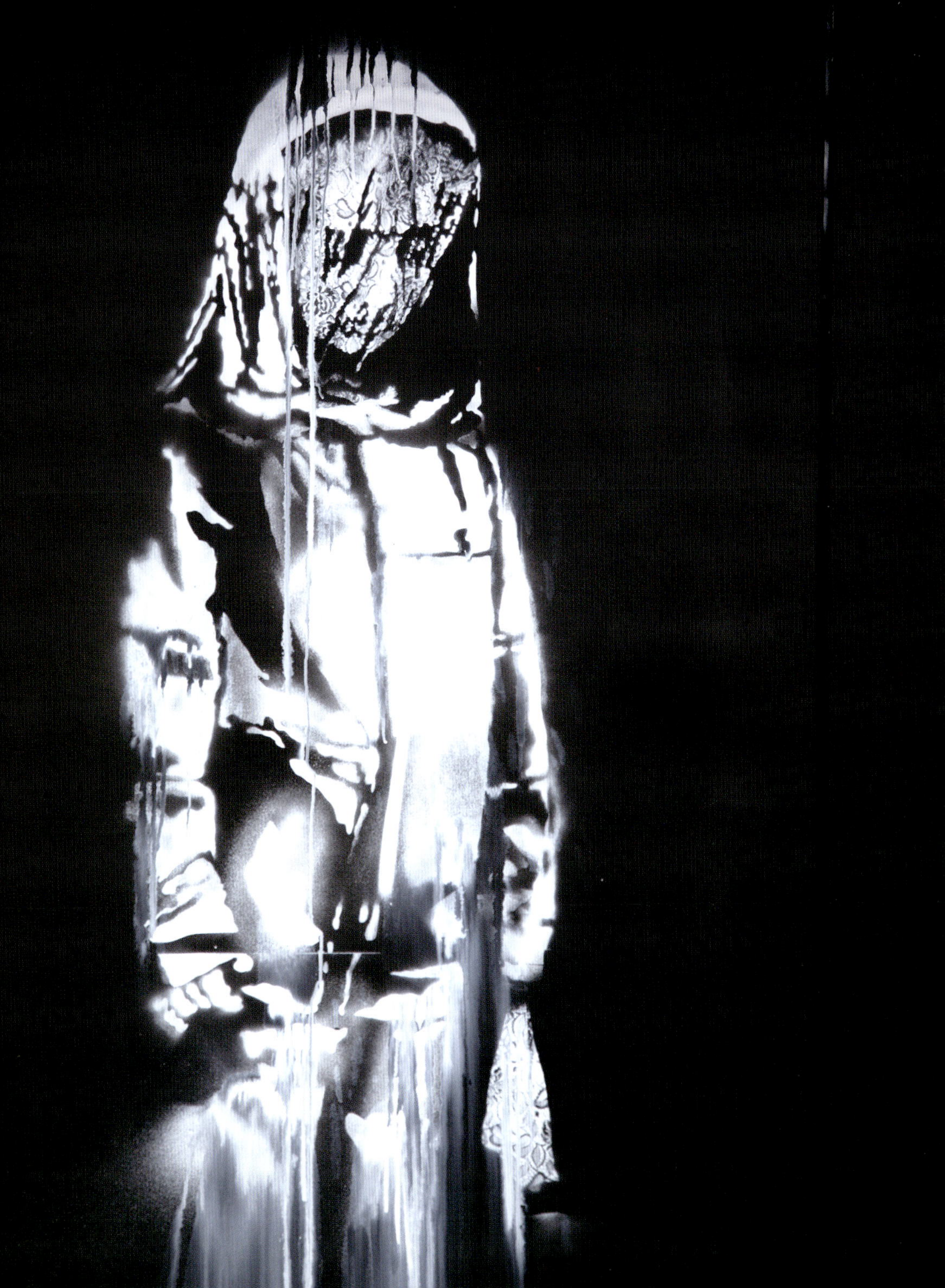

What makes Banksy a modernist, is a refusal to stop struggling, and like Baudrillard give in to the death of any relationship between signs and signifiers, to embrace the end of meaning, to drown oneself in a warm bath full of post-truth banalities and a simulacra rubber duck.

Like all good modernists, Banksy is primarily a sloganeer.

His rats are slogans disguised as paintings.

His installations are slogans disguised as installations.

Everything he writes is a slogan.

Everything has a punchline.

Like comedian Peter Kay once said 'I want to tell jokes that my nan would get'. Banksy wants to make art that some bloke who staggers out of the pub and goes for a piss in a back alley would get.

But even jokes, for Banksy, are instrumental. They are meant to bring down dictators. Like the story he lovingly recounts of the 1989 revolution in Romania, Banksy believes that you can laugh down Babylon. The right joke at the right time can topple dictators. Stand up comedy as a revolutionary project. Modernism again.

Banksy's particular style of sloganeering comes from a British punk tradition, going back to the situationists, French proto-punks of the mid-century. Their contribution to Banksyism was a critique of urban space. Paris was the first modern city. The situationists saw how the urban environment was like a solidified expression of capitalism, designed to make people behave in certain ways, the laboratory in which consumerism was invented.

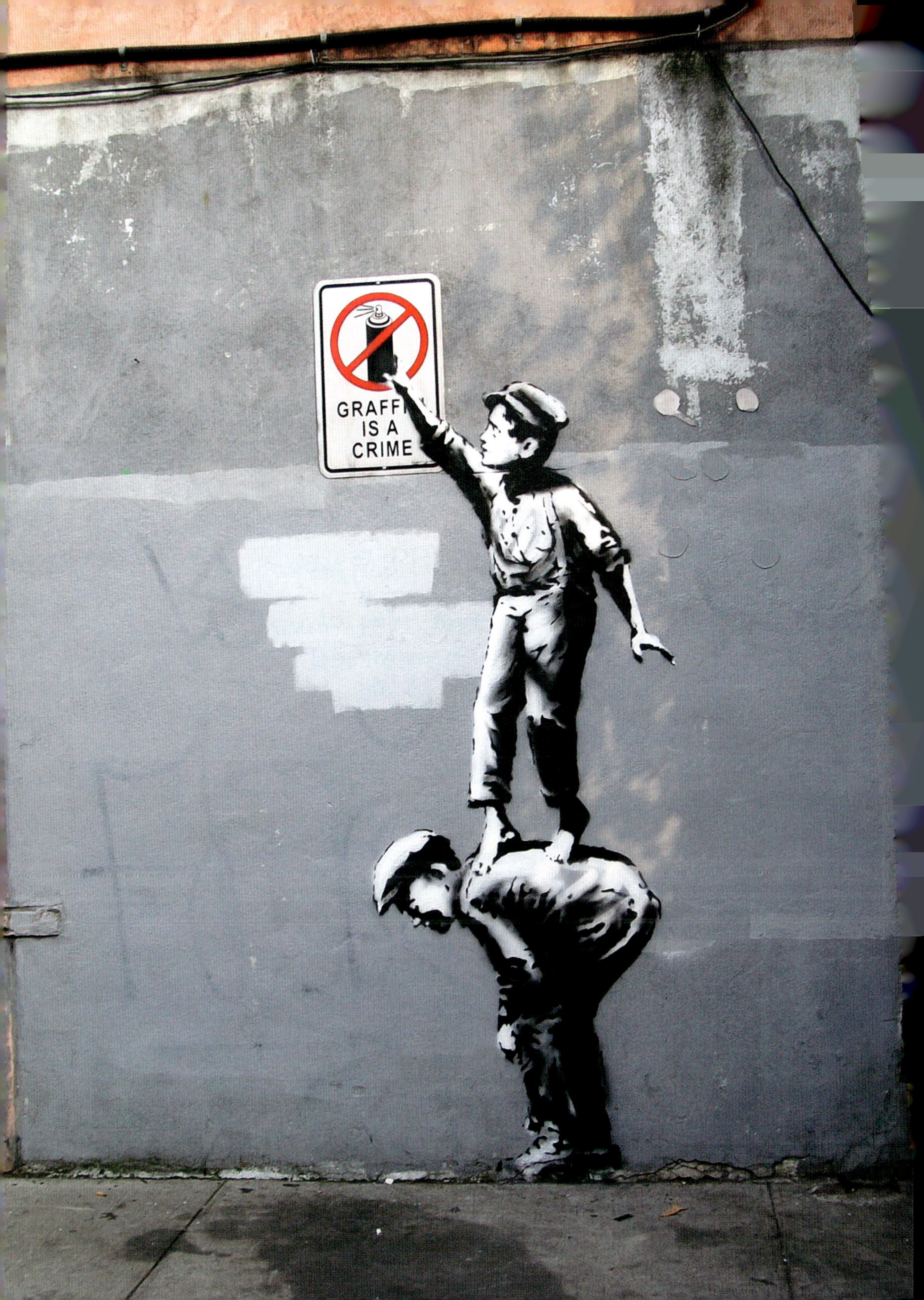

GRAFFITI
IS A
CRIME

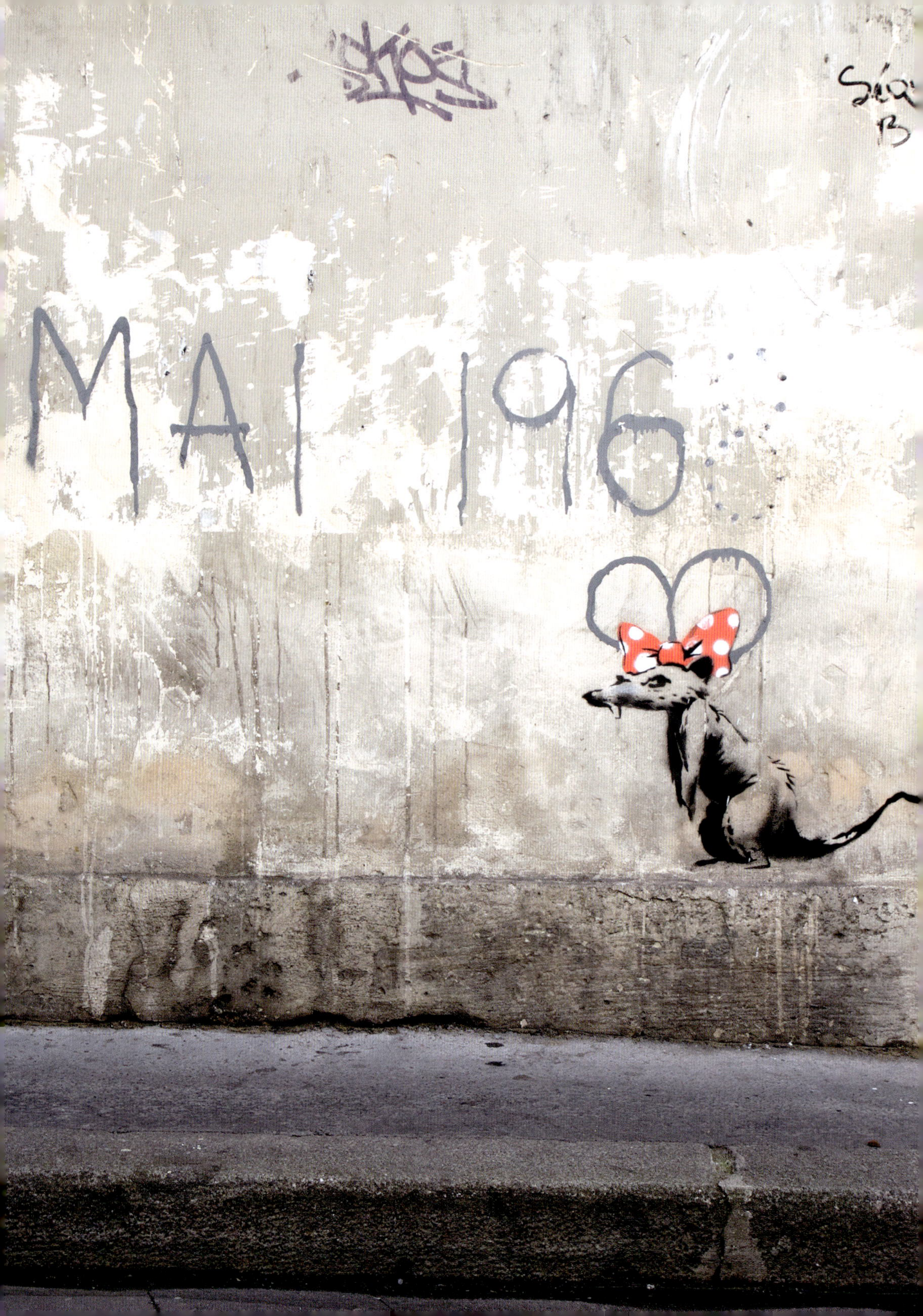

MAI 196

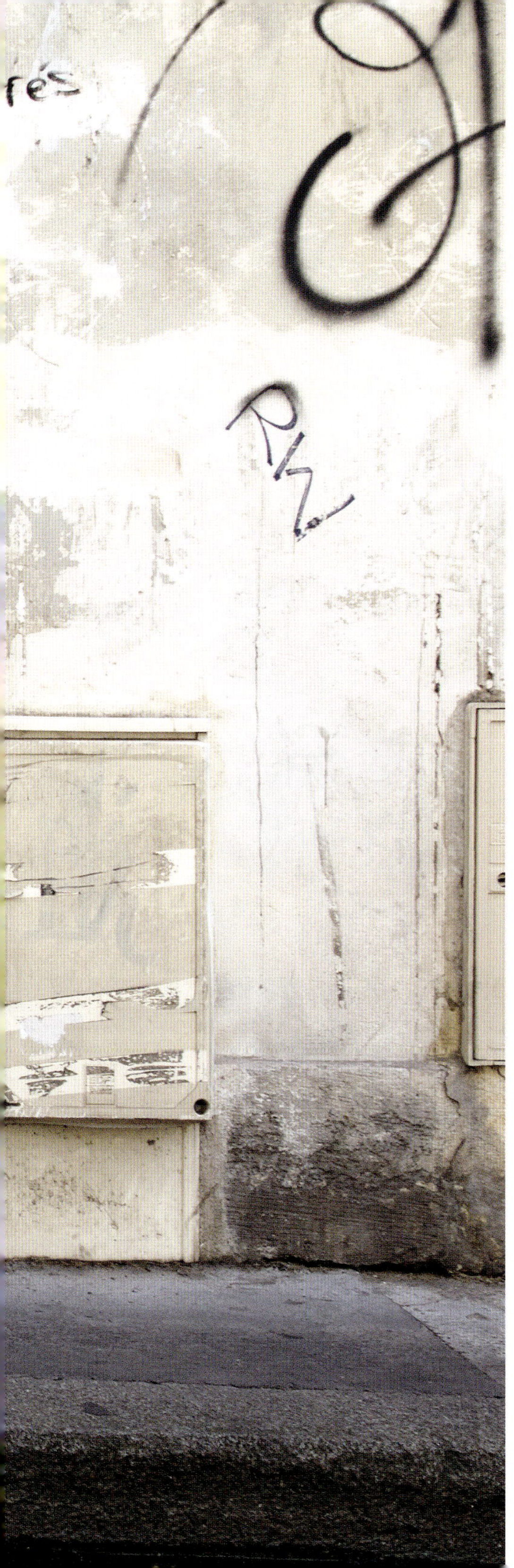

"In the spectacle the eye meets only commodities and their prices"

- Guy Debord

They talked a lot about ways in which you could subvert that, ways in which you could make 'real life erupt within the spectacle'. Their writings informed a generation of young French rebels who wrote some of the best political graffiti in history during the late 1960's. They also cut up adverts and remixed pop culture to make their own propaganda, blending an attack on the failure of traditional socialism with an aggressive critique of bourgeois 'culture'.

"Boredom is counter revolutionary!"

- Situ Graffiti, 1968

Everything that was described as culture was suspect, part of the machinery that kept the spectacle alive. Everything they made was intended to be corrosive to everything that existed. A tall order to maintain.

"Be realistic, demand the impossible!"

- Situ Graffiti 1968

One of Banksy's most iconic images is the rioter throwing flowers. This is an image so situationist in it's flavour it could have come from the pages of the Situationist International. It's even based on a photograph of a Parisian student rioter. Banksy's an anti-intellectual who is happy to study art history and then pretends he hasn't.

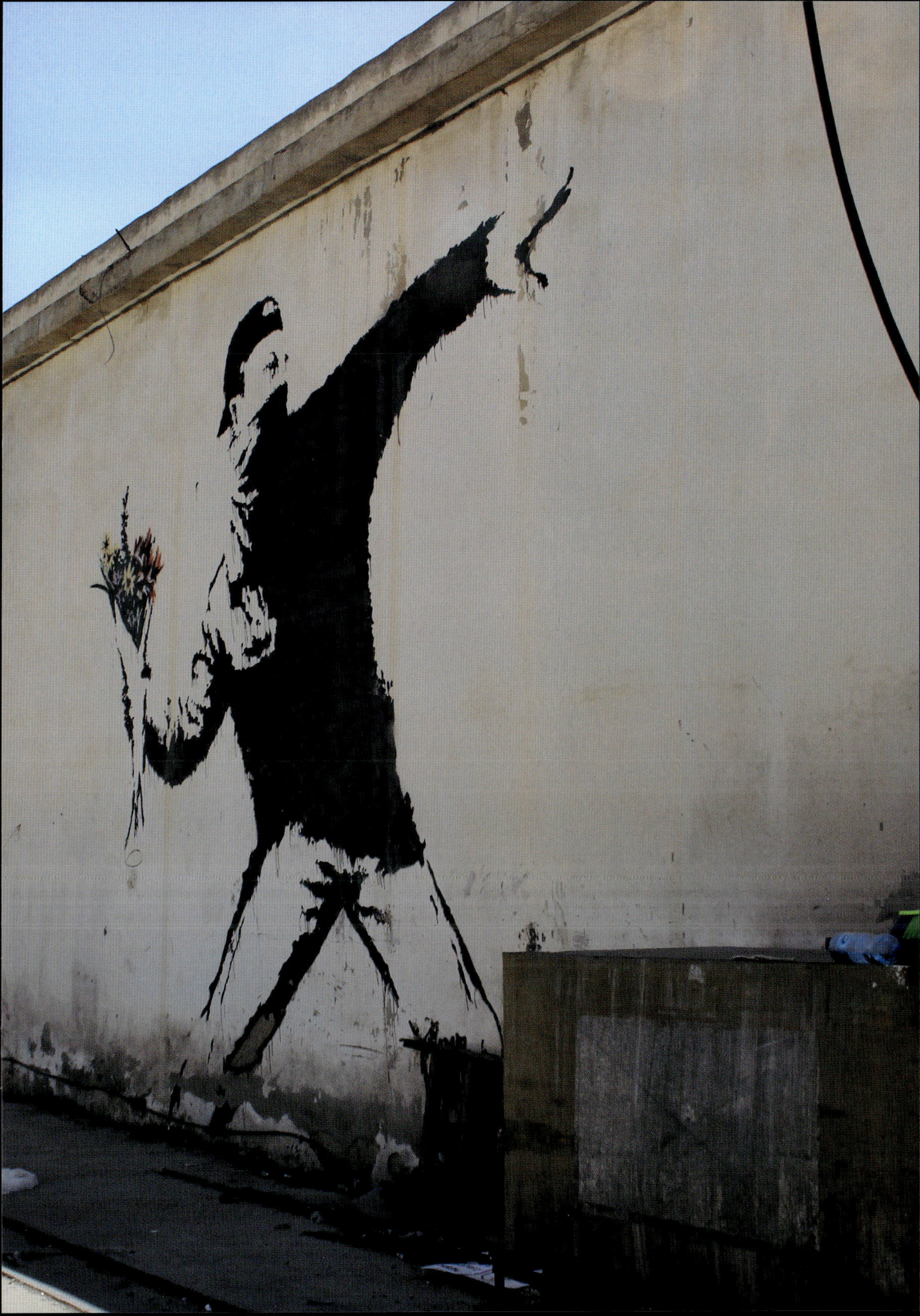

"Never work!"

- Situ Graffiti 1968

Play, games, revolution as a type of carnaval, a serious commitment to not being serious, silliness with subversive intent, all of these were hallmarks of the situ movement, the punk bands it influenced and hallmarks of Banksy's art.

Banksy's girl hula hooping with a bicycle tire is an example of this, applying the logic of play to thinking about urban space. Banksy uses children a lot, to symbolise a direct, spontaneous and playful response to the reality we find ourselves in. She doesn't know that she's supposed to be feeling gloomy about urban decay and the collapse of local industry, she's just having a great time with the tyre.

The situationsts influenced Malcolm McLaren and their ideas entered into British youth culture through the Sex Pistols lyrics such as 'no future in England's dreaming'. Later another situationist fan, Tony Wilson brought the situ slogan 'The hacienda must be built' to life in an infamous Manchester warehouse (now a block of lux hipster flats). Blek le Rat's stencil graffiti work in Paris owes a clear debt to Situ 'detournement' aesthetics.

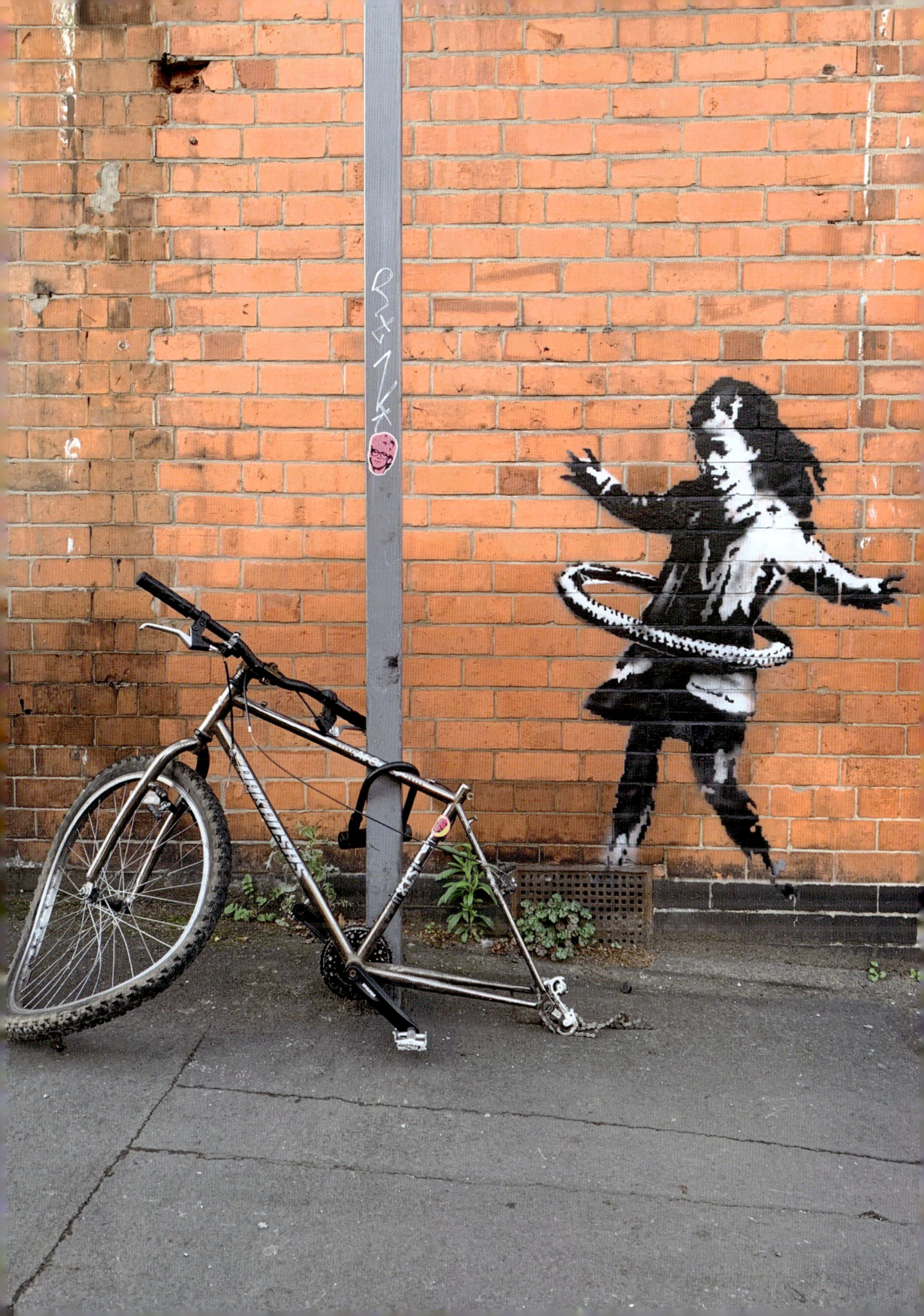

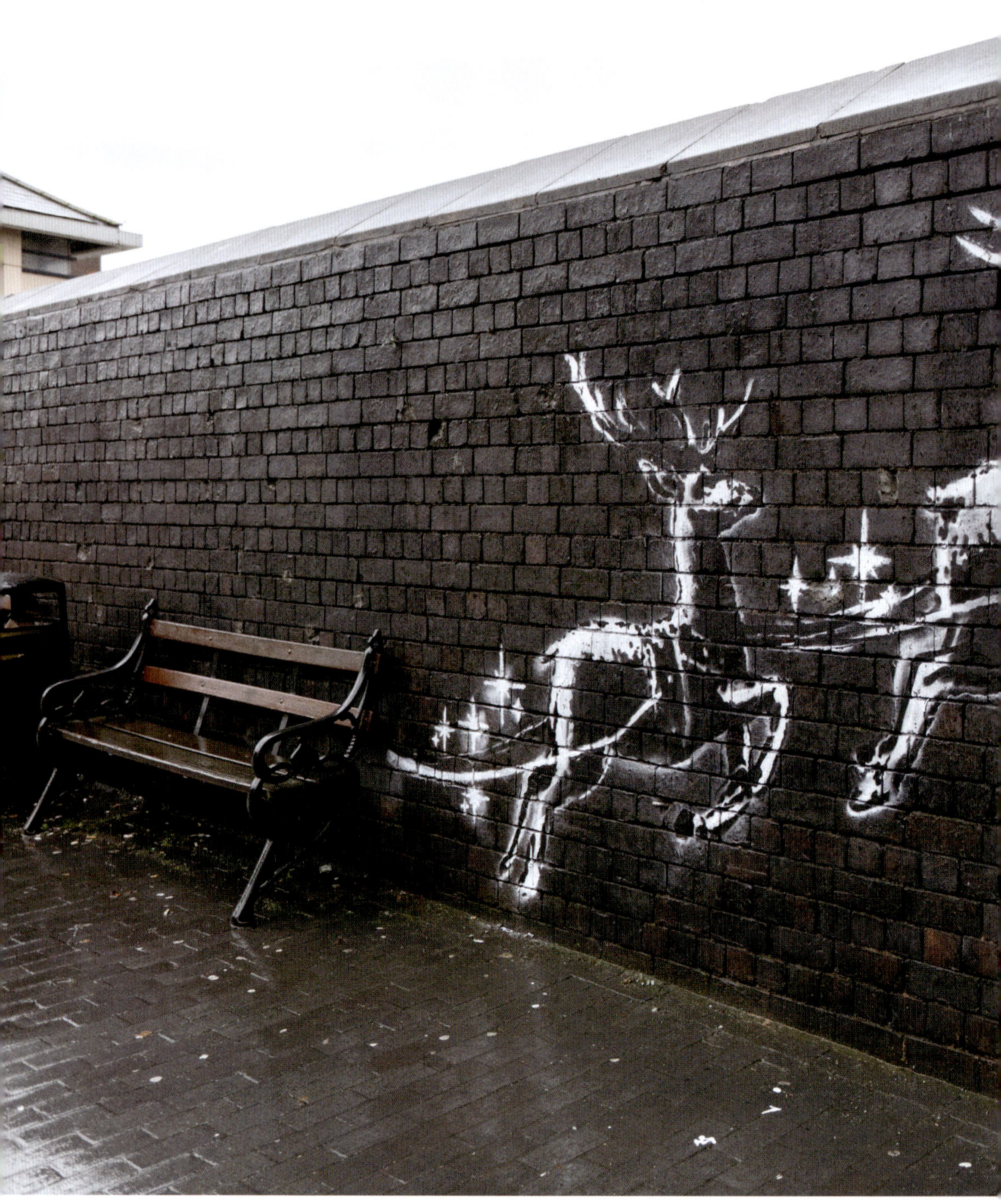

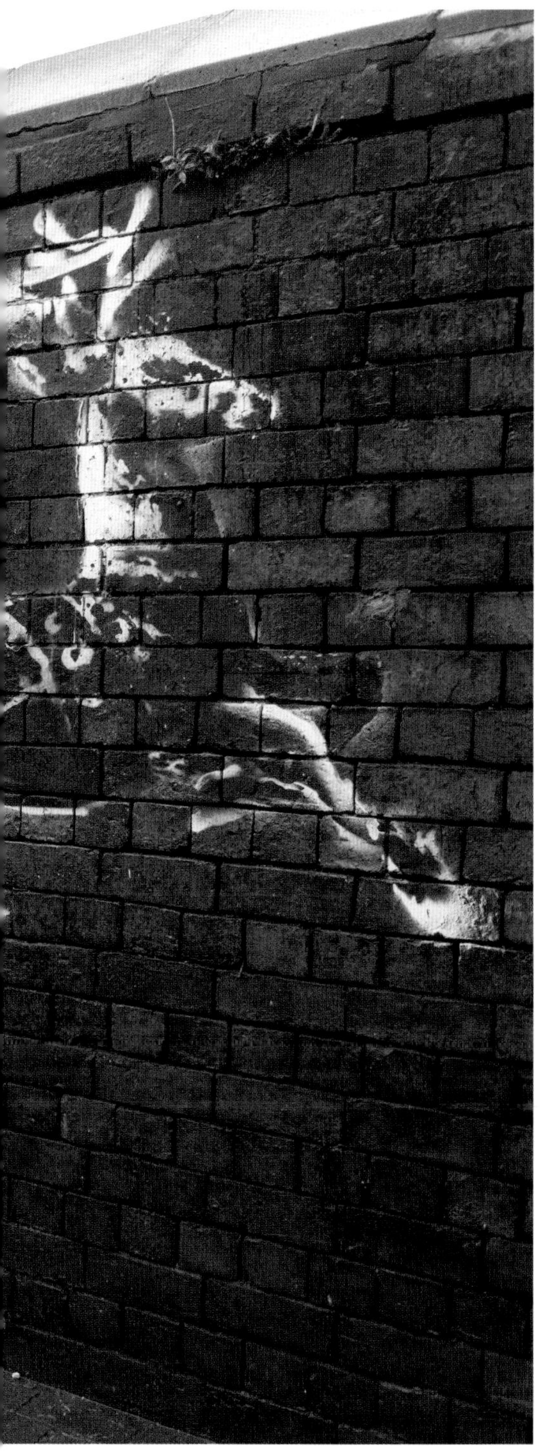

Penny Rimbaud and Crass were never convinced by the Sex Pistol's revoultionary stance. They claimed that while McLaren was selling revolution to get rich, they were the true revolutionaries. Banksy offers a similar critique with his image of a mum getting her punk anarchist son ready for his riot.

"Wealth is a ghetto." - CRASS

Penny Rimbaud named himself after the French Poet Arthur Rimbaud, a late 19th century bohemian who inspired the situationists and many other avant gardes. The poetic flavour of situ sloganeering echoes Rimbaud. He was a prototype of the romantic rebel figure, who loved the underdog, the rats of society. There are rumours that Banksy might have spent some time with Crass members Penny and Gee Vaucher (with whom he collaborated) at Dial House, the self-sustaining open house promoting cultural and political projects that was also the home of the anarcho-punk band Crass.

Reclaim the Streets emerged in the late 1990's as a protest group with a strong connection to situationist thought. Banksy was at the May Day 'riots' painting some of his most famous ealy works (Mona Lisa with rocket launcher on a boarded up shop) while at the same time the Metropolitan Police were also getting creative with their new invention 'kettling.'

Banksy was part of something, a current in British subculture going back generations. And the slogan that united this ragtag alliance of misfits was pure modernism 'Another World is Possible'. Ideas that re-emerged several years later in the occupy movement, where again Banksy was present and making work while the year of 'dreaming dangerously' played out in 2011, the peasants of London rioted, Eygptian football hooligans brought down a government and the Spanish youth hijacked their own democracy.

Banksy took that moment to champion an underdog, the graffiti writer TOX, perhaps asserting a classic left position that real change can only be driven by the underclass.

Because shining through in every Banksy piece, even through the encrusted layer of world weary irony, is the light of a very old fashioned hope, the belief that art can change the world. Even when he says, nothing changes anything, it's clear that he still thinks it might, in some inexplicable way, by speaking directly to people who are so often patronised and abused and hypnotised by messaging that is designed to turn their own instincts against them, that by speaking to people who have been raised to be the perfect consumers, in a visual language that they understand, that simplifies complex realities, at precisely the right moment, that those people might be shocked out of the merry-go-round of working to make the money to buy shit they don't need to make them feel better about working to make money to buy shit they don't need. Art as a shock to cure hiccups. Turn the corner, see the unexpected image, fall into a space of reflection, realise something. Maybe.

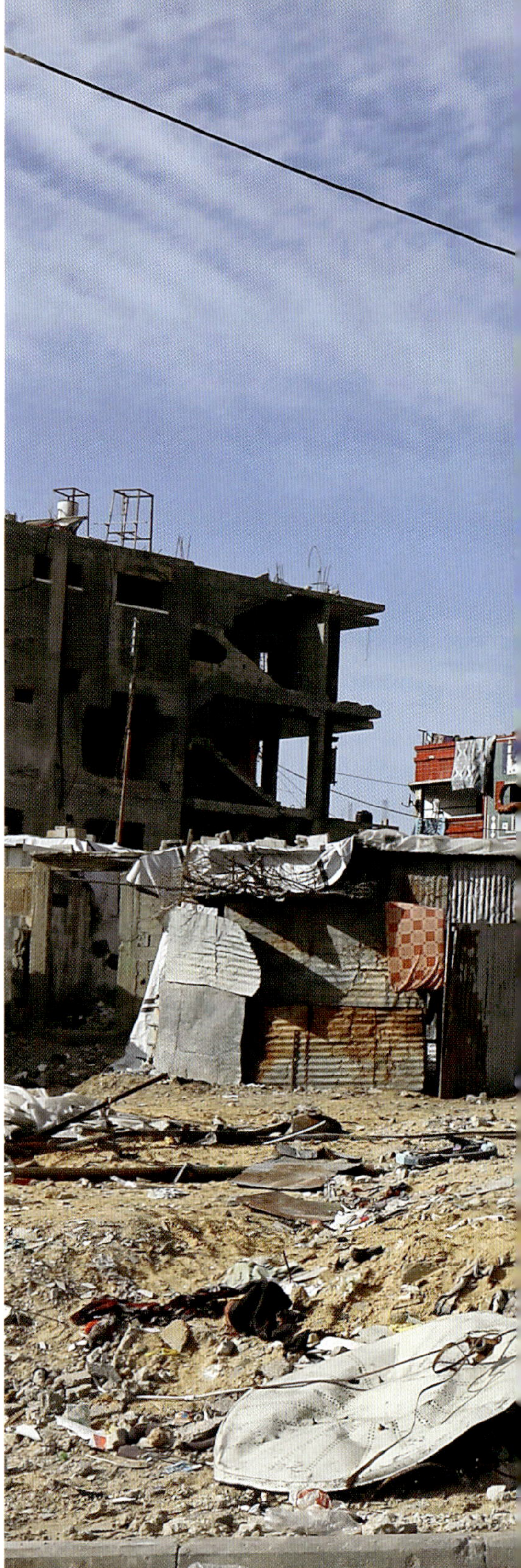

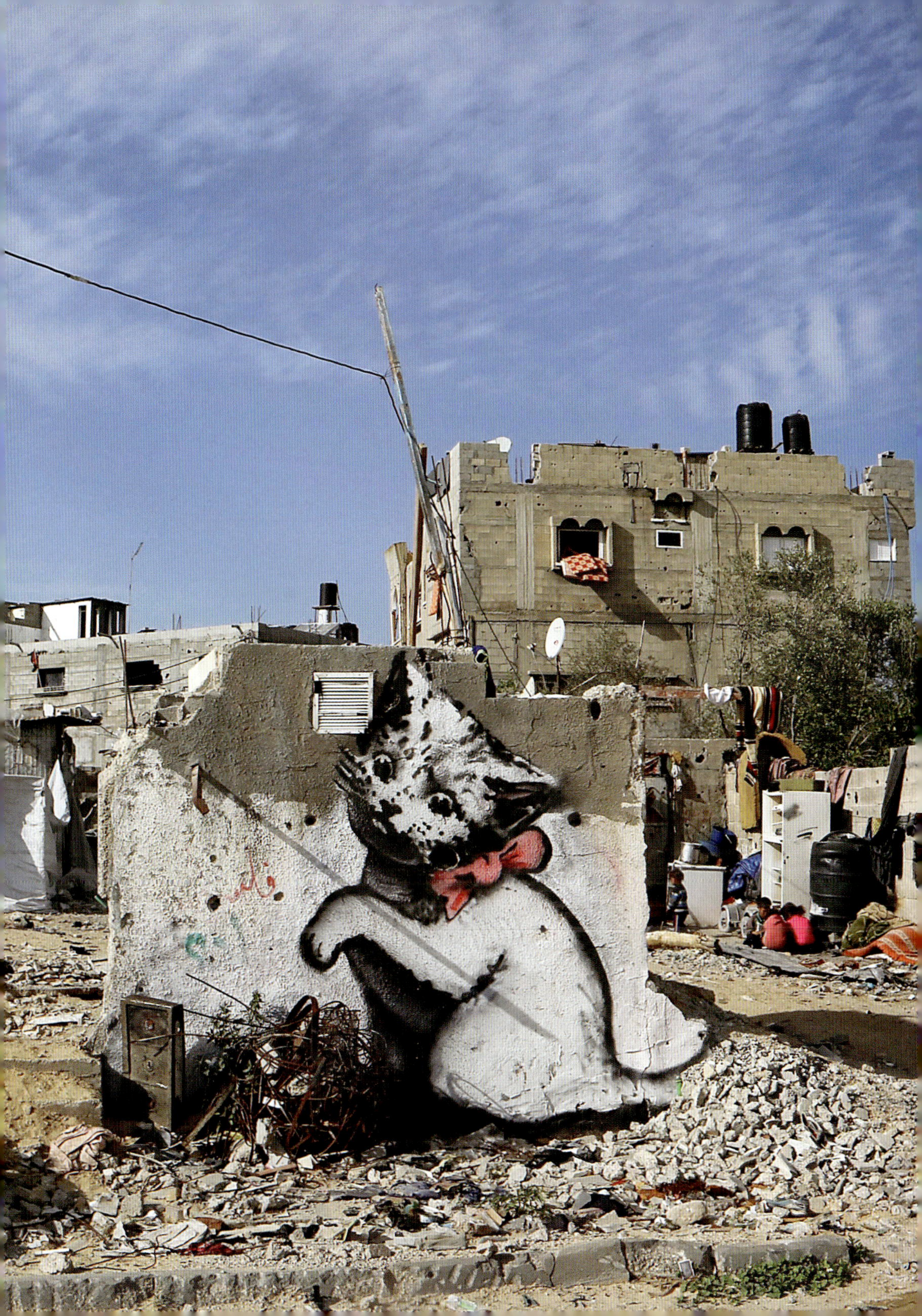

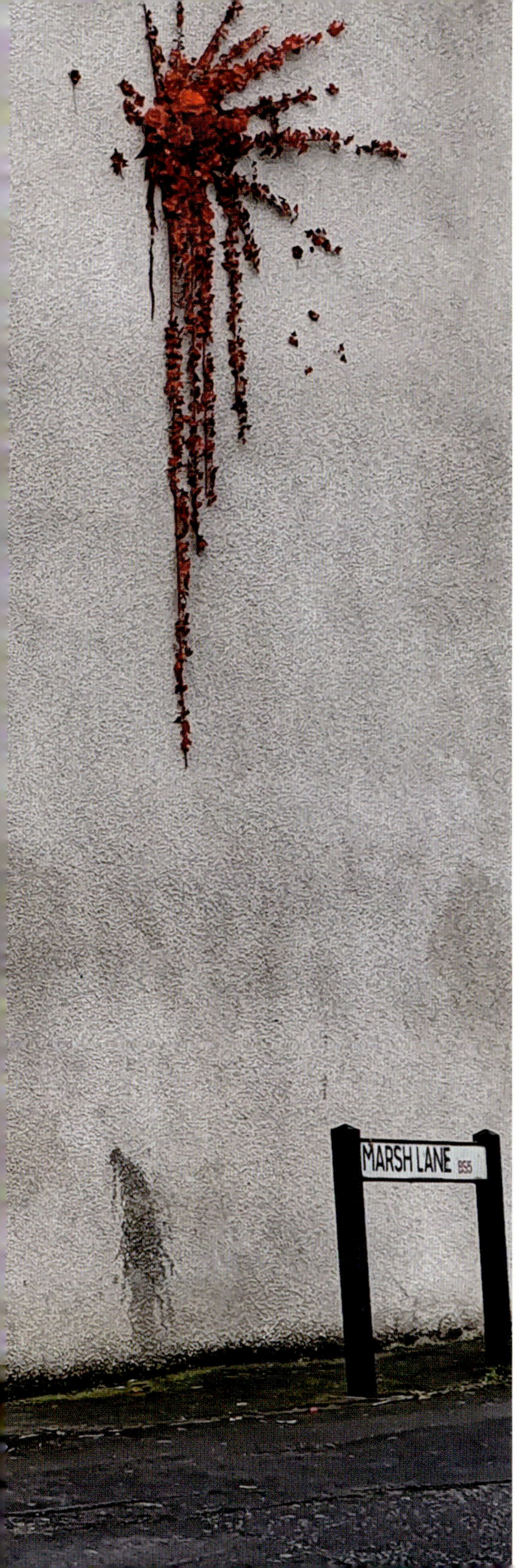

The old belief in the power of agit-prop, agitational propaganda.

And is it so silly to believe that? Because isn't our world still very much dancing to the beat of the propagandist's drum? Although of course, it was long ago rebranded as marketing.

Maybe it is naive to believe that art can change the world, now that the game has shifted in some fundamental way, to a game where disorientation is the goal, a kind of deliberate erosion of the relationship between meaning and communication, allowing everything to be equivocal, of equal value.

My opinion is just as valid as your research, and yet my opinion is not even really an opinion, it is a fragment of something that maybe once meant something, but now I cannot keep focus on anything for long enough to recognise whether it has any continuity or not, because all fragments are equal when you think about them for less than a few seconds.

All that is solid melts into air.

Blame the internet as the parade of images scrolls past the flickering eye, who can still think in sentences?, who even in full words? As the food processor of the digital age throws everything into hyper rapid disintegration. There is a monstrous ball that rolls around the world, absorbing all that was analog, into the zeros and ones.

Banksy is what he is only because of the birth of the internet. The Banksy phenomenon is as much social media as it is street culture. In the digital Banksy is omnipresent.

And in the internet, somewhere in the tangled undergrowth of buried server farms, shimmering with the heat of the energy they consume, endless halls of flickering lights, where the data that is Banksy's presence in the world culture is strewn across the world physical, in this geographical space that is sold to us as non-geographical, the cloud, out there is where Banksy's power resides, not in the streets, in the billions of combinations of zeros and ones that make up every mention, every post, every share that exists, over which the meat bag that is Banksy no longer has any control.

To become part of the cultural alphabet, to become a symbol is both reduction, and elevation to a religious state. When the man in the street knows BANKSY, then BANKSY has become something that will never die, but its eternal life will be reduced to a greeting card with a girl with a red balloon on it.

Even your nan, knowing who Banksy is, and coughing spray paint.

And how is Banksy coping with his beatification as the nation's favourite artist OF ALL TIME? Insistently. Where many artists in their middle years would be sliding into ever more complex progressive variations, seeking some kind of new plane, Banksy resolutely sticks to his guns, making the kind of work that he would have made in 2002, still in 2021.

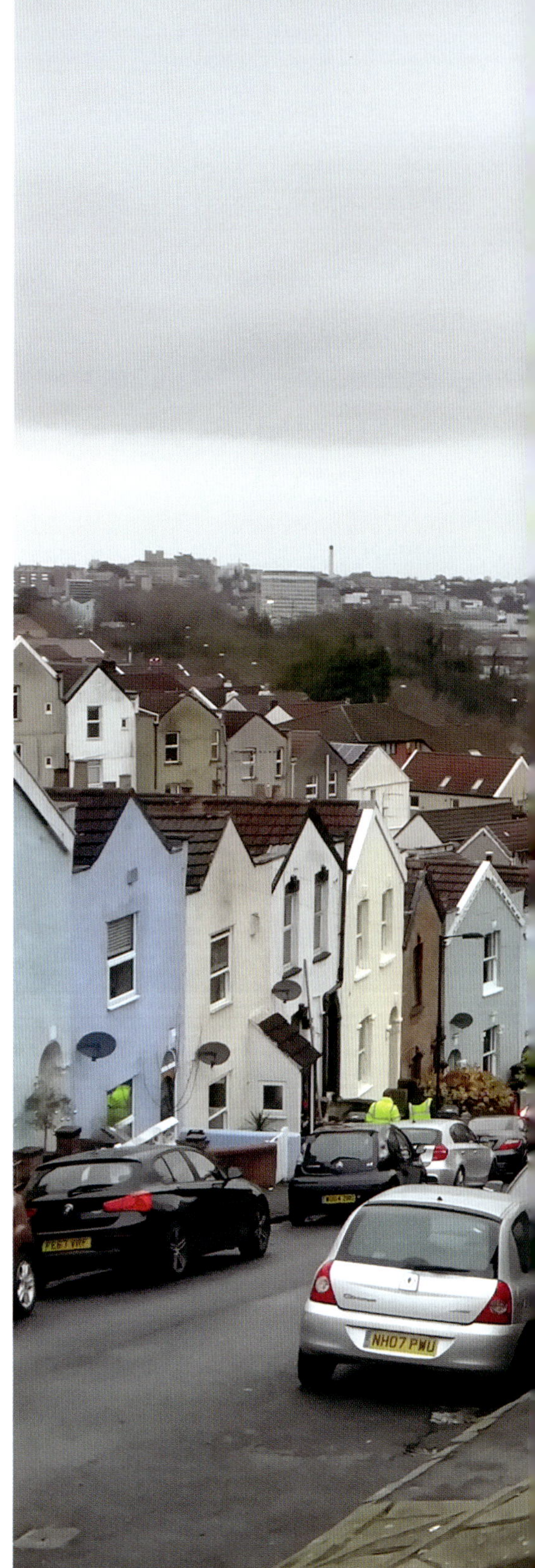

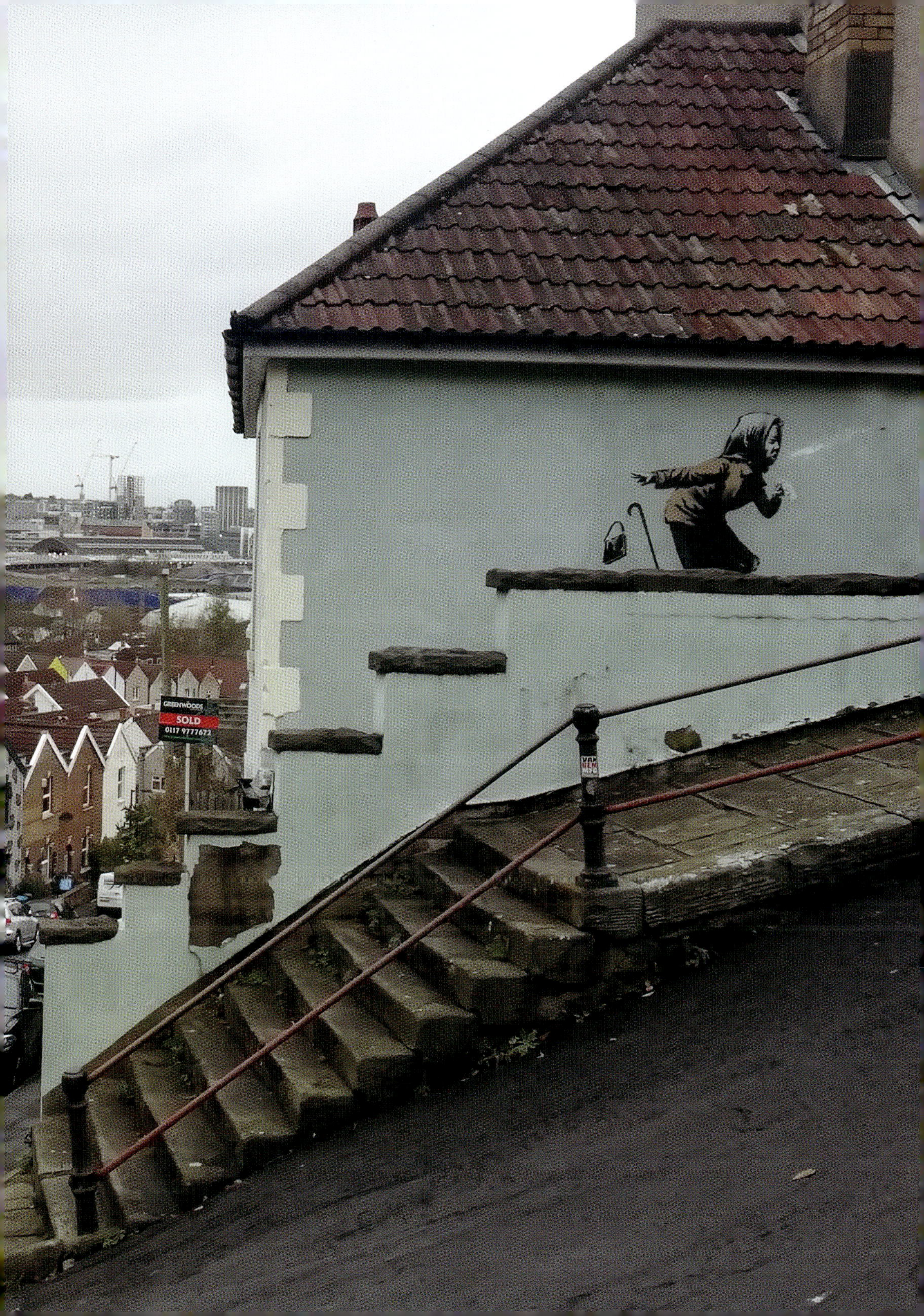

GREENWOODS
SOLD
0117 9777672

Because like a guitarist friend of mine once said, why would I learn any more chords? I'd just turn into a prog rock wanker.

Banksy shows glimmers of his frustration with being in his current position. His penance for having become a brand after being an anti-branding warrior, is to semi-secretly do charitable works, in defence of groups that are overlooked by some in mainstream society, like refugees. In this way he is still very much true to his original message, one day the rats will take over.

So, little has changed with Banksy, politically, even though he couldn't resist attempting to defend his own copyright, in spite of his rageous anti-copyright stance in his early career, his political messaging is so consistent it demands a kind of admiration. And in some ways you can view his whole career as an artist trying to find fresh ways of saying the same thing, to wit 'cunts still rule the world'.

The left has long believed that there is power in the marginalised groups, the people who have been left out and despised, and art can give those people a voice, maybe provide a focal point around which they can organise, and build a brave new world in the cracks of society.

March 2021. HM Prison, Reading.

Likely depicting Oscar Wilde, who was an inmate in 1895 imprisoned for 'gross indencency' a prosecution against gay men. In 1898 Wilde pens 'The ballad of Reading gaol'.

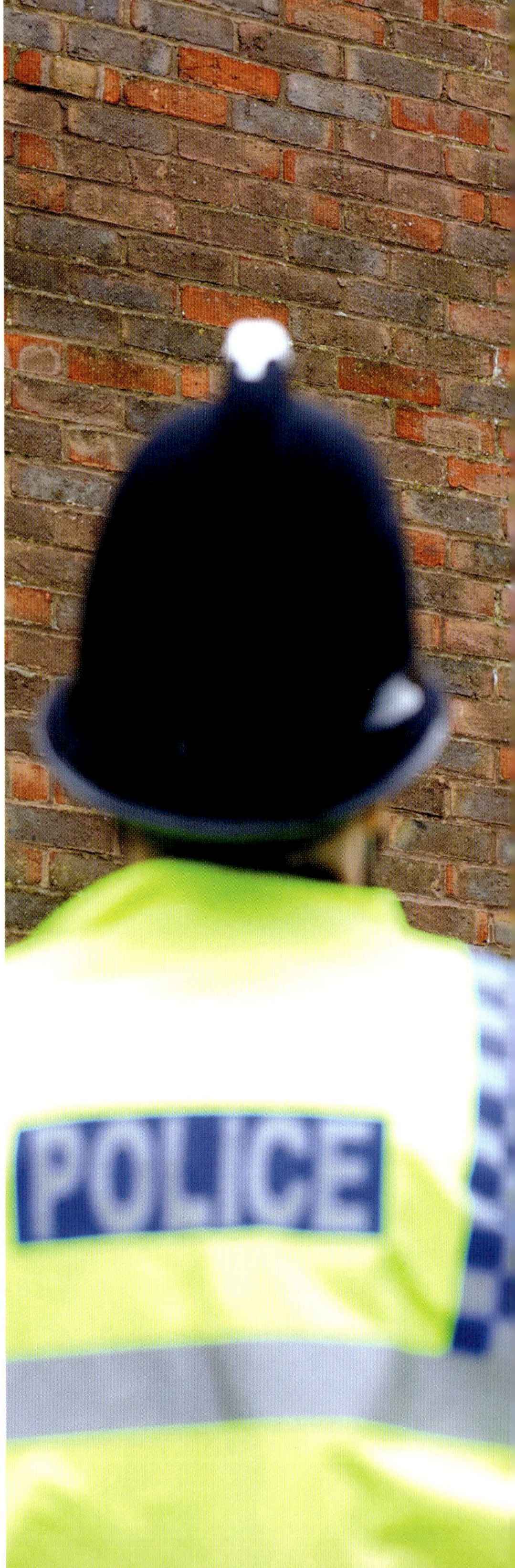

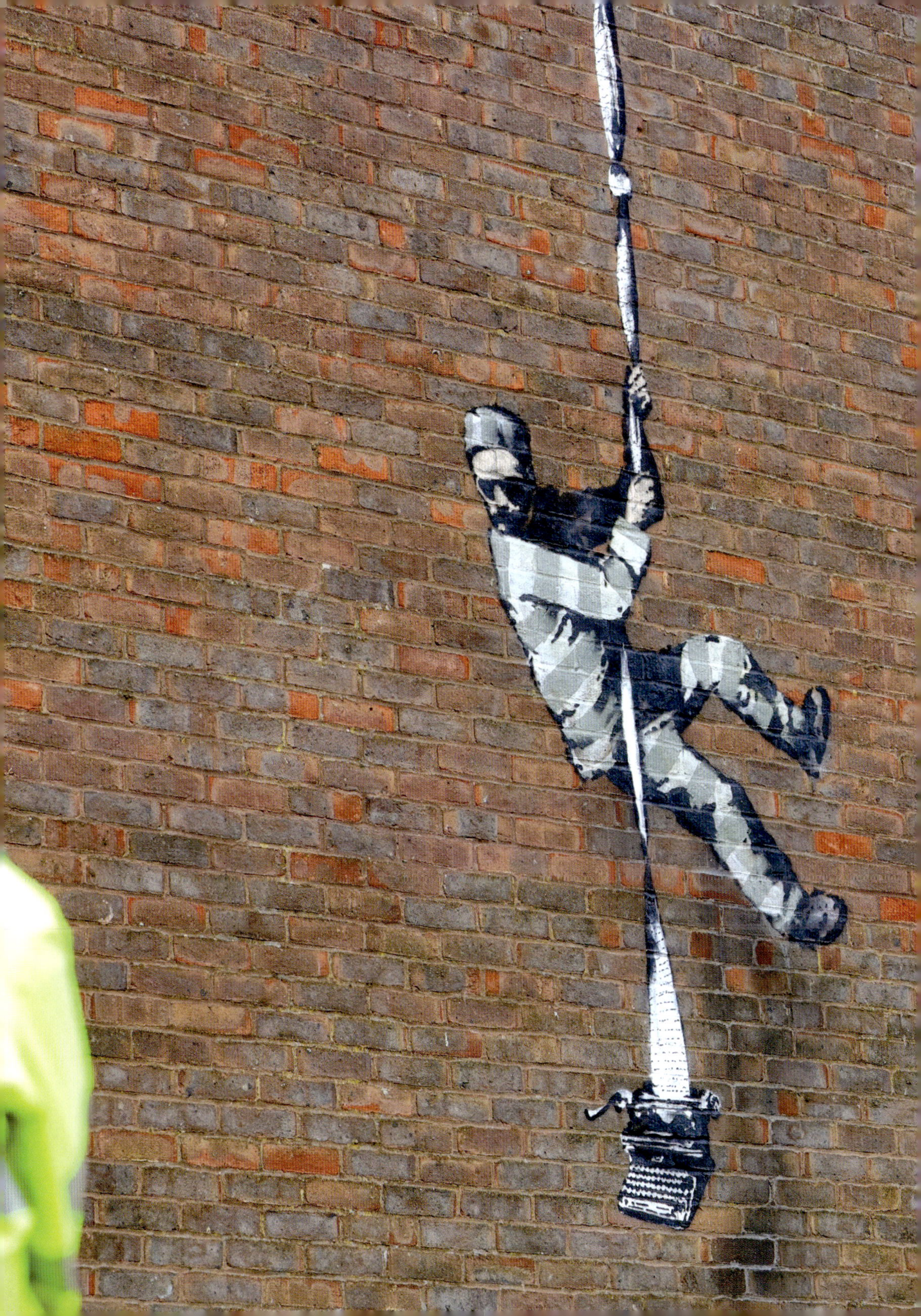

It is a powerfully romantic view, that 'the man controls the day, and we will control the night', ironing out all the complexity, Robin Hood politics. It ignores our complicity, our shared responsibility in recreating the very world that we say we despise.

But maybe it is a necessary starting point, prioritising action over reflection, actually saving people from drowning instead of arguing over immigration policies, arguing over something called 'economics' which apparently decides who gets to drown in the Mediterranean and who gets to go on holiday there.

You can write a brilliant thesis about refugees drowning or you can buy a boat and go fish them out.

Above all, Banksy wants you to do something. It's the only outcome that saves Banksy from becoming another ism. Because the only way that art can change the world, is by getting someone else to actually change the world.

So a kind of anti-intellectualism based on a mistrust of armchair liberalism, exists in Banksyism, but also, a belief that there is a unified BIG OTHER, there is an enemy that can be brought down by a unification of the common rat.

The people who are destroying the world have names and addresses.

Banksyism has at its root a faith in the great unwashed. So what happens when the great unwashed unify behind another kind of vision? When killer clowns waving national flags find it easier to channel the anger of the underclass than leftist street artists?

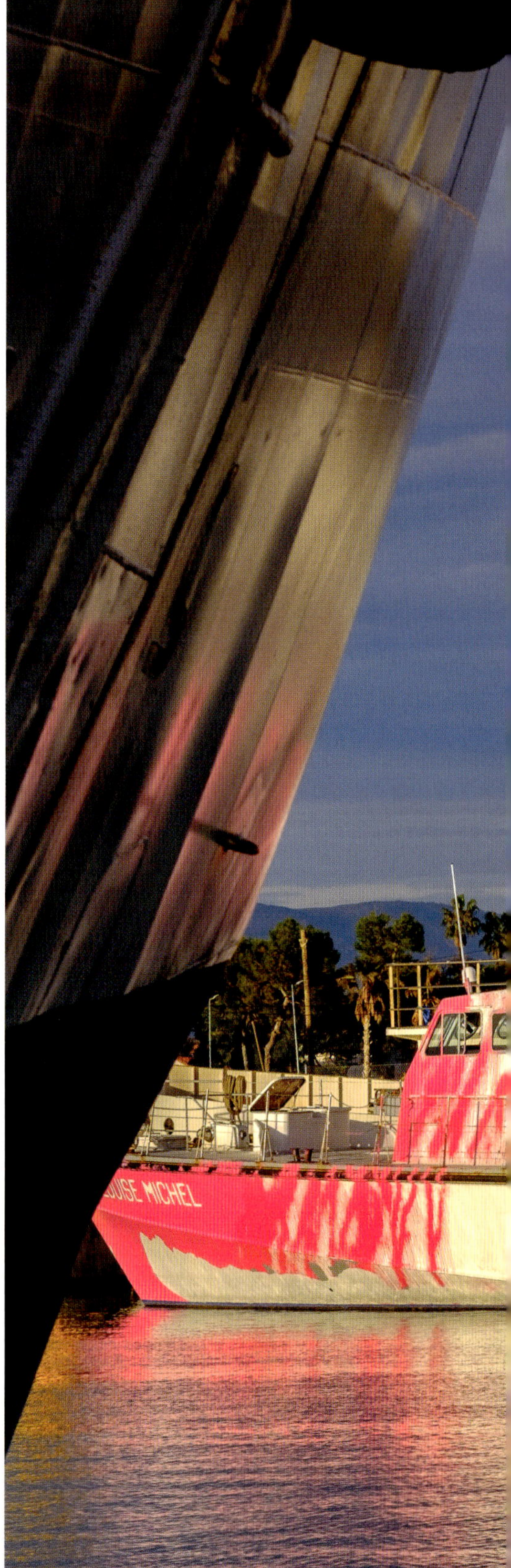

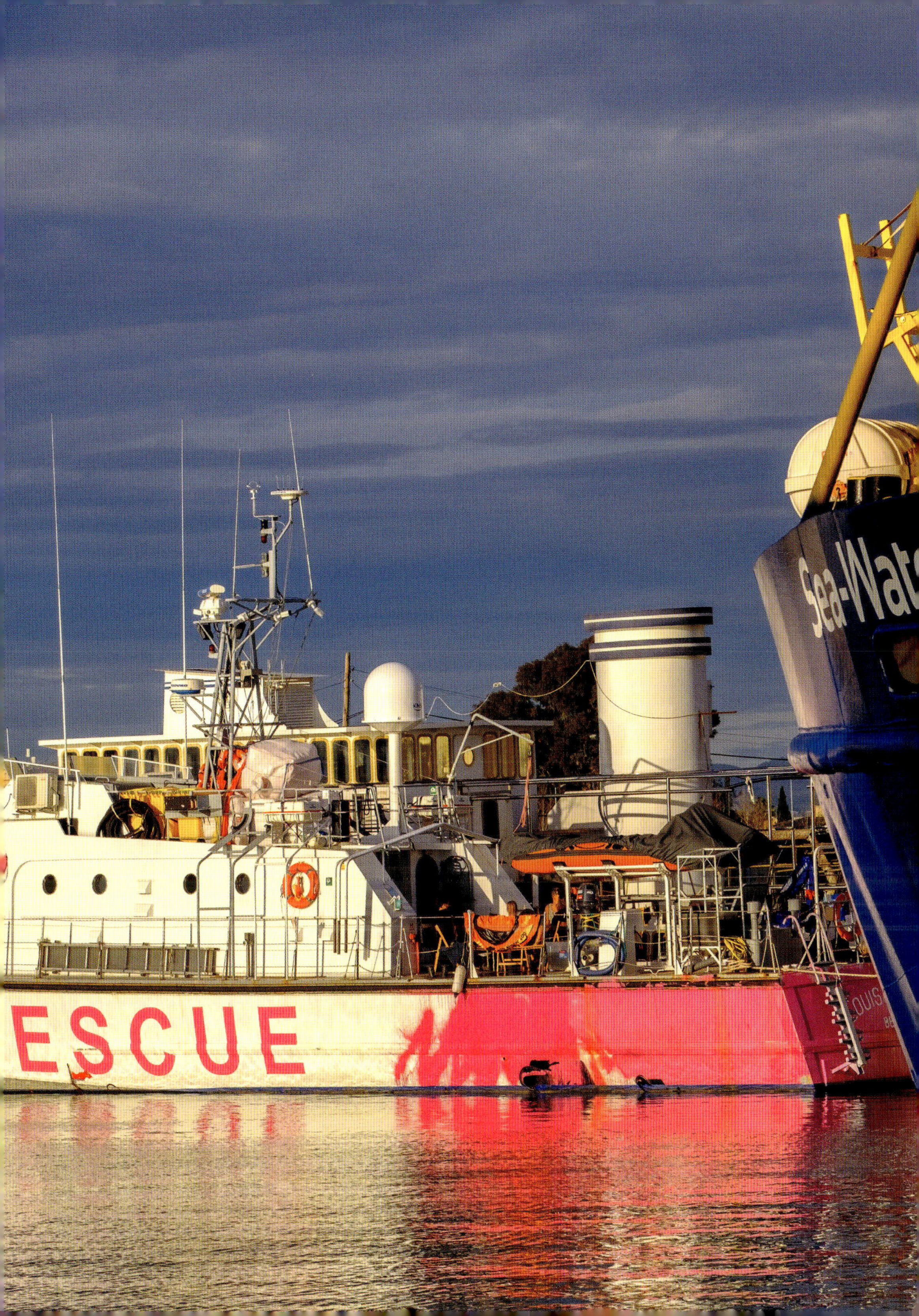

Sea-Wat
ESCUE

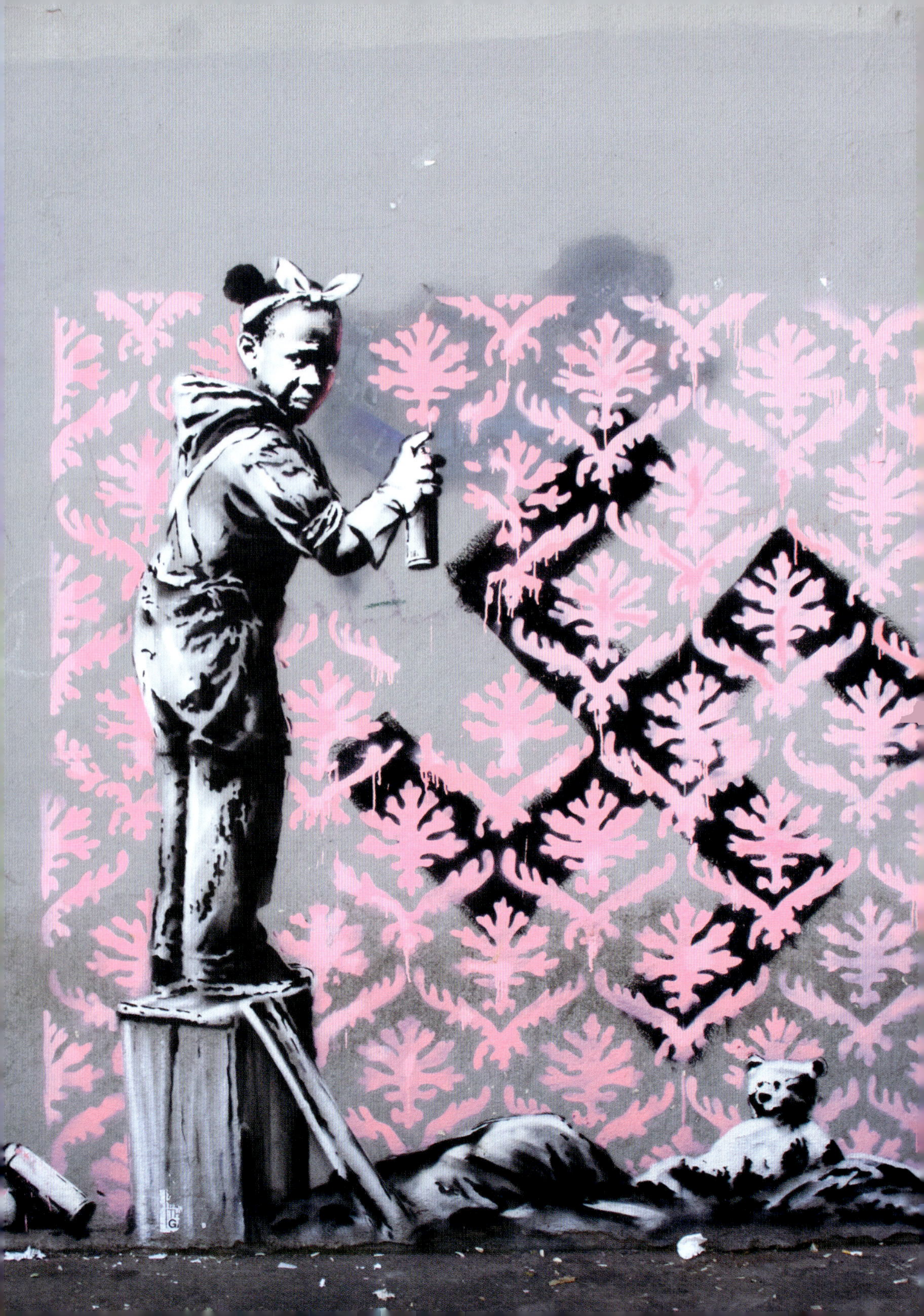

Banksy's image of a young black girl spray painting over a swastika is striking. The return of the far right has made the liberal world uneasy. But the swastika is being covered up by what looks like an elegant victorian wallpaper design. Facism gentrified, made acceptable to the middle classes perhaps? What part has the liberal world played in creating this resurgence of fascisim?

Banksy continues to address the mythical common man, hoping against hope that a sense of fairness and love of irreverent comedy will overcome an attraction to nostalgic patriotism.

This book is full of Banksyisms, a type of word play that Banksy makes his own, often a one two punch of irony and anger, a political statement remixed as a joke. And through the gathering of all the best examples, you might hope to uncover a Banksyism, an ideology of Banksy, an idea of what it is exactly that this particular Robin Hood is fighting for.

Maybe there is a Banksyism, maybe there isn't. Maybe he's written an accidental manifesto only visible looking back on his thirty years of art crime, or maybe he's a secret genius. It doesn't really matter, because the number one rule must surely be, don't assume that your rulers are secret geniuses. Don't buy the idea that culture is above you. And above all don't assume that those who rule the world couldn't be brought down by a well placed rat.

Another world is possible, but there's no guarantee that we'll want to live in it.

"Il faut être absolument moderne."

(We must be absolutely modern.) Arthur Rimbaud

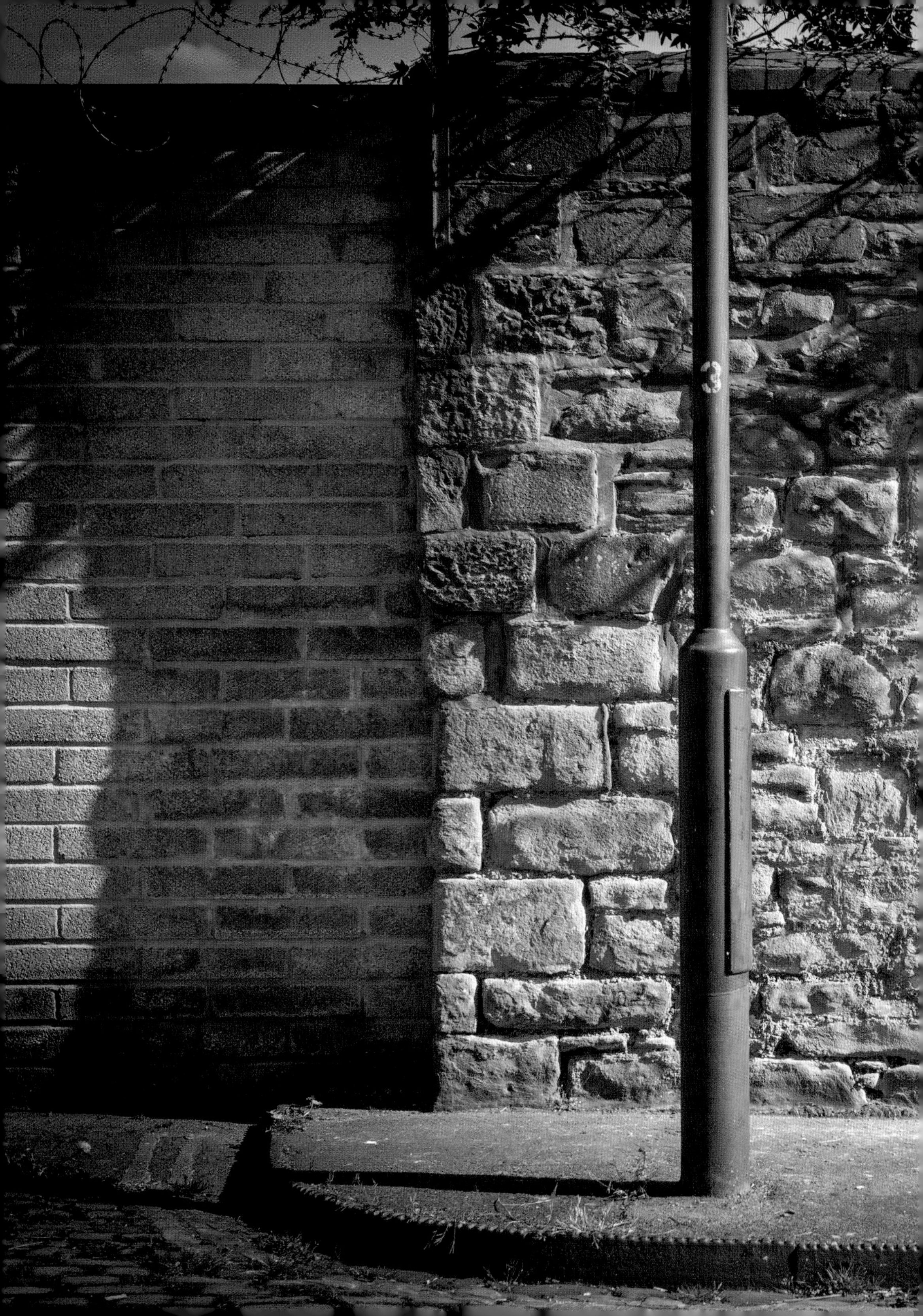

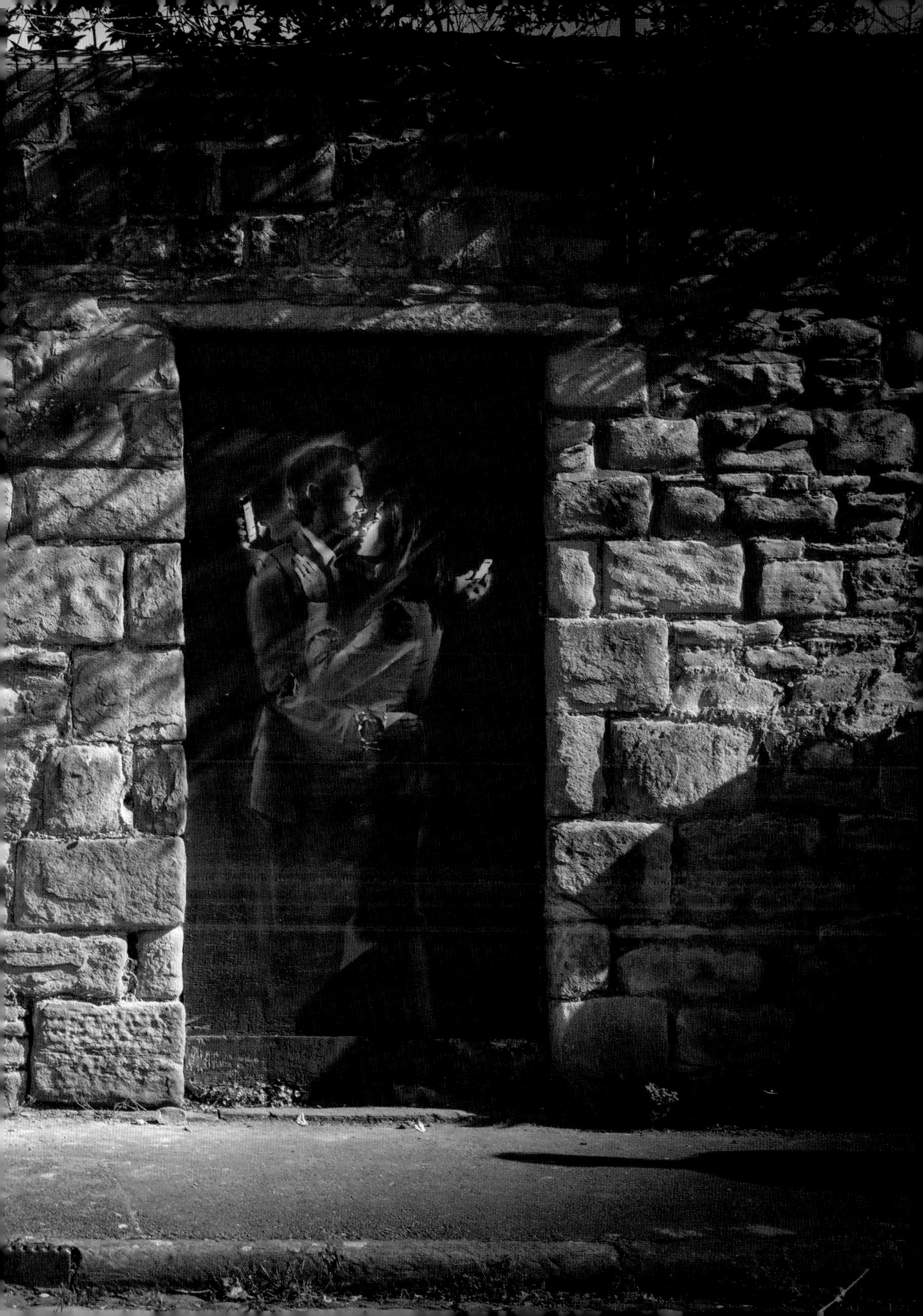

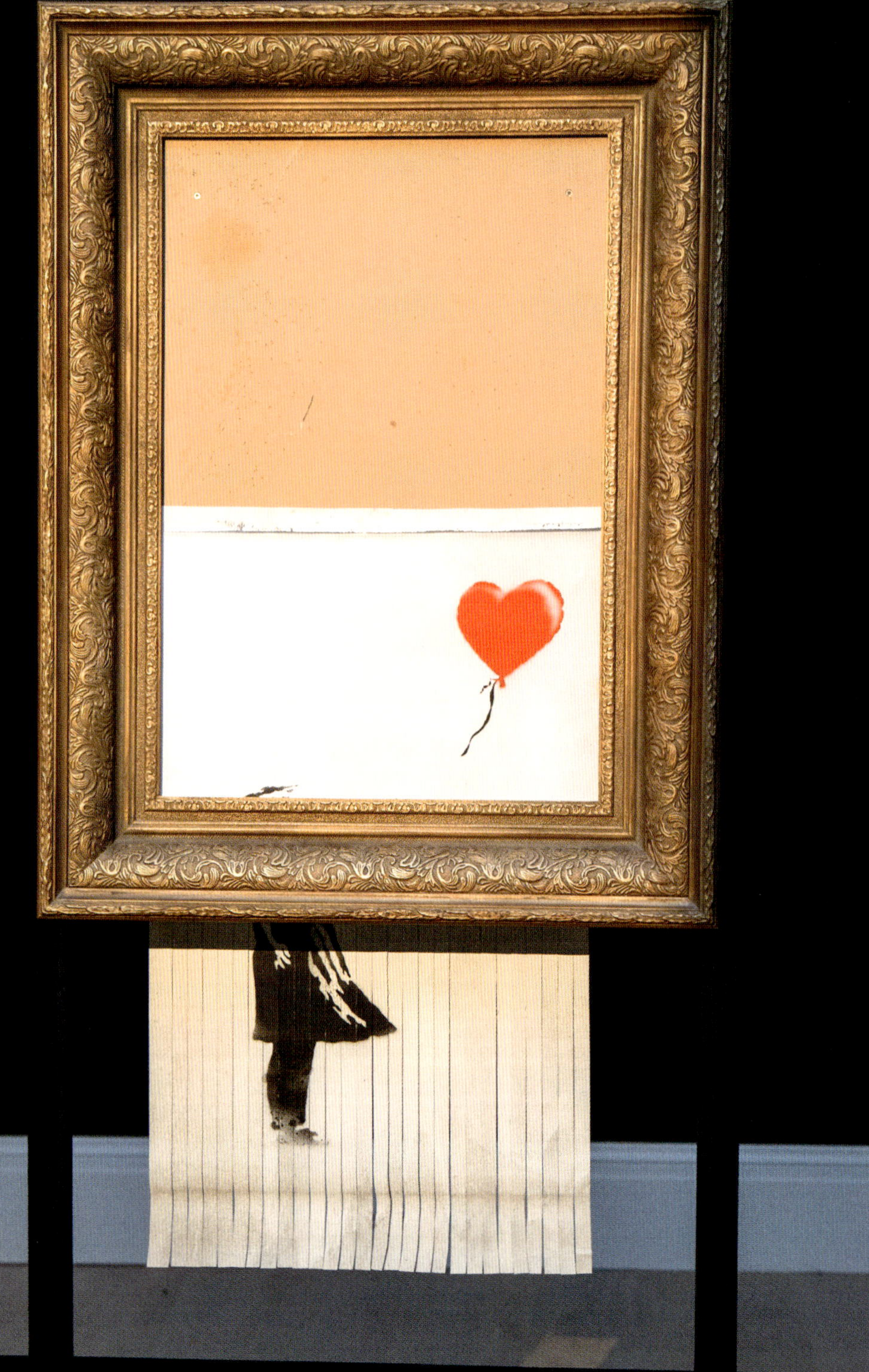

TL;DR
WTF IS BANKSY?

Imagine if you'd never heard of Banksy. Imagine if your nan had never heard of Banksy. How would you describe him?

PRE-EMPTIVE OBITUARY

Born most probably around 1975, somewhere in Bristol, a maritime city in the West Country area of England, Banksy discovered graffiti culture as a schoolboy in the 1980's. In Bristol, Robert del Naja was painting as 3D, capturing the imaginations of Banksy, some ten years his junior.

The potent Bristolian cocktails of Soundsystem culture, punk and West Indian influences, anarchist politics, new age travellers and free parties, and the new sounds of Trip-Hop and Drum and Bass all had an impact on Banksy's 'fluffy and angry' style. His pranks, jokes, black humour and trickery are deeply rooted in English outlaw traditions from Robin Hood to Johnny Rotten.

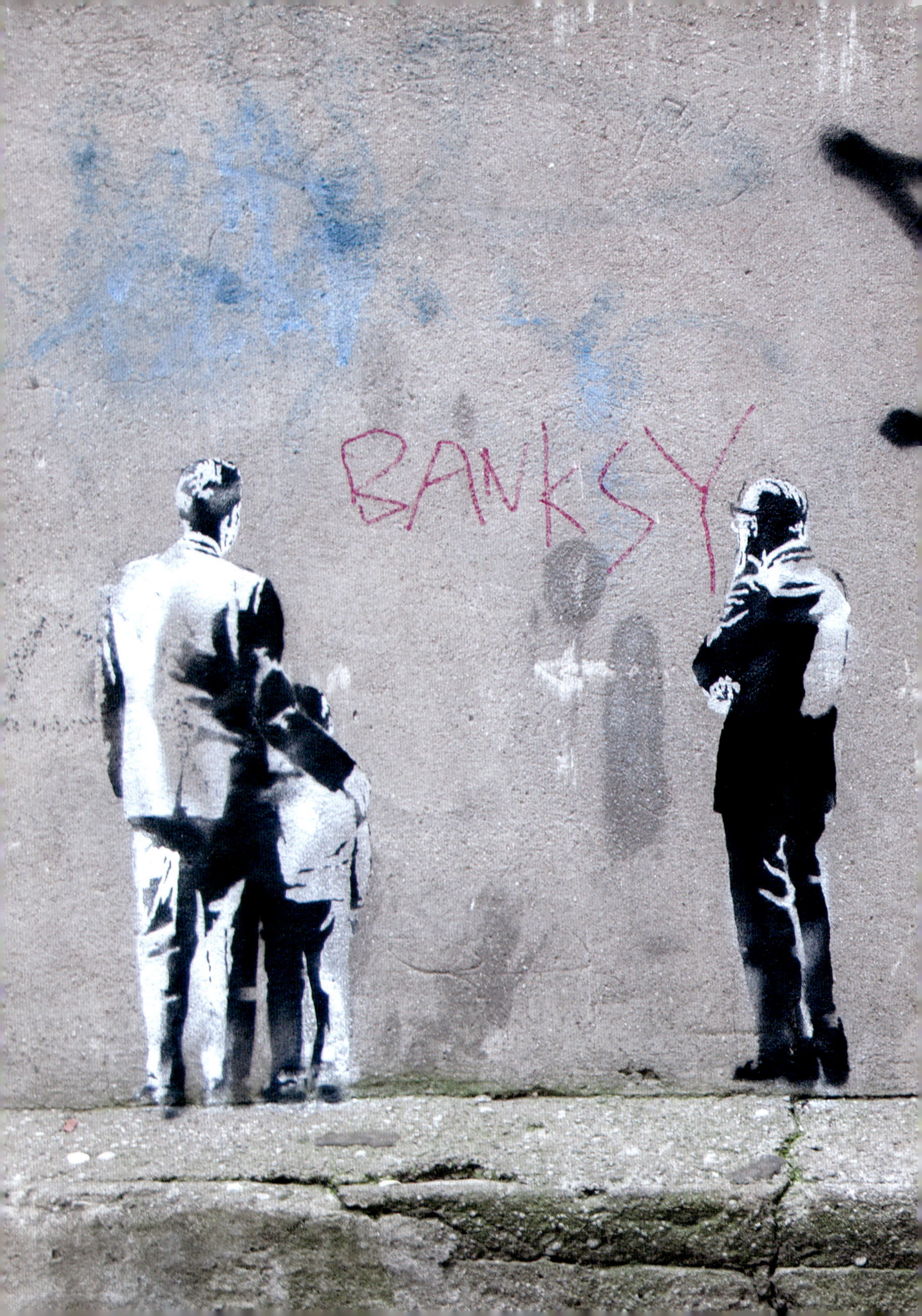
BANKSY

At some point, while hiding from police under a rubbish truck, Banksy was struck by the idea of using stencils to speed up his work and reduce risk. He then began a prolific campaign, travelling across the country and the world, growing ever more audacious in his targets and scale.

Somewhere between 1998 and 2003 Banksy's prolific work, his sense of humour and style and his flashes of righteous anger catapulted him to a level of fame way beyond that of any prior UK street artist. With success came a tricky to navigate relationship with commerce and the art world. Banksy started organising his own art exhibitions in 2003, and with money came ever more elaborate stunts.

From 2003 until the present Banksy has consistently turned out street and gallery work, interspersed with large scale events like his trips to Palestine, Los Angeles, New York, Venice, New Orleans and his opening of twisted leisure facilities like Dismaland, The Walled Off Hotel and the New York Pet Store and Charcoal Grill. Being adopted as the artist of choice for art collecting celebs from Christina Aguilera to Brad Pitt helped to cement his newfound fame.

In spite of (because of?) all his hatred for the Art World, the Art World loves him to death. In 2019 an original Banksy painting sold for 9.9 million pounds. Even when he tried to flick two fingers up at Sotheby's with a self-destructing art work, they only went and sold the half shredded work of art for a higher price.

In spite of his criticisms of Brexit the flat-capped tea-swilling British commoner just loves him too. A YouGov poll in 2019 had Banksy voted as Britain's favourite artist, and a 2017 poll showed Girl with Balloon was the nation's favourite painting. Far from being in danger of arrest, Banksy's work is now protected by local councils, fought over, stolen, chipped off walls and sold. It is so valuable that it provokes a kind of gold fever wherever it appears.

Banksy has attempted in the past to sell his artworks at affordable prices to ordinary people either by doing surprise pop-up sales or using complicated bidding processes as with his recent Croydon shop - however he has an agency dedicated to authenticating his work for anyone lucky enough to find an old print in the attic.

Banksy, an artist who has always hated the power of Big Brands, has with bitter irony become the Biggest Brand of them all. However, he still continues to try and operate according to a value system that he defines, even as he struggles to cope with increasing levels of copyright infringement. As someone whose entire career is theoretically illegal, he can't exactly turn up in court.

But this struggle to remain authentic is something we all experience, as we try to find ways to make money without losing our humanity to it, because with all the best will in the world, there ain't gonna be a revolution tonight.

Sadly, Banksy was run over by a rubbish truck last week. Several paint cans exploded in his knapsack, creating a stencil out of his flattened corpse. Council workers chipped it off the road, it's expected on sale at Sotheby's sometime soon.

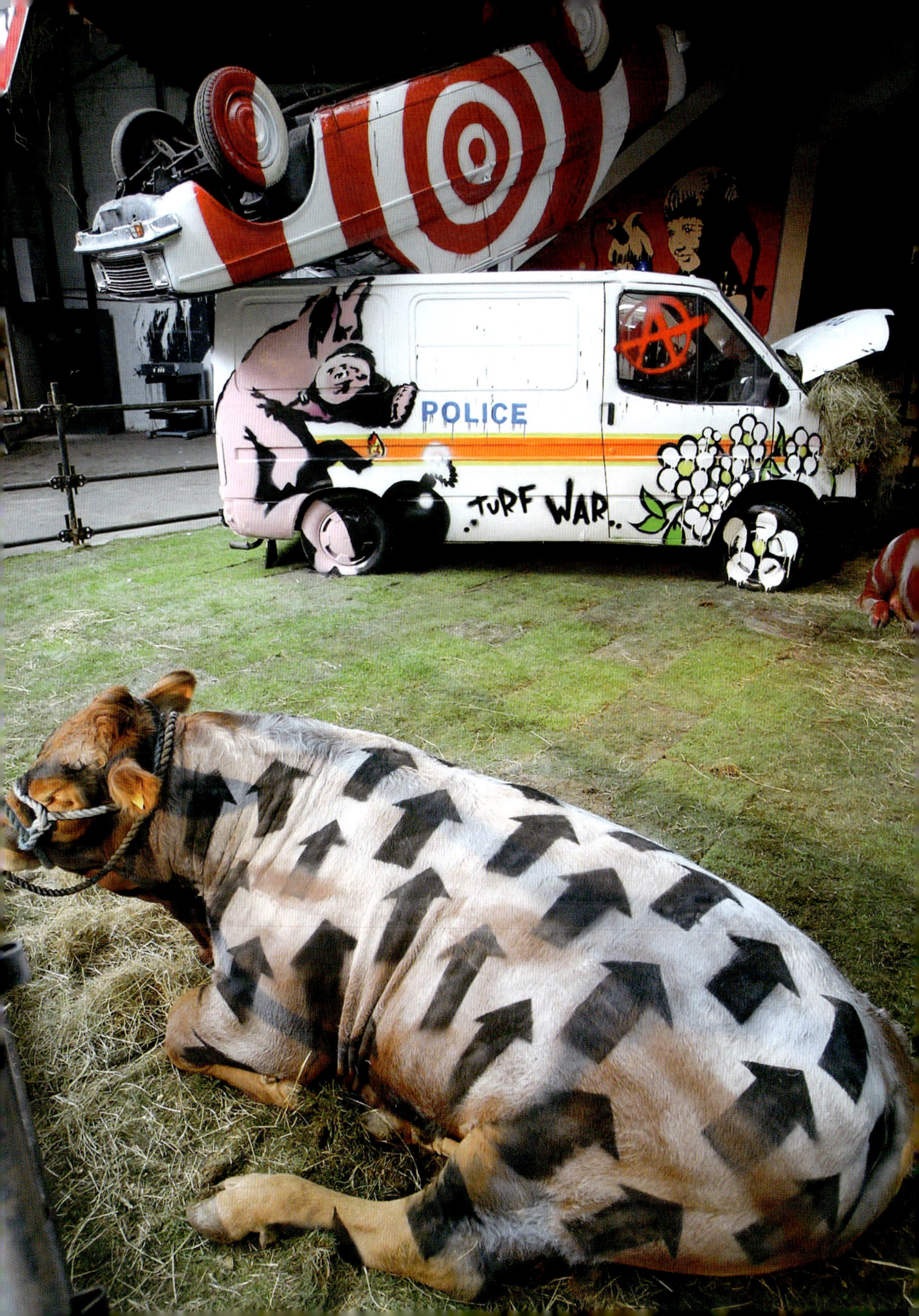

POLICE
TURF WAR

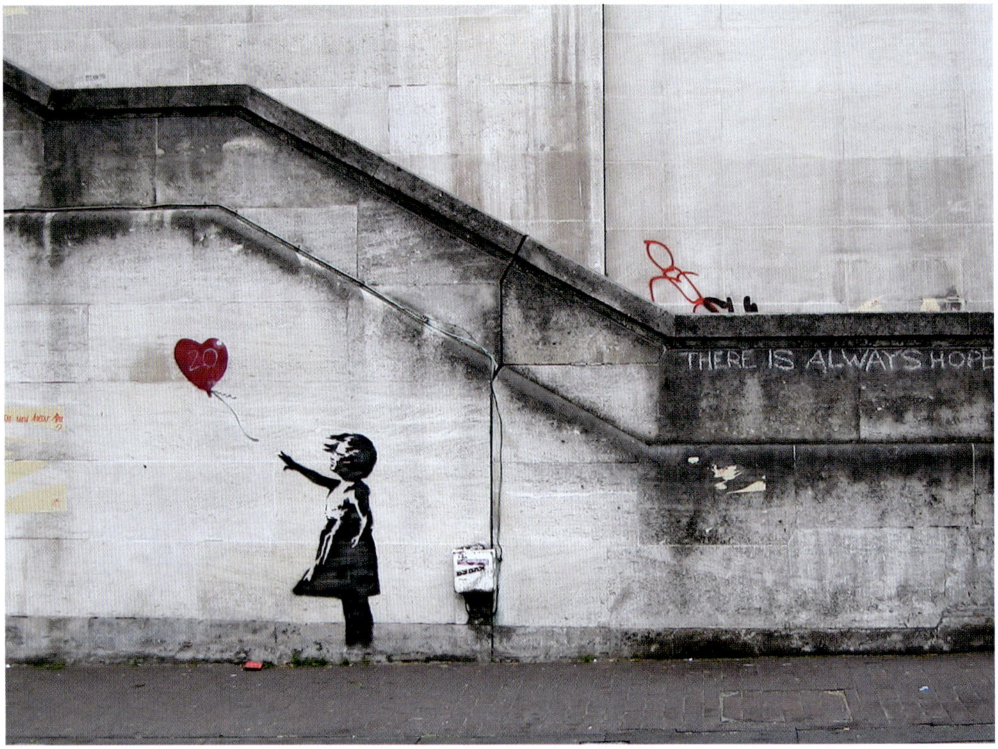

THERE IS ALWAYS HOPE

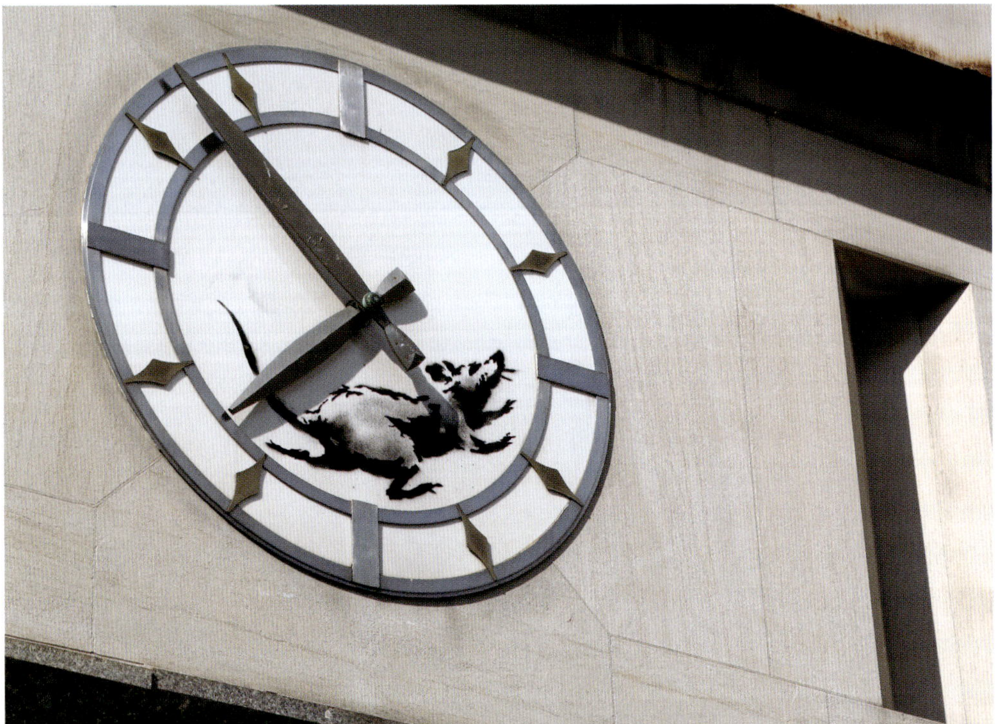

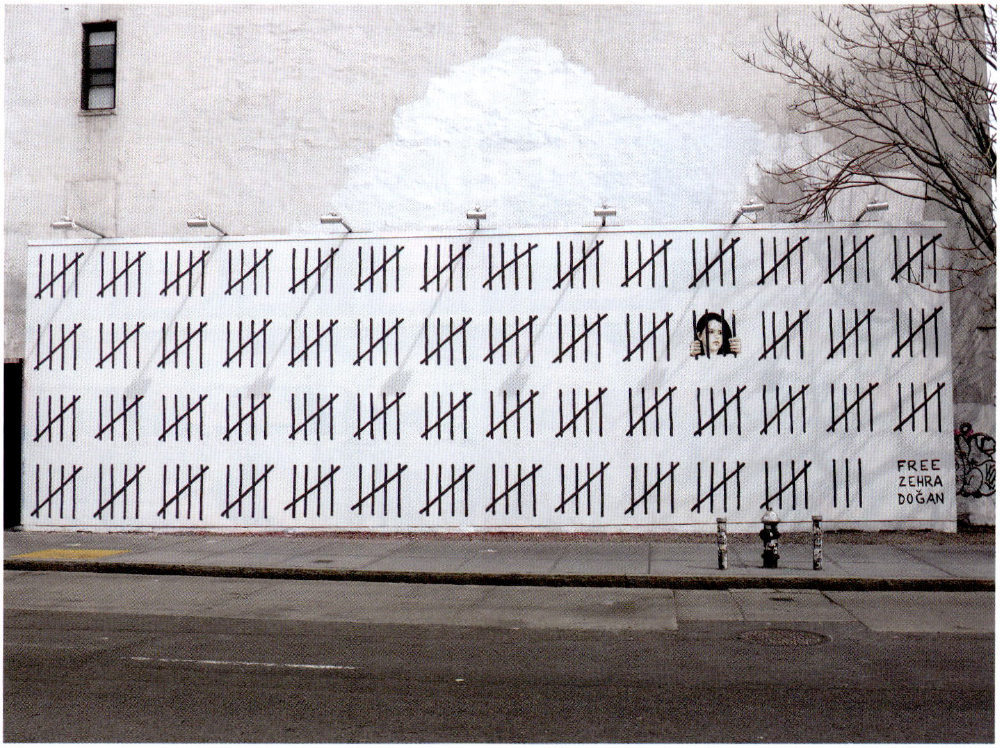

FREE
ZEHRA
DOĞAN

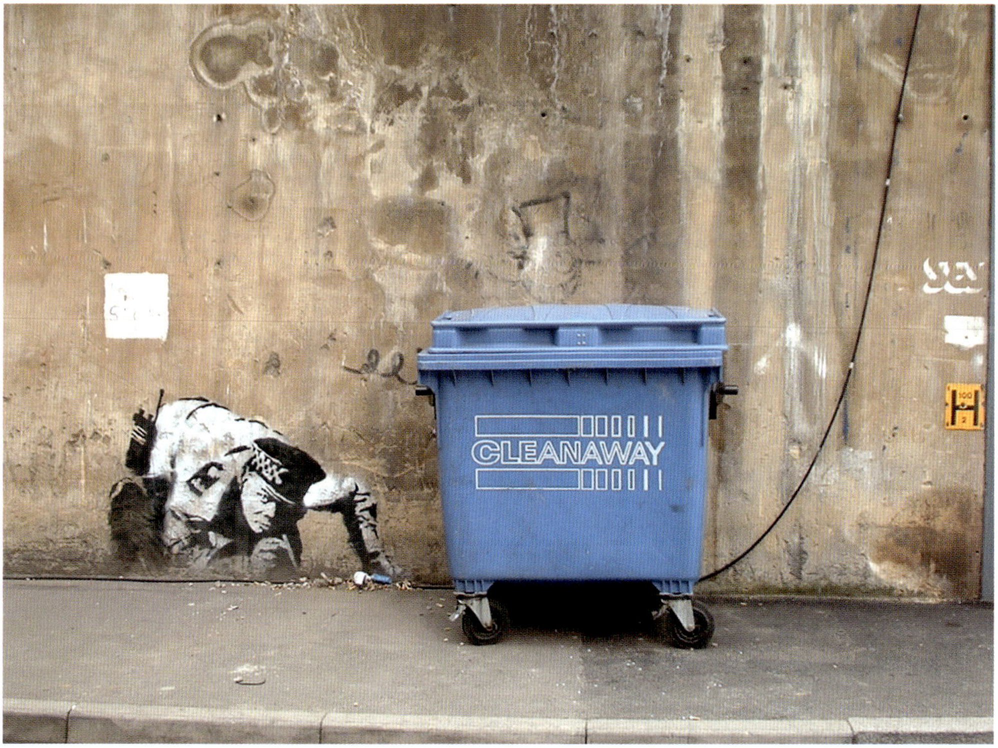

CLEANAWAY

BANKSY TIMELINE

Born **1975** **(?)**	(Robert del Naja AKA '3D' was born ten years earlier.)	**1983**	Rock Steady Crew tour Europe. Hip Hop culture arrives in the old World.
1980 **(?)**	Sister is reported to have thrown a load of his drawings away. "Not like they'll end up in the Louvre."	**1988** **–** **1990**	Ducking and Diving "I was a bootlegger for three years." (A bootlegger who made money out of pirating band merchandise, tapes, CD's, T-Shirts and posters etc)

1989 | Operation Anderson. A major police operation raided the homes of 87 graffiti artists in Bristol, Cardiff, Exeter and Bath. Banksy's friend Inkie was arrested.

1992 | Dial-up internet arrives.

1985 – 1989 | Banksy frequents the Barton Hill Dug Out youth club where remnants of some of his earliest stencil work can be found.

1990 – 1994 | DryBreadZ Crew. So called because they were too poor to butter their toast. Old-school free-hand spray graffiti crew.

1994 | Quentin Tarantino's second smash hit movie 'Pulp Fiction' cements his position as a 1990 icon. Banksy later takes the protagonists as inspiration for one of his most famous murals in London.

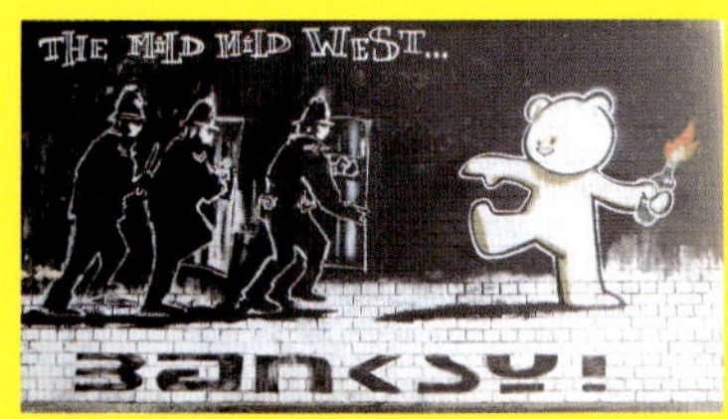

1994 - 1997 — Banksy must have been busy during this period, but it's difficult to find any evidence of this. We know that he was painting his trademark stencil BANKSY, and that he had garnered fame in Bristol by **"spraying his name on the railway bridge over the M32 and cleverly on the railings at the Eastville M32 roundabout junction."** - Bristol Live

1999 — The Mild Mild West. Again, apparently in broad daylight, Banksy demonstrated his growing ambition by painting another large mural in a strategic spot. This iconic Banksy celebrates the anarchists of the 1990's Stoke Croft rave scene, represented by the teddy bear throwing a petrol bomb. It was a response to police intervention at a rave at Winterstoke Road.

1998 — Banksy and Inkie organised a Street Art exhibition at Bristol Docks with permission from the City Council. In broad daylight, wearing a crap disguise, Banksy painted a mural depicting wildstyle graffiti dying on a surgeon's operating table, surrounded by mourning figures. The hoardings were later stolen. Graffiti is dead, long live graffiti.

1999 — First of the 'Reclaim the Streets', May Day Riots in London

2000

During another outburst of fluffy anarchist 'rioting' in Parliament Square London, a 25 year old ex-soldier from Cambridge, James Matthews, vandalised the statue of Winston Churchill with a can of red spray paint and someone capped it off with a chunk of turf as a green mohican. Banksy, who possibly was there, later immortalised this image as a print called 'Turf War'.

2001

I'm pretty sure that Banksy was at the May Day riot this year, because I was and I saw his great big Mona Lisa with a bazooka painted on the boarded up windows of the one of the shop fronts. This was the year of the 'wombles', an amusing group of heavily padded revolutionaries.

2000

Banksy does a front cover for the hipster magazine Sleazenation - it's a Busta Rhymes Stencil.

2001

Banging Your Head Against a Brick Wall. Banksy publishes his first little black book, looking like an anarchist zine and sold in all your anarchist hotspots

2002

Existencilism. Banksy puts his second book out, and you can begin to see how prolific he actually was.

2002 | Banksy went to Glastonbury festival and pulled a number of stunts including painting his parachute rats on a wheel clamp.

2003 | Turf War (Banksy print referencing the May Day 2000 'riot'.)

2003 | The Tate Britain Stunt. Banksy installs "Crimewatch UK Has Ruined The Countryside For All Of Us" while disguised as a pensioner.

2003 | The Guardian interview with Simon Hattenstone.

2003 | Creates the Blur Think Tank album cover.

2004 Banksy puts up 'Mona Lisa Smile' an acid house remix of the original.

2004 The Drinker. Banksy gets into sculpture, using the money from his early success to fund more ambitious street projects. The statue, mocking Rodin's Thinker, was 'kidnapped' by AK47 and held to ransom. It was later stolen again.

2004 Di-Faced Tenner.

2004 "Banksus Militus Ratus" is smuggled into the Natural History Museum, London, near to some ancient artefacts. A stuffed rat with a spray can housed in glass-fronted box its accompanied by a deadpan description card.

2004 CUT IT OUT, the third and final of Banksy's little black books, was published just as he stood on the cusp of breaking into mainstream fame. It shows how much he travelled during this period, boasting work in cities across the globe. The same year, Facebook was launched.

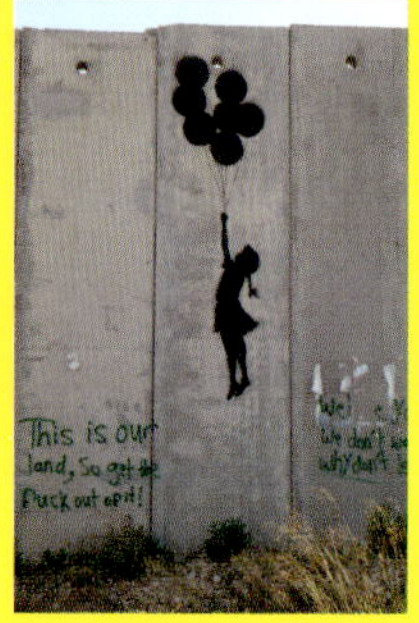

Aug 2005   First Palestine trip. Banksy took a group of artists to paint the division wall between Israel and Palestine.

2005   Banksy publishes a coffee table book 'Wall & Piece' with Century. It was to be his last book. Small wonder that he stopped publishing at this point. With professional photographers hunting his work and the smartphone camera, mobile internet revolution just around the corner - he had no need to document himself anymore.

2005   First LA exhibition, Barely Legal. Banksy courted the West Coast art scene with an extravagant indoor show including a live elephant. After his Elephant moment, Banksy got an increasing taste for sculpture and performance art.

2005   The City of New Orleans was devastated by flooding.

2005   The Paris Hilton CD stunt.

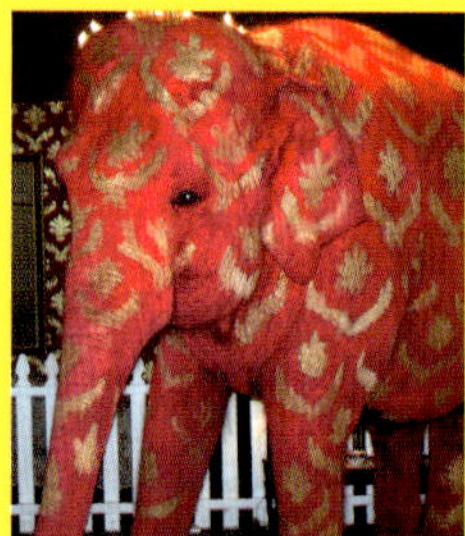

2005 'Peckham Rock' Banksy's take on Cave Painting lasts 3 days stuck to the wall of a gallery in the British Museum.

2006 The Disneyland, Guantanamo stunt. An inflatable doll dressed up as a Guantanamo detainee is deposited alongside the Rocky Mountain Railroad.

2006 Death of a Phone Booth. Banksy expanded his repertoire of sculpture with a murdered telephone box.

2006 Christina Aguilera bought a painting of Queen Victoria enjoying some oral pleasure. Banksy had landed firmly on the A-List.

2006 Banksy painted Well Hung Lover. It was the first Banksy to be retrospectively legalised by Bristol Council. The legalisation of Banksy had begun.

2007 Brad Pitt and Angelina Jolie spent a small fortune on a Banksy original. The Banksy Effect was in full swing. Apple launched a little touch screen phone with a built in camera that was about to change everything.

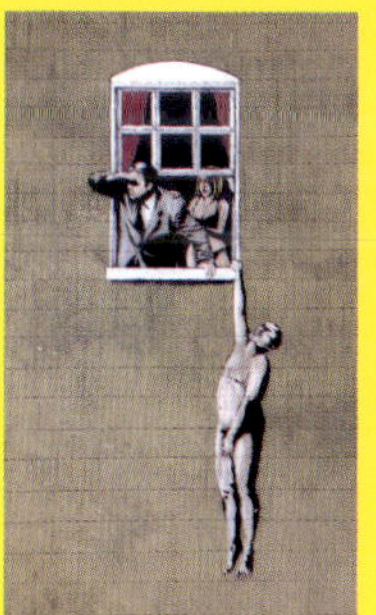

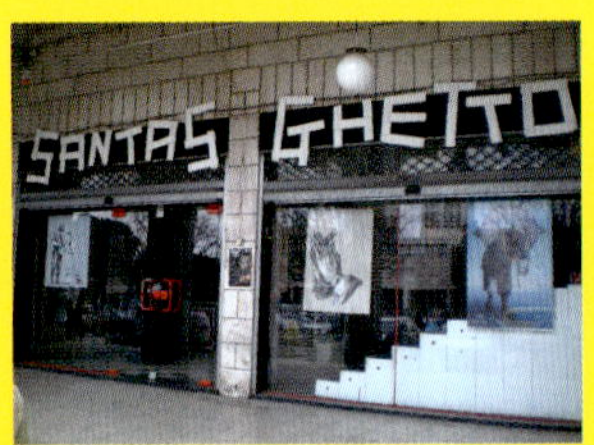

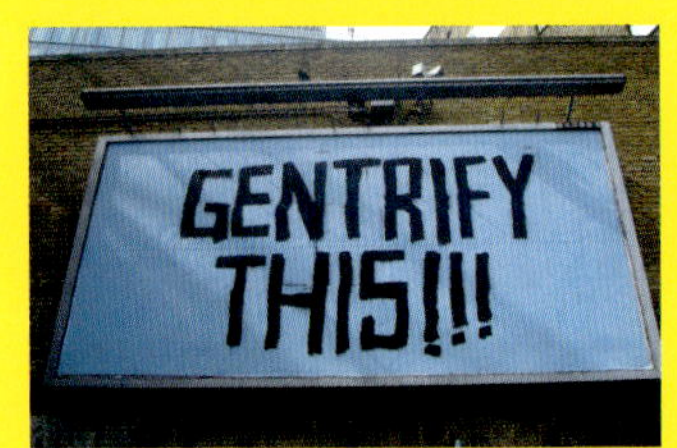

2007 | Banksy relocates the annual Santas Ghetto 'squat art concept store' to Manger Square, Bethlehem. Artists featuring include Ron English, Faile, Bast, Blu, Antony Micallef and Kennard/Phillips alongside local artists

2008 | CANS FESTIVAL. Banksy hired a tunnel near Waterloo Station, London, and invited the top names in noughties Street Art, including Blek le Rat, to fill it with an Exhibition. A man refusing to confirm or deny being Banksy gave an in depth interview to a Daily Mail reporter by the name of Lee Coan.

2008 | Banksy toured New Orleans in an attempt to boost efforts to rebuild.

2008 | Village Pet Store & Charcoal Grill. Banksy moves into performance art installation with his New York pet shop stunt. He used kinetic sculptures to expose our weird double standards about animals as food and as pets. There was also a swipe at fishing practices with a Dolphin caught in a net.

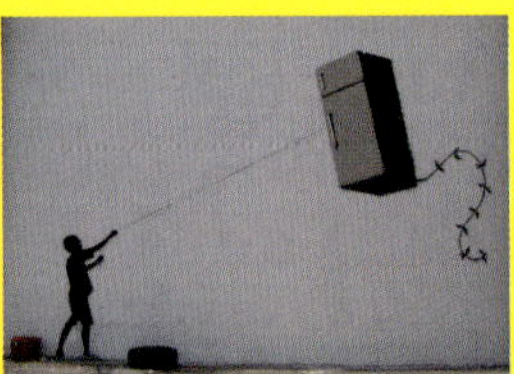

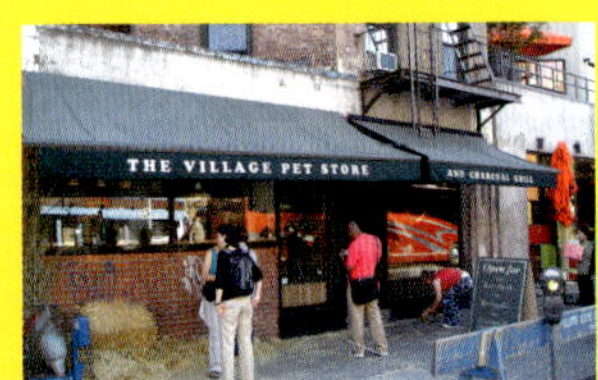

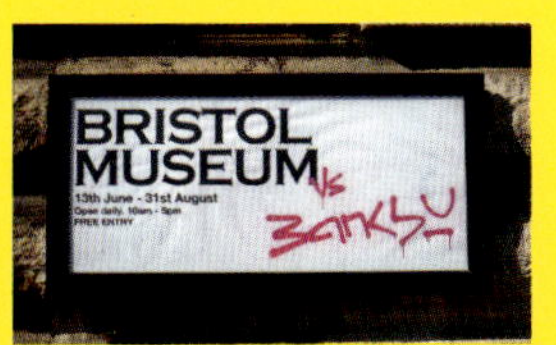

2009   Bristol Exhibition. Banksy painted his largest canvas painting 'Devolved Parliament', originally called 'Question Time' depicting the MP's at question time in the House of Commons all as chimpanzees. Ten years later it sold for nearly £10,000,000 at Sotheby's auction house.

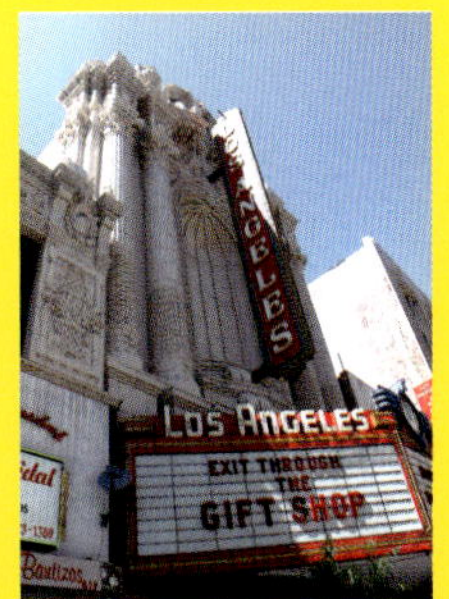

2010   Banksy released his feature length mockumentary 'Exit Through the Gift Shop'. A bizarre yet somehow uplifting practical joke, factual documentary, acutely observed parody of the hipster art world or some mix of all three. It launched the career of Mr Brainwash. The film features the top Street Artists of the moment, including Shepard Fairey.

2009   Banksy set up 'Pest Control' to authenticate his own works **"This process does not make a profit and has been set up to prevent innocent people from becoming victims of fraud."**

2010   Salt Lake City. Banksy paid a visit to the Mormon capital presumably to promote 'Exit Through the Gift Shop' at the Sundance Film Festival.

2010   Banksy made the opening credits couch gag for an episode of The Simpsons.

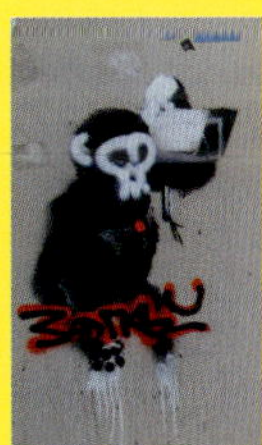

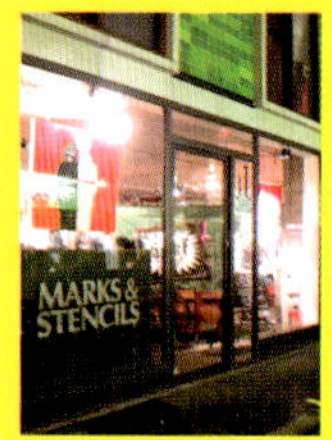

| 2010 | Instagram arrived on the iPhone. | Dec 2010 | Banksy's pop up shop "Marks & Stencils" opens in Soho, London. | 2011 | Banksy releases a print of a petrol bomb featuring Tesco's Value Range branding. In a reference to the Stokes Croft riots, it raises money for the legal defence of people involved. **"It's available exclusively from Bristol's Anarchist Bookfair this coming Saturday. All proceeds go to the People's Republic of Stokes Croft and associates."** |

| 2011 | Google trends shows 2011 as the high water mark for interest in Street Art as a search term. The Street Art craze began to enter a slow decline. Banksy however, remains the one street artist that your mum knows about, probably forever. | 2011 | Stokes Croft Riots, Bristol. On the 21st of April police raided Telepathic Heights. The squat had become the HQ for a campaign to resist the arrival of Tesco on Cheltenham Road. A week later, riots broke out and the new Tesco Metro shop was targeted for attack. |

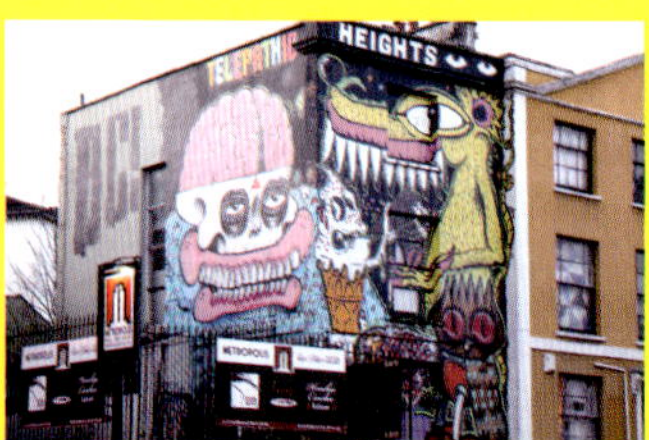

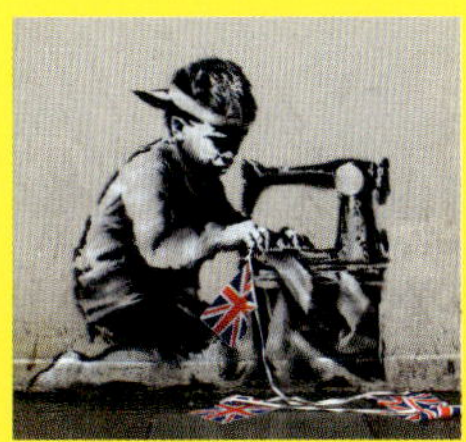

2012 Wood Green, London. Banksy painted a picture 'Slave Labour' of a child labourer sewing Union Jack bunting on the side of a Poundland in protest against sweatshop manufacturing for the Diamond Jubilee and London Olympics.

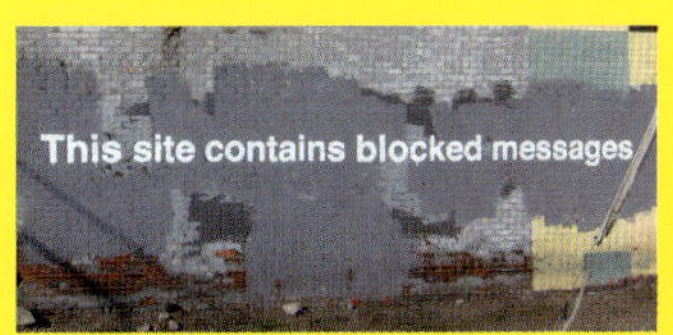

2013 'Better Out Than In' Banksy held his first month long 'residency' in New York painting a large number of works, displaying two altered vehicles (Sirens of the Lambs and a 'moving truck of paradise') and one pop up art sale in which he shifted a load of canvases for 60 dollars a pop before anyone realised that they were authentic Banksy. He also donated an original painting 'the banality of the Banality of Evil' to a thrift store (charity shop).

2013 'Slave Labour' was removed, stolen and shipped to Miami for auction. After complaints lodged by residents of Wood Green the sale was cancelled and the piece returned to London, where it was then sold at auction anyway. Banksy's statement on this sort of thing was: **"For the sake of keeping all street art where it belongs I'd encourage people not to buy anything by anybody unless it was created for sale in the first place."** Daily Mail

2014 Mobile Lovers. Seven years after the iPhone was released, Banksy was taking aim at our brave new state of digital alienation. He painted two lovers looking over each other's shoulders at their smartphones.

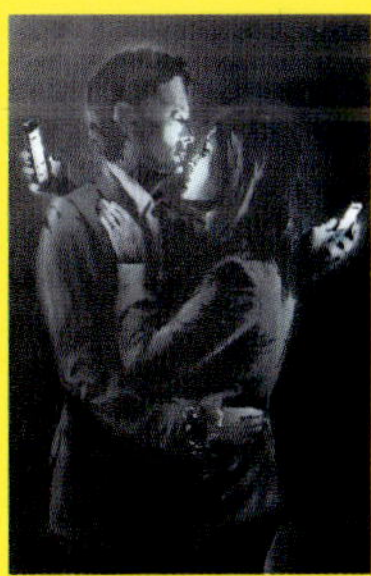

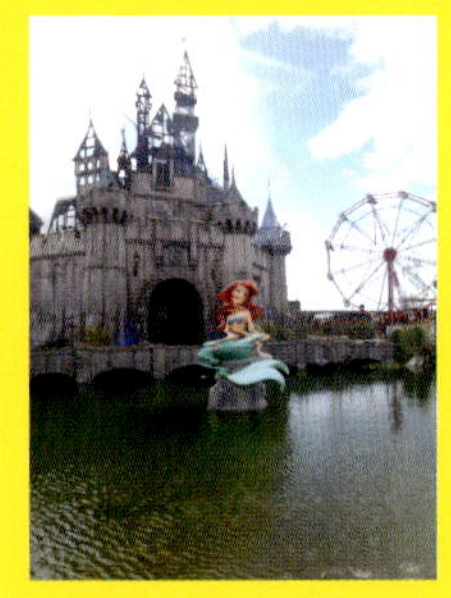

2014 Banksy went back to Glastonbury with his animal rights piece 'Sirens of the Lambs' a truck packed with squealing soft toys, en route to the abattoir.

2015 Dismaland, Weston-super-Mare. Banksy pulled off his largest outdoor installation to date with a miserable theme park. The attraction involved a huge collaboration, featuring 58 artists including ten Banksy originals.

2014 The Summer War, Israel punished Palestine for the terrorist murder of three Israeli teenagers, with a seven week campaign of airstrikes and ground bombardment. Hundreds were killed.

2015 Back to the Gaza Strip. In the aftermath of the Summer War Banksy returned to draw attention to the plight of the Palestinians now living in the rubble.

2016 Les Mis. In a heartfelt response to the suffering of migrants in Calais, opposite the French Embassy in London, Banksy painted the famous image of the girl from the musical Les Miserables, eyes streaming with tears, shrouded in the smoke from a tear gas canister. The piece featured a QR code linking to a video of french police using tear gas on refugees.

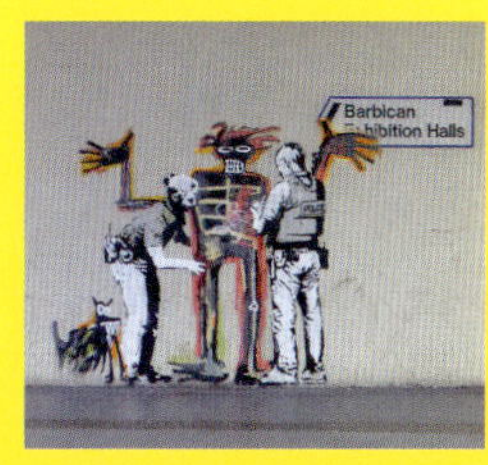

2016 After a campaign marked by disinformation and appeals to popular fears of immigration, the British voted to leave the European Union 52% to 48%.

2017 Boom For Real. As homage to street art pioneer Jean Michel Basquiat during a retrospective exhibition In London. Banksy puts up two works close to the Barbican in London.

2017 Brexit, Election Souvenir Special. Prime Minister Teresa May pulled a snap election that exploded in her face and Banksy commemorated the moment with a mural in Dover showing a man chipping one of the stars off the European flag. Dover is significant as a gateway to Europe, being the busiest passenger port to France and a Leave (62%) stronghold.

2017 Walled Off Hotel. The most ambitious and thoughtful of Banksy's long term installation projects - the Walled Off is a real hotel situated in Bethlehem, where many of the rooms feature a view of the division wall itself. The hotel opened in the centenary year since the British took control of Palestine after WW1 and drew attention to the British imperial blundering that triggered the century-long conflict in the region.

2017 Girl With a Balloon was voted Britain's Best-Loved artwork

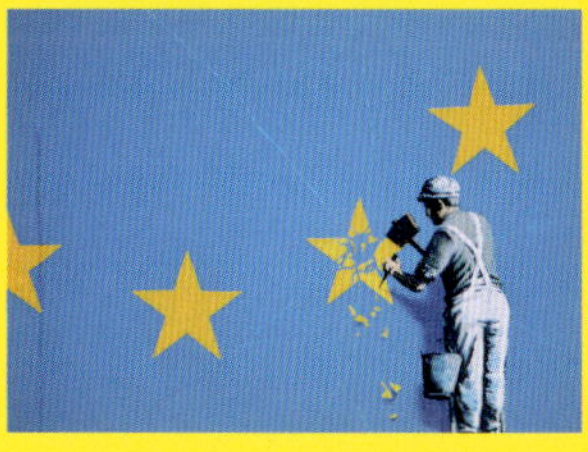

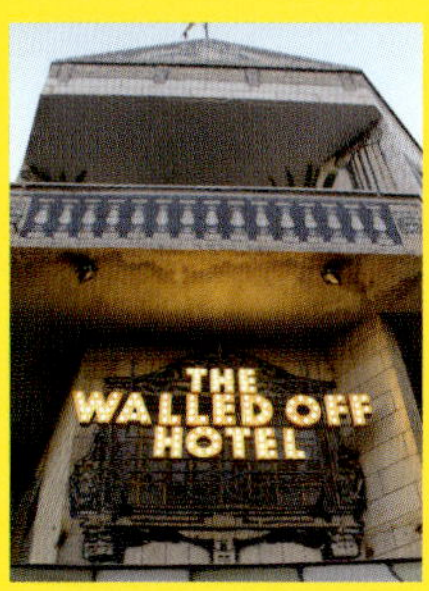

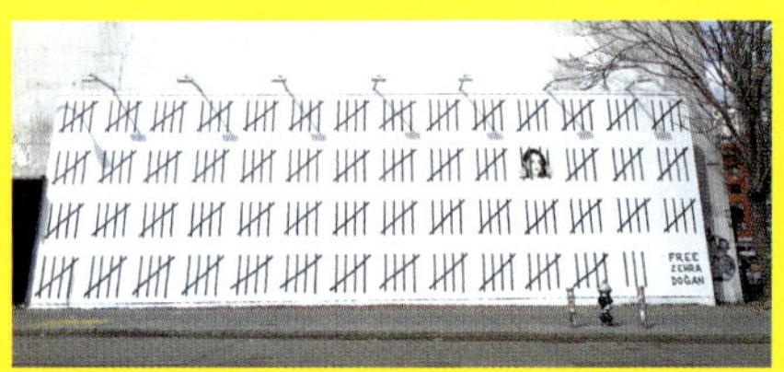

2018 | Second New York 'Residency'. Banksy paints a series of works across NYC including the stock broker whipping fleeing families with a red arrow, and a mural protesting the imprisonment of Zehra Dogan.

2018 | The Self-Destructing canvas. In the middle of an auction at Sotheby's the print for sale, a framed Girl with Balloon, was minced by a hidden shredder inside the frame itself.

2019 | Stormzy wore Banksy's stab proof vest for his triumphant Glastonbury headline set. The vest, painted with a grungy Union Flag, references the rising rate of knife crime in the greater London area.

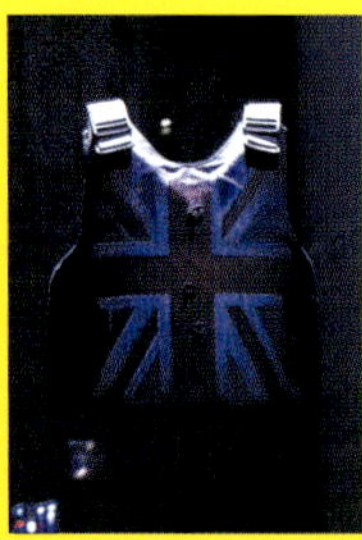

2019 | Gross Domestic Product. Banksy opened a shop that never opened in Croydon (perhaps not coincidentally, the hometown of Stormzy). The shop functioned as a defence of his intellectual property. It was also an attempt to sell Banksy originals to ordinary people at affordable prices, using a lottery ticket system to sell the artworks on display in the shop.

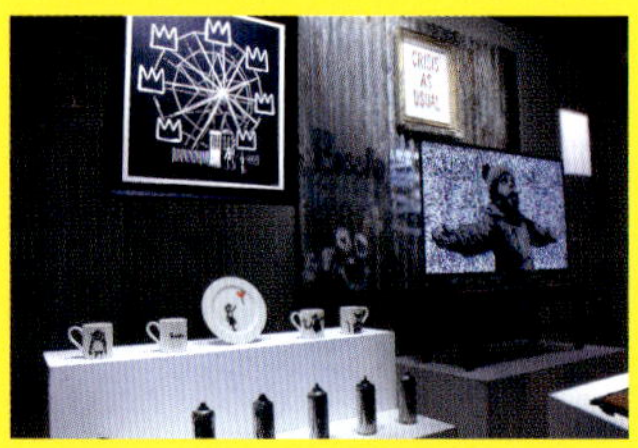

2019 | Banksy was voted Britain's favourite artist of all time in a poll run by YouGov, beating a list of big hitters including Claude Monet, Vincent Van Gogh, John Constable, Leonardo Da Vinci, JMW Turner, Pablo Picasso, Salvador Dali, LS Lowry, Michelangelo.

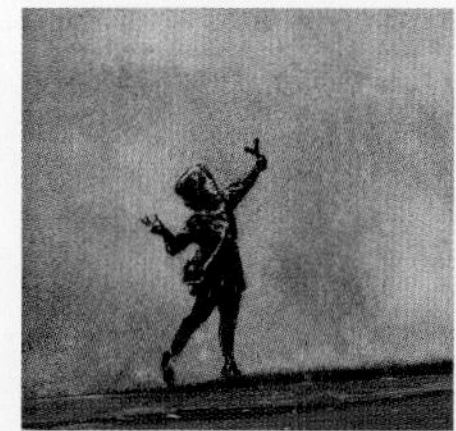

2020 | Valentine's Day. Banksy revisited his most iconic image, the Balloon Girl with an artwork depicting the Balloon Heart shot down by a girl with a catapult. A few short weeks later, the nation was in lockdown under the COVID-19 pandemic.

Mar 2020 | The UK goes into lockdown in response to the COVID-19 Pandemic.

May 2020 | Banksy unveils a large painting at Southampton General hospital showing a small boy ditching his superhero toys to play with a toy nurse.

Apr 2020 | Banksy tweets an image of his own vandalised bathroom with the message 'My wife hates it when I work from home'.

Jul 2020 | Disguised as a maintenance worker Banksy appears on a tube train and paints a tag in drippy snot green along with a few rats. The tweet was captioned 'If you don't mask you don't get'.

Jul 2020

Banksy donates a tryptich painting 'Mediterranean Sea View 2017'. It's a reworked romantic oil seascape with a political message previously displayed in the lobby of the Walled Off Hotel featuring washed up life jackets highlighting the migrant crisis. It's sold to raise funds for BASR hospital in Bethlehem towards building a new acute stroke unit and rehabilitation. The work sells for £2.2m at auction.

Sept 2020

Art Attack's Neill Buchanan rebuts a conspiracy theory that he is in fact Banksy.

Aug 2020

Banksy funds the 31m high speed lifeboat 'Louise Michel' patrolling the Mediterranean Sea to rescue refugees.

The former French Navy boat features a modified painting of 'Girl with Balloon' but with the balloon converted to a safety float. Named after a 19th Century French anarchist it's captained by a crew with a 'flat hierarchy and a vegan diet'

'We answer the SOS call of all those in distress, not just to save their souls - but our own'.

Oct 2020

Banksy loses his copyright battle after refusing to reveal his identity to Judges in the EU trademark ruling over 'Flower Thrower'.

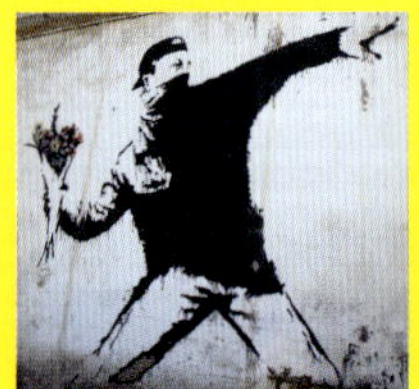

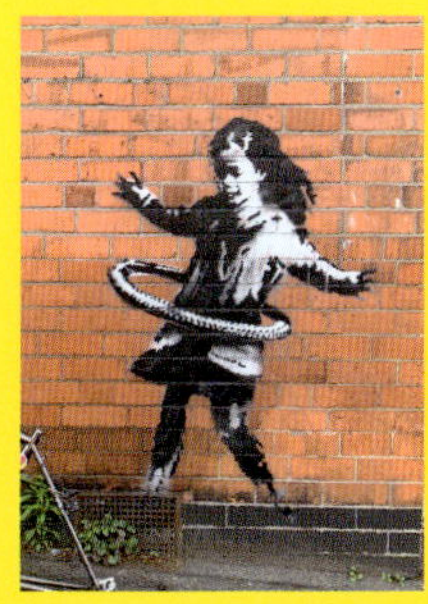

Oct 2020

Hula Hoop Girl appears in Lenton, Nottingham. An installation piece featuring a hula-hooping girl with a bicycle tyre, alongside a bike chained to a metal post missing its back wheel.

Oct 2020

'Show Me The Monet' sells for £7,551,600 at Sothebys. A re-imagining of Monet's impressionist water lilies featuring shopping trolley and traffic cone. It becomes his second most expensive work sold to date.

Dec 2020

'Aachoo!!' appears on the side of a house for sale in Totterdown, Bristol. An area famous for its Easter Sunday egg rolling contest. The piece depicts an old woman sneezing and her dentures taking flight.

In a new high of hysteria the media estimates that the price of the £300,000 house could now be worth an extra £5m.

Feb 2021

Nottingham's Hula Hoop Girl mural is removed and sold to a collector for a six figure sum, much to the frustration of local residents.

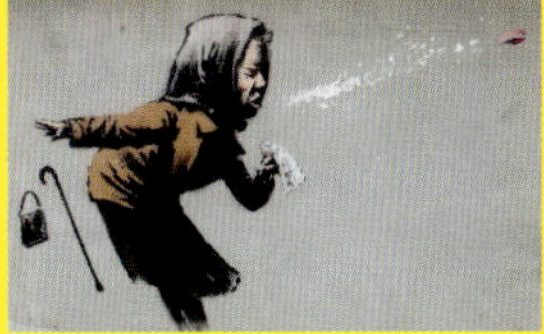

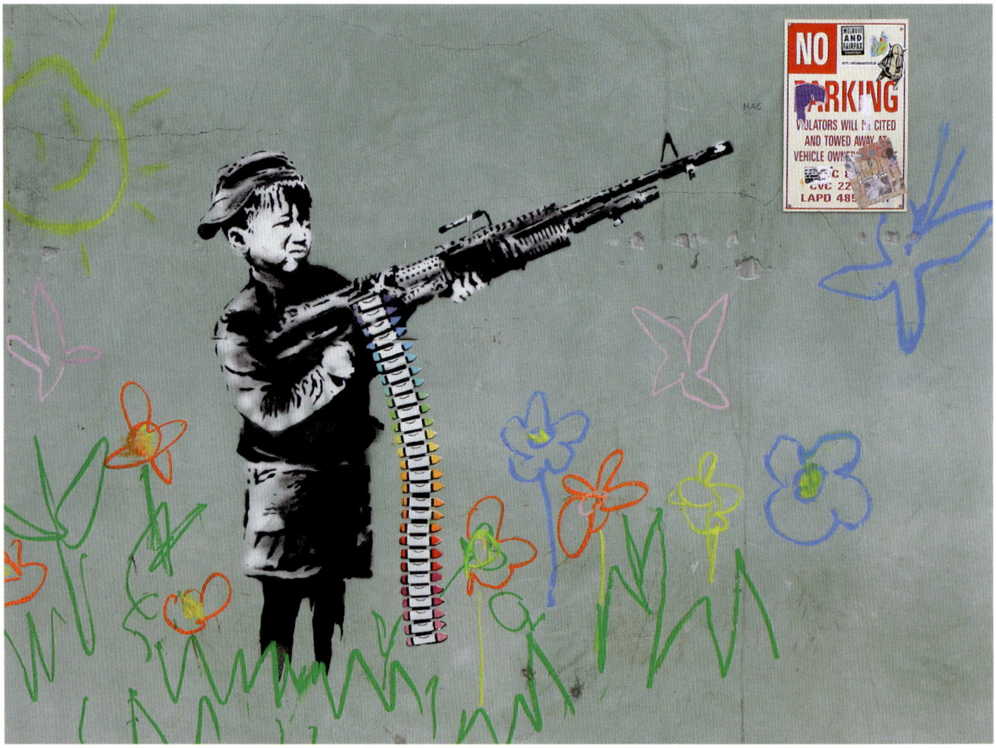

MELROSE
AND
FAIRFAX
NO
PARKING
VIOLATORS WILL BE CITED
AND TOWED AWAY AT
VEHICLE OWNER
CVC 22
LAPD 485

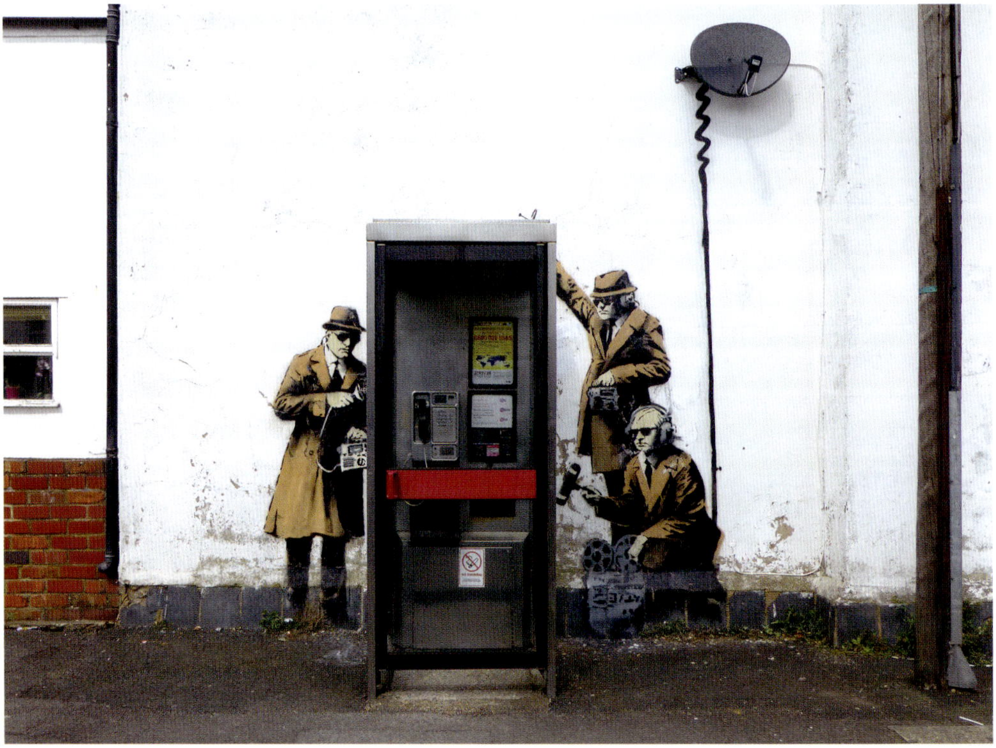

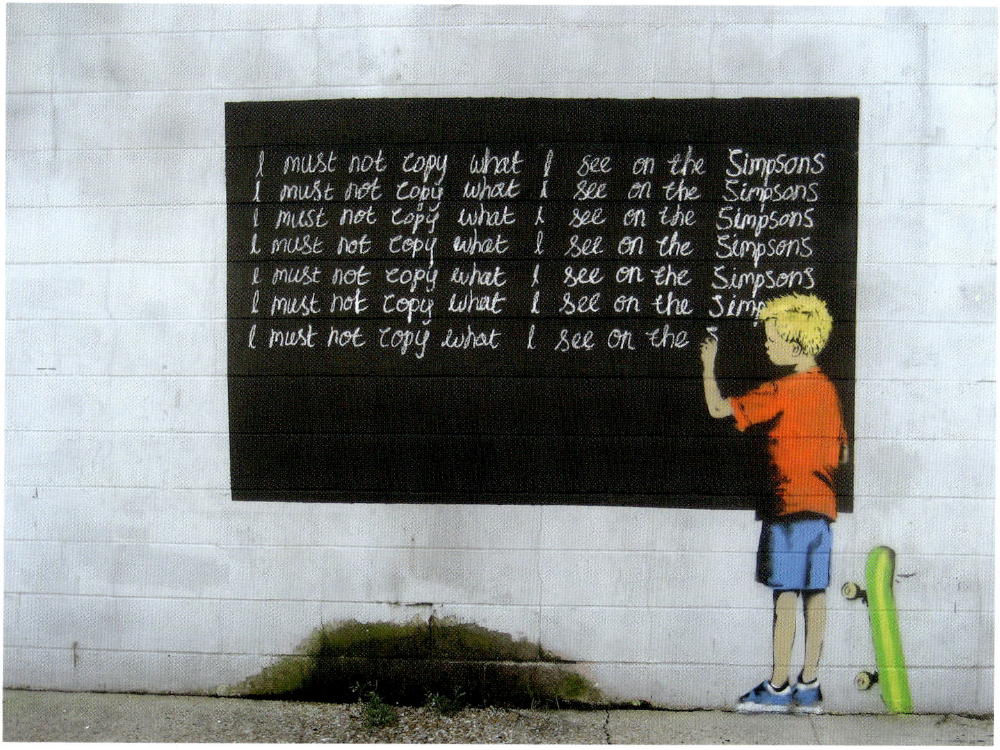

I must not copy what I see on the Simpsons
I must not copy what I see on the Simpsons
I must not copy what I see on the Simpsons
I must not copy what I see on the Simpsons
I must not copy what I see on the Simpsons
I must not copy what I see on the Simp
I must not copy what I see on the S

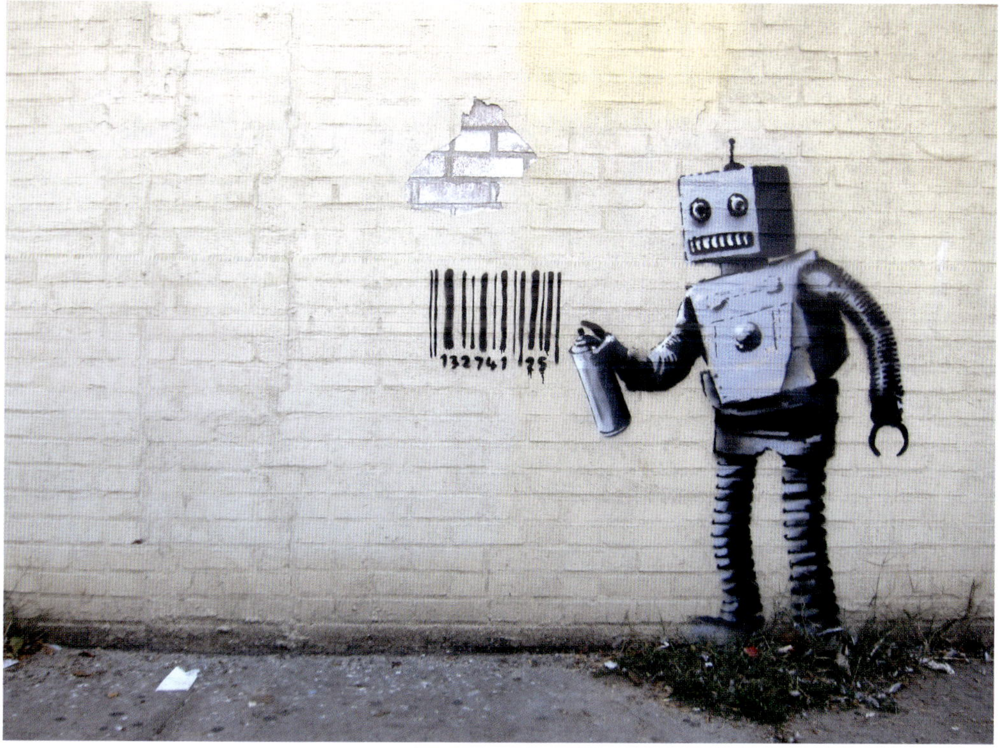

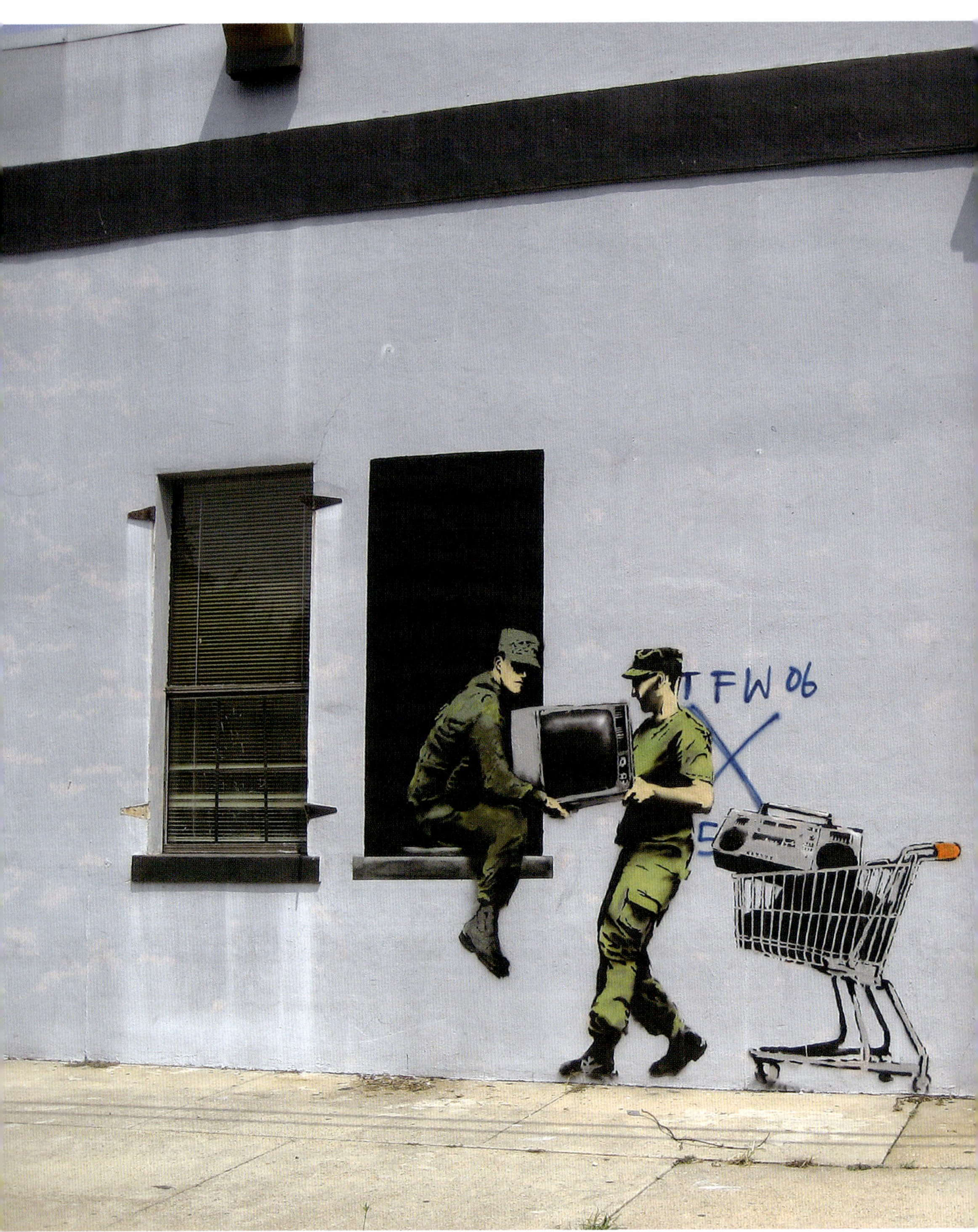
T F W 06

KEEP LEFT

This is a call...

Once upon a time I was a young man who wanted to change the world. At the time it seemed to me that nobody else did. It was the time of Tony Blair, and the End of History. We lived in the best of all possible worlds, they said. And I saw Banksy's work, and it gave me hope, naive as I was, that there was an underground, that there was a resistance. And when I found his little black books, I devoured them, alongside the Schnews and all kinds of other anarchist small press. I believed in it all fanatically. But I never figured out a way to change the world. And the world still needs a changin'. So I want to dedicate this book to young people who believe they can change the world. Because, sooner or later, maybe some of them will be right...

This is dedicated to the wild eyed young rebels, hopped up on hope and the dizzy high of holy angers. Those who clutch, like a sacred text, the pamphlets of old revolutionaries, trying to extract every drop of hope that the underground still lives, that the resistance is real. Scouring the works of revolutionary artists, trying to find out how to push the dream of another world forward, right here, right now, against all odds.

Hurry! Before the cynicism grows, before the knowing of the world turns your rebellion into another British sneer, another biting black comedy.

Every generation carries the promise of a new world, and then thirty years later, it's all mortgages and pensions, defeated and broken. But this is not some force of nature. It is engineered. And just maybe, your generation will be the one that frees us all from this gloom and banality.

Many campaigns have been fought. Many have fallen. This is the story of one such.

From Banksy to Banksyism.

Patrick Potter

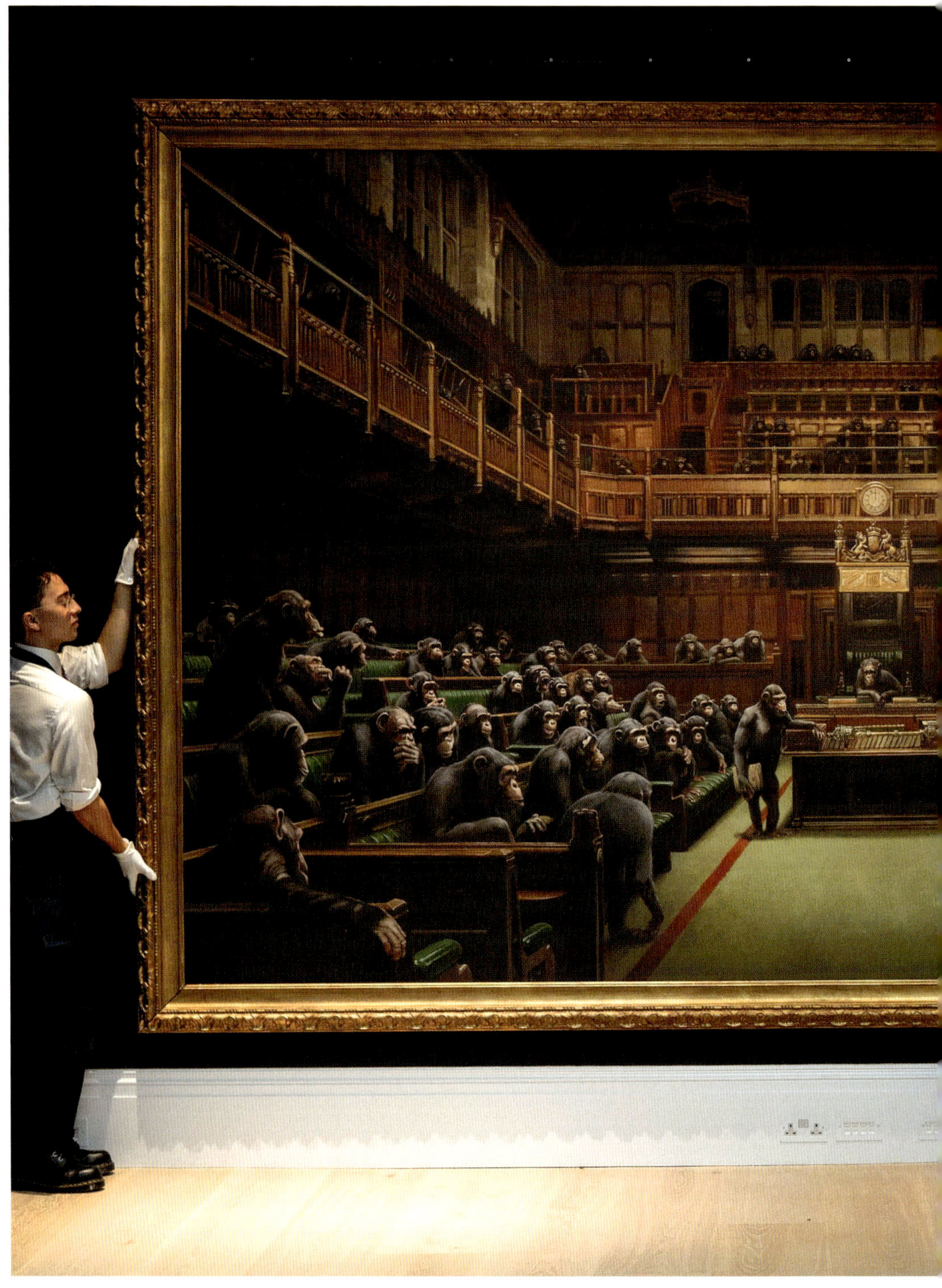

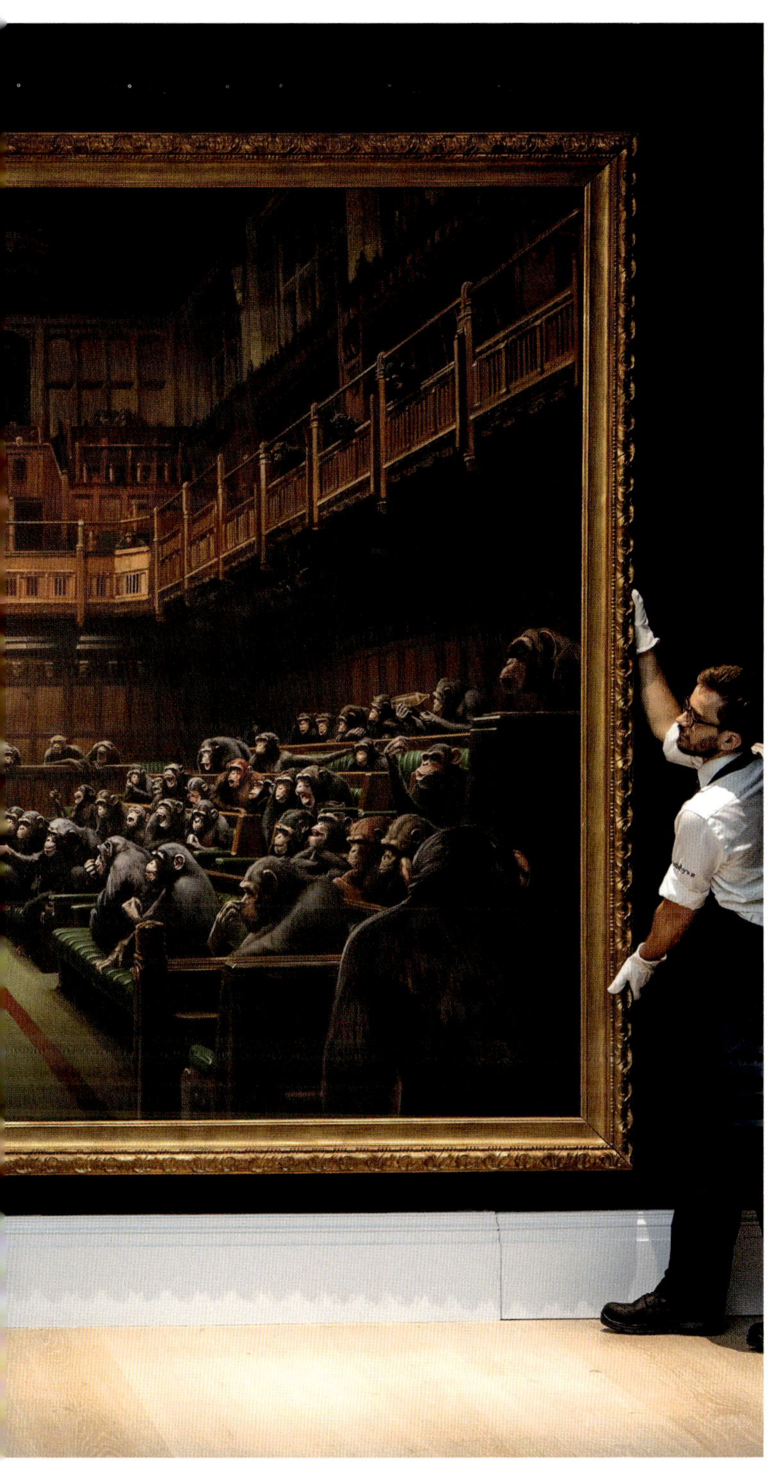

Devolved
Parliament,
painted in 2009.

When first shown at
the Bristol Museum &
Art Gallery takeover
in 2009 it was titled
Question Time. Sold in
2019 at Sotherby's for
£9.9 million.

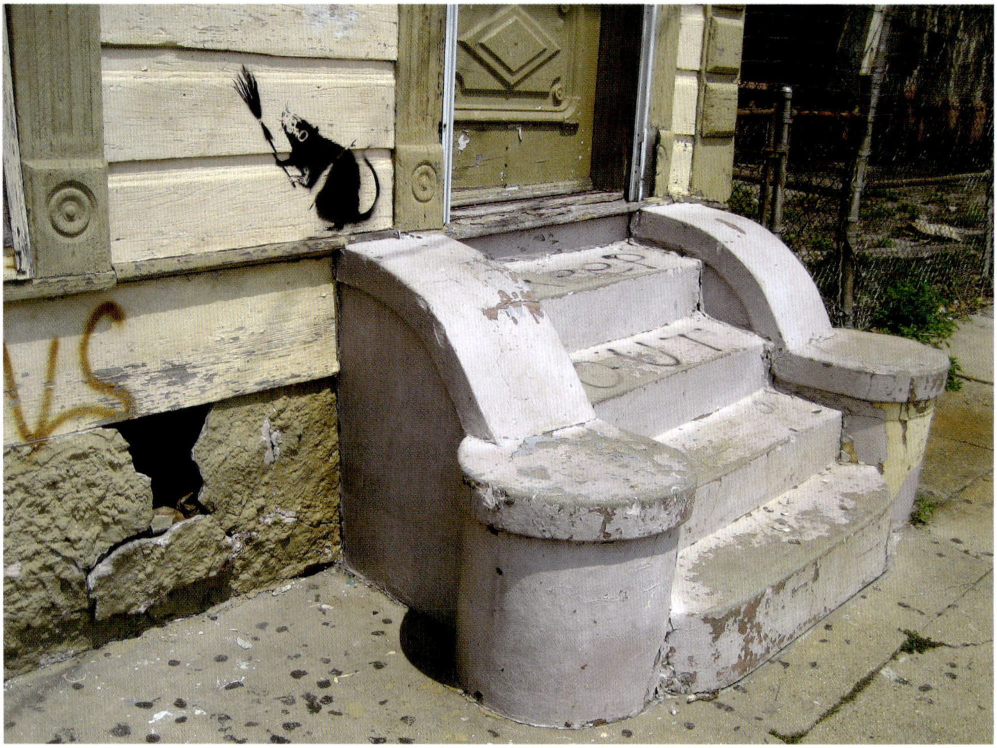

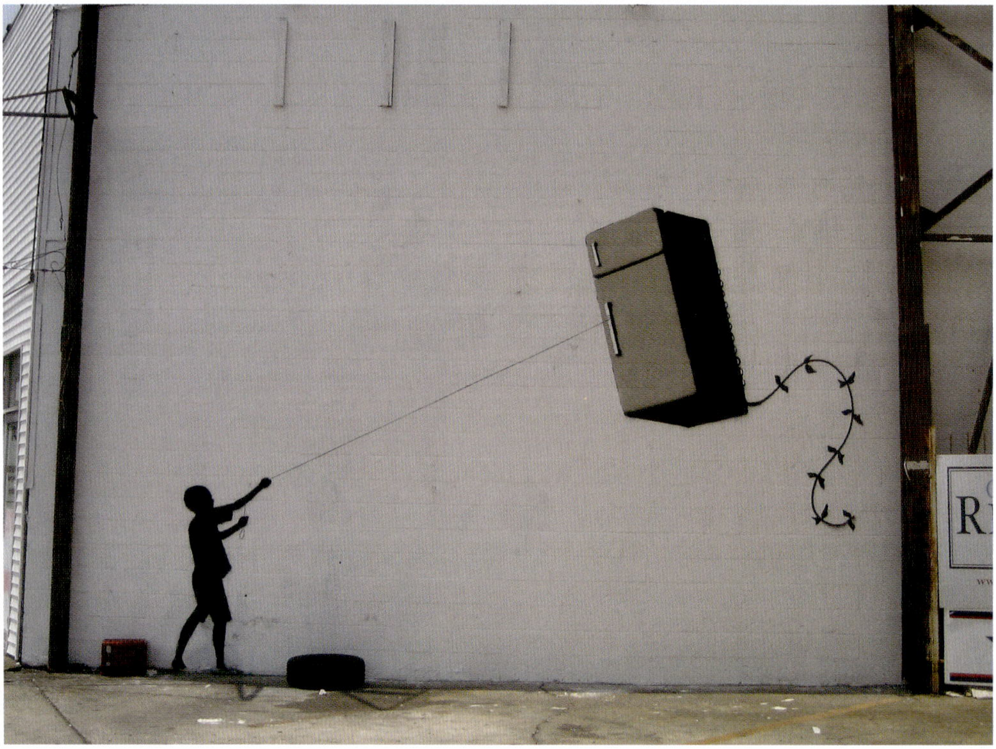

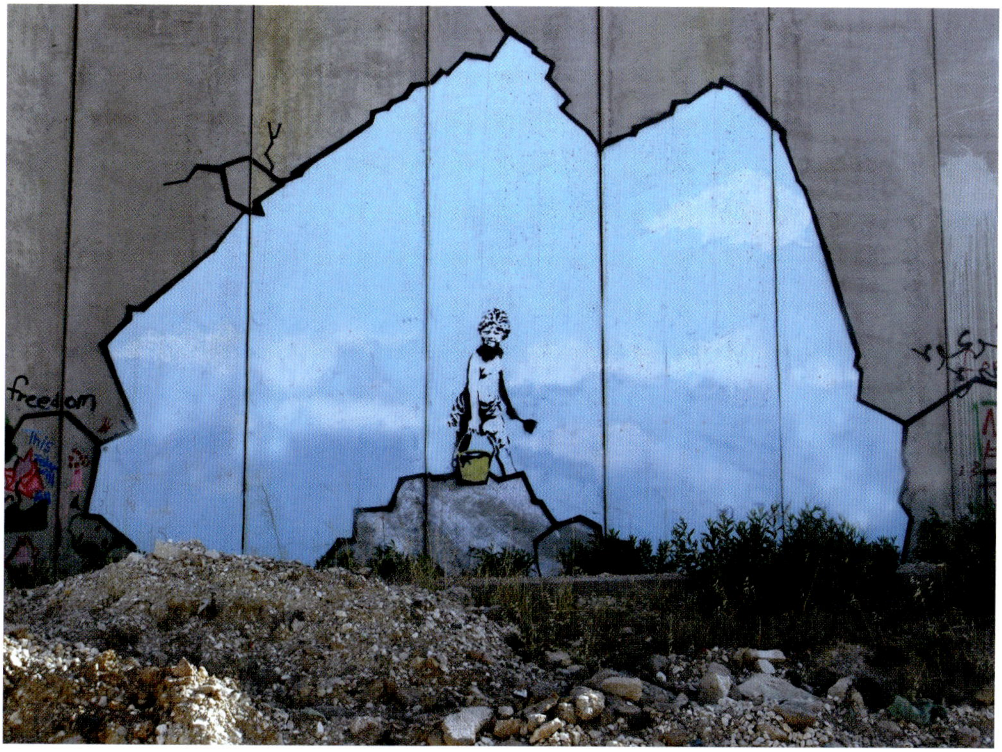

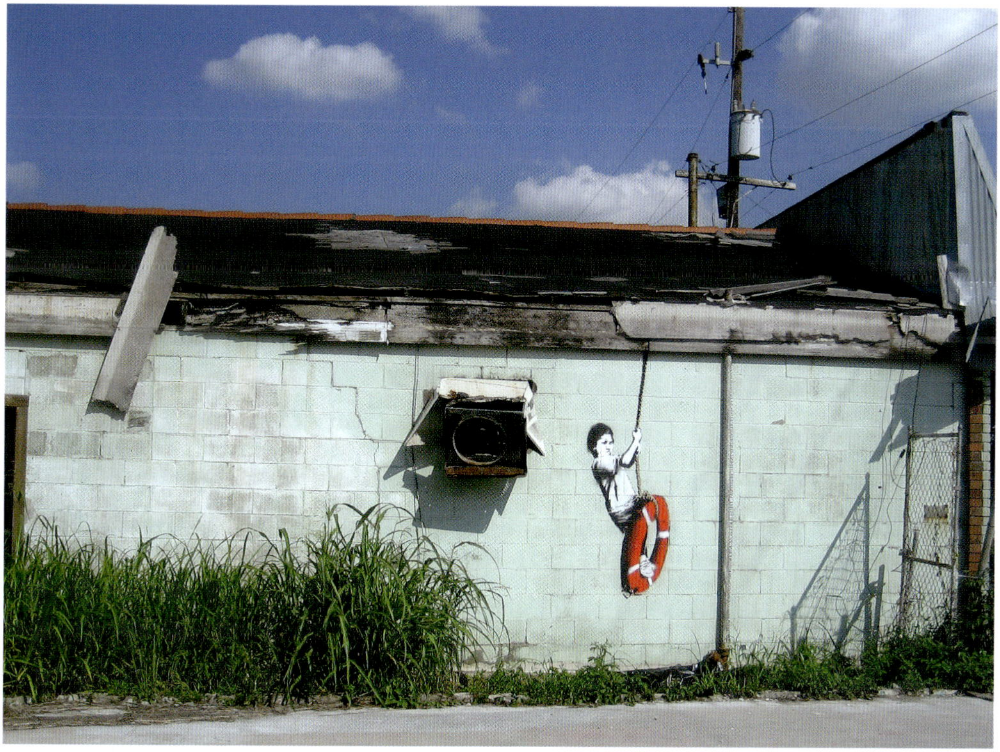

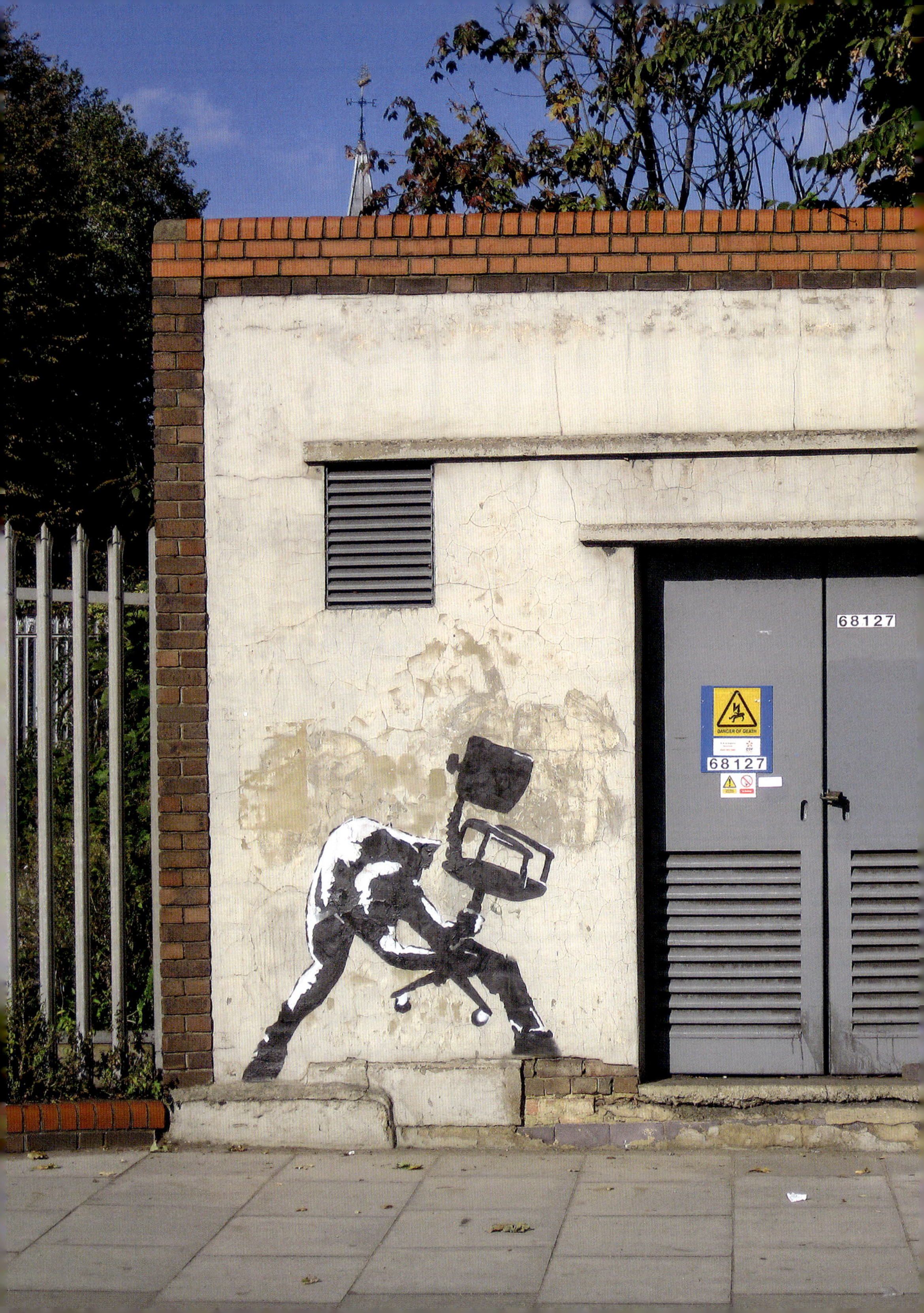
68127
DANGER OF DEATH
68127

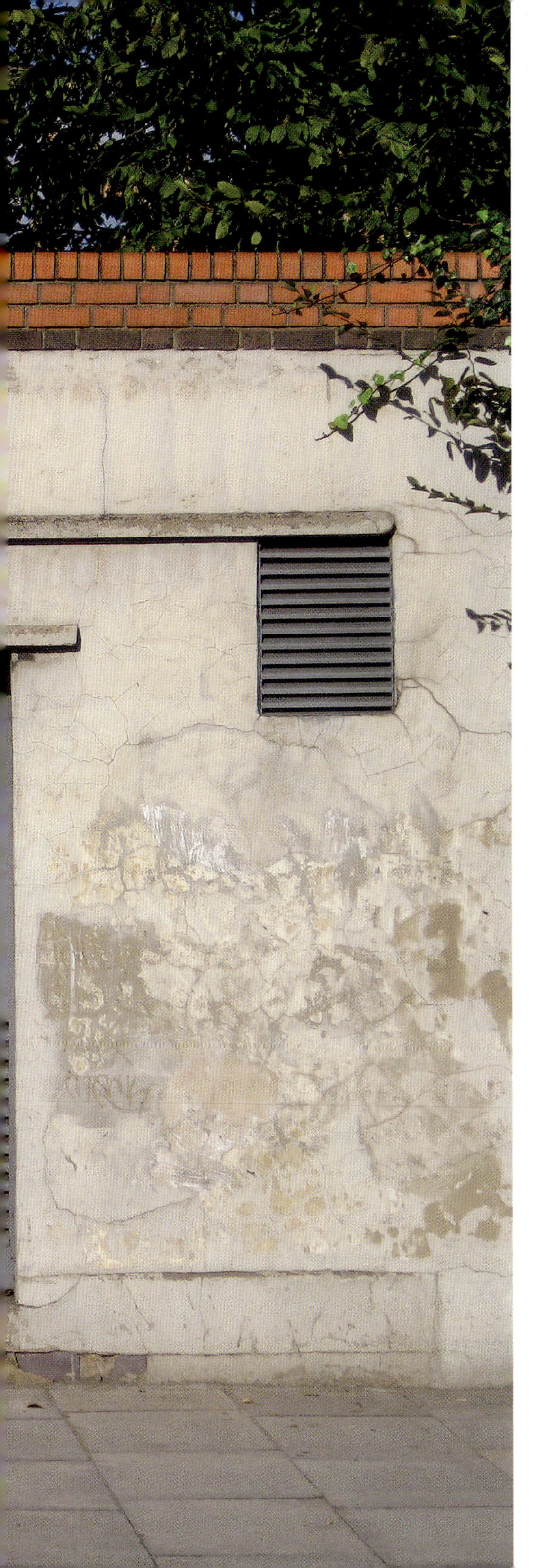

ANOTHER ANGRY YOUNG MAN

Once upon a time, in a different world called Britain in the 90's, an angry young man started a campaign of his own. A tremendous act of blind faith, to go out and paint illegally, for years on end, living on nothing but friendships and dry bread. He was enraged, intelligent, funny and tenacious. He was also a bit of a smart arse, a practical joker. He was deathly afraid of wasting his life on the sofa, talking armchair revolution, like so many other Bristolian stoners. He had to act. And he used stencils, a voice for the voiceless.

Banksy was a revolutionary. And if anyone didn't get that, he told them so in a short series of little black books, zines really - the kind you could only find at trestle tables in far out Brighton nightclubs or sold alongside Anarchist magazines at Rave Parties in East London.

Mayday Riots and Reclaim the Streets, Resistance to Capitalism 1990's style. What later became known as 'anti-capitalism' a movement for a generation that could agree that they hated capitalism but not on what they wanted to replace it with.

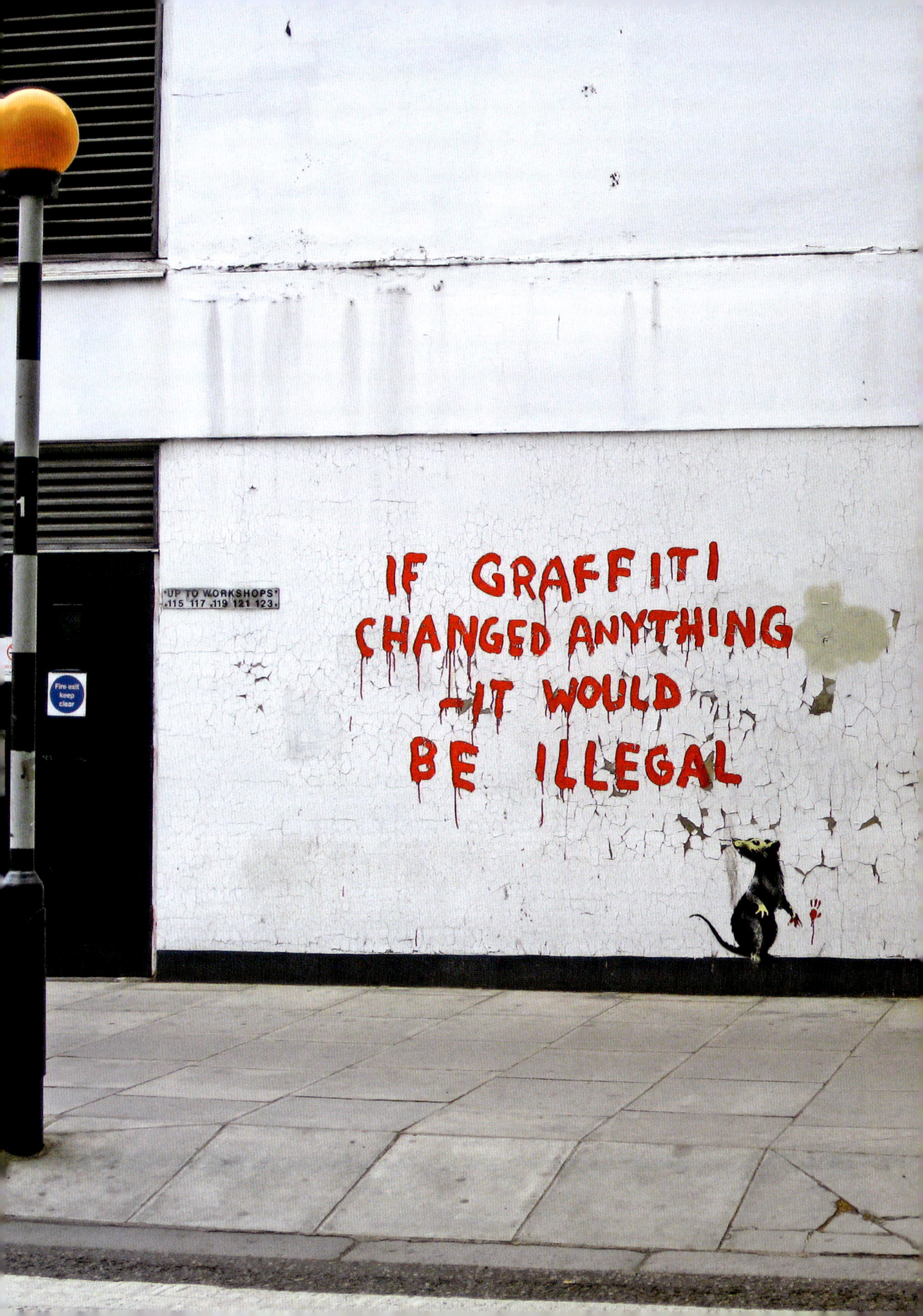

IF GRAFFITI
CHANGED ANYTHING
-IT WOULD
BE ILLEGAL

"UP TO WORKSHOPS"
115 117 119 121 123.

Fire exit
keep
clear

Even when he is taking the piss, Banksy's art only makes sense because he believes that another world is possible. And in the thirty years that have passed, fungus grows on your Pulp Fiction references, and the Girl with the Balloon has become a Valentine's card, and everything, literally everything has got worse for those that cling to any hope for a life after capitalism.

But Banksy is not dead yet. And neither is the desire for another world.

When Banksy says 'If Graffiti changed anything, it would be illegal' what he means is that he firmly believes that Graffiti can and does change things, that's precisely why it is illegal.

No wonder he's still going.

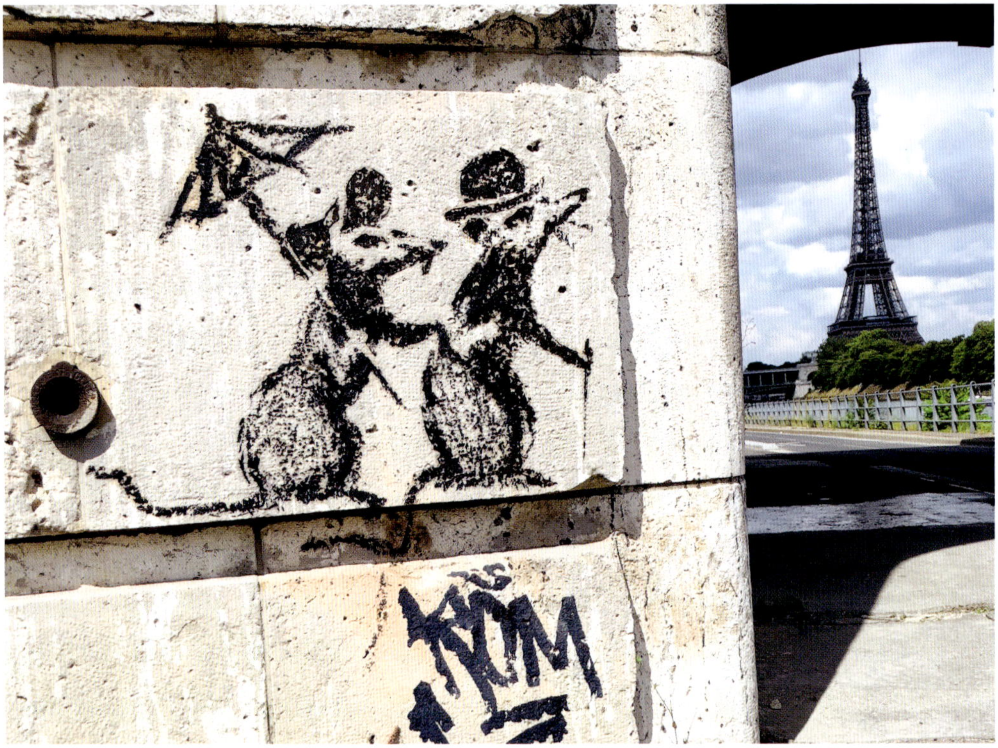

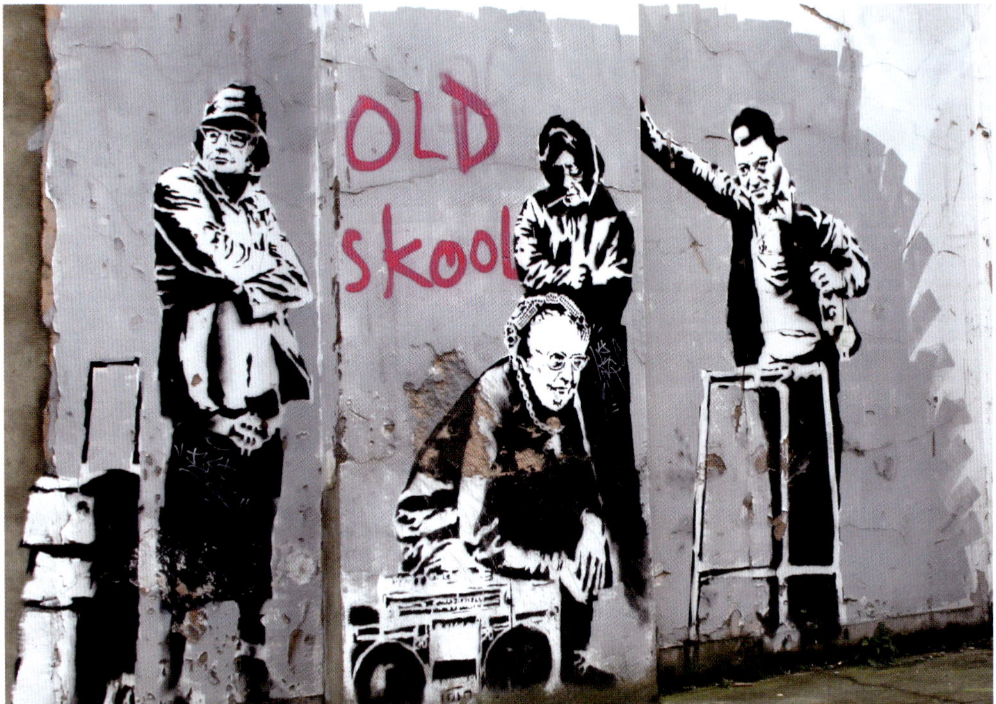

OLD
skool

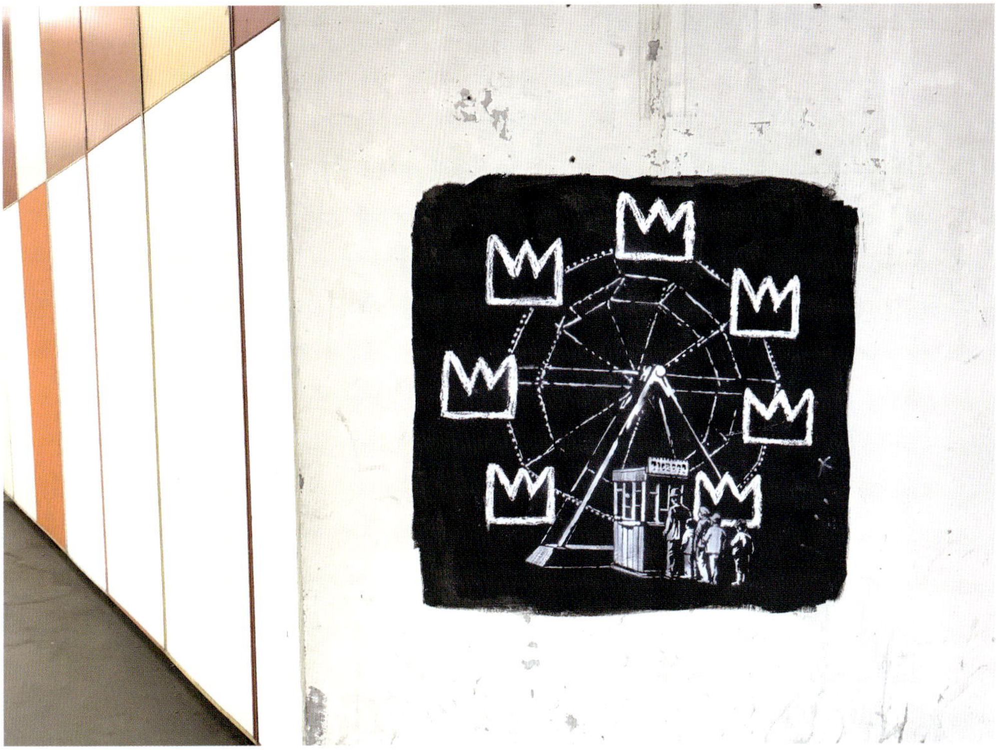

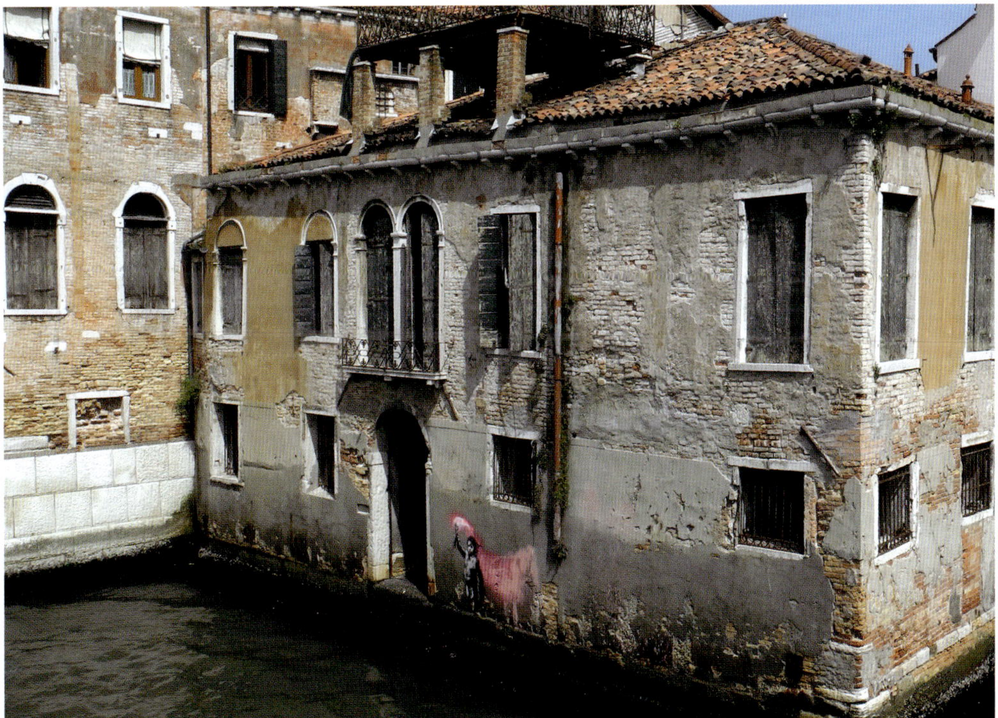

RESISTANCE IS FUTILE?

Banksy contemporary Charlie Brooker, another angry young maker of satirical Zines in the 1990's, summed up the paradox of being a revolutionary in modern Britain beautifully. In a nation where everyone from the marketing mogul to the hedge fund manager thinks of themselves as a revolutionary, revolution is a very cool product to sell.

In episode two of Brooker's Black Mirror, 'Fifteen Million Merits' a young man on a reality show uses a piece of jagged glass to threaten to commit suicide, forcing the producers to let him criticise their fascistic society live on air. The producers think it is brilliant and they offer him a show. The angry voice in the wilderness is just another channel on the infinite TV show of post-modern life. For Banksy the jagged piece of glass, the key to his position and voice, is his anonymity and the 'illegal' nature of his work.

Capitalism loves the counter-culture. Nothing is more hip than resistance to capital. Nothing is more saleable than the revolutionary artist

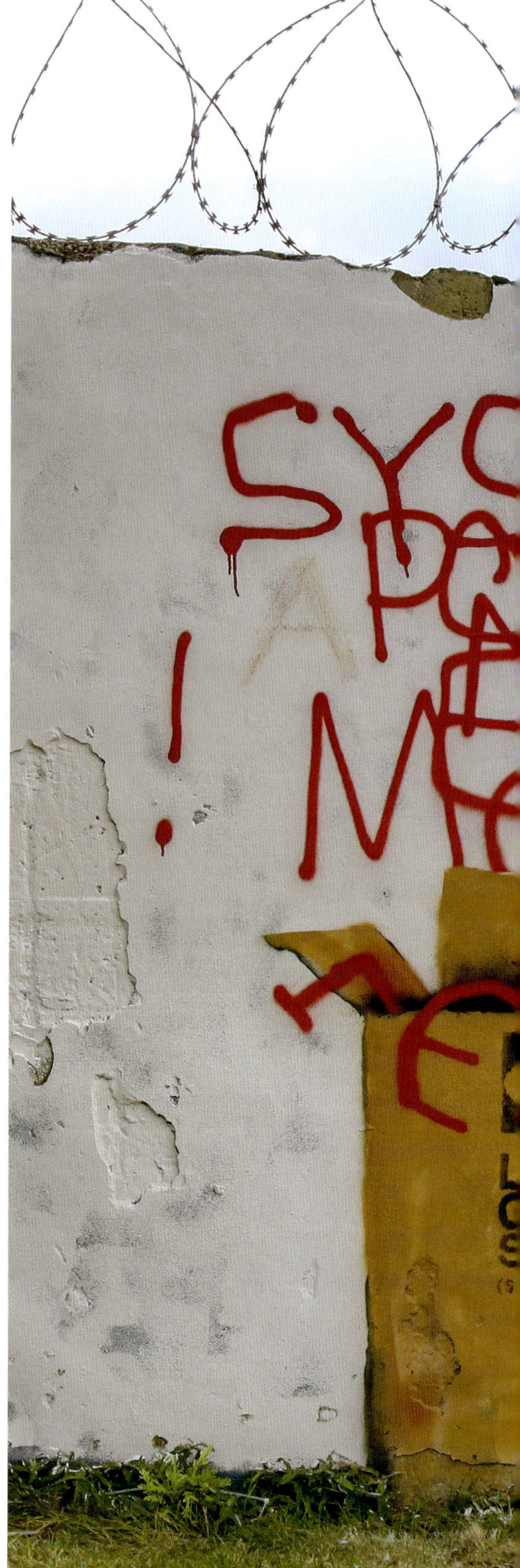

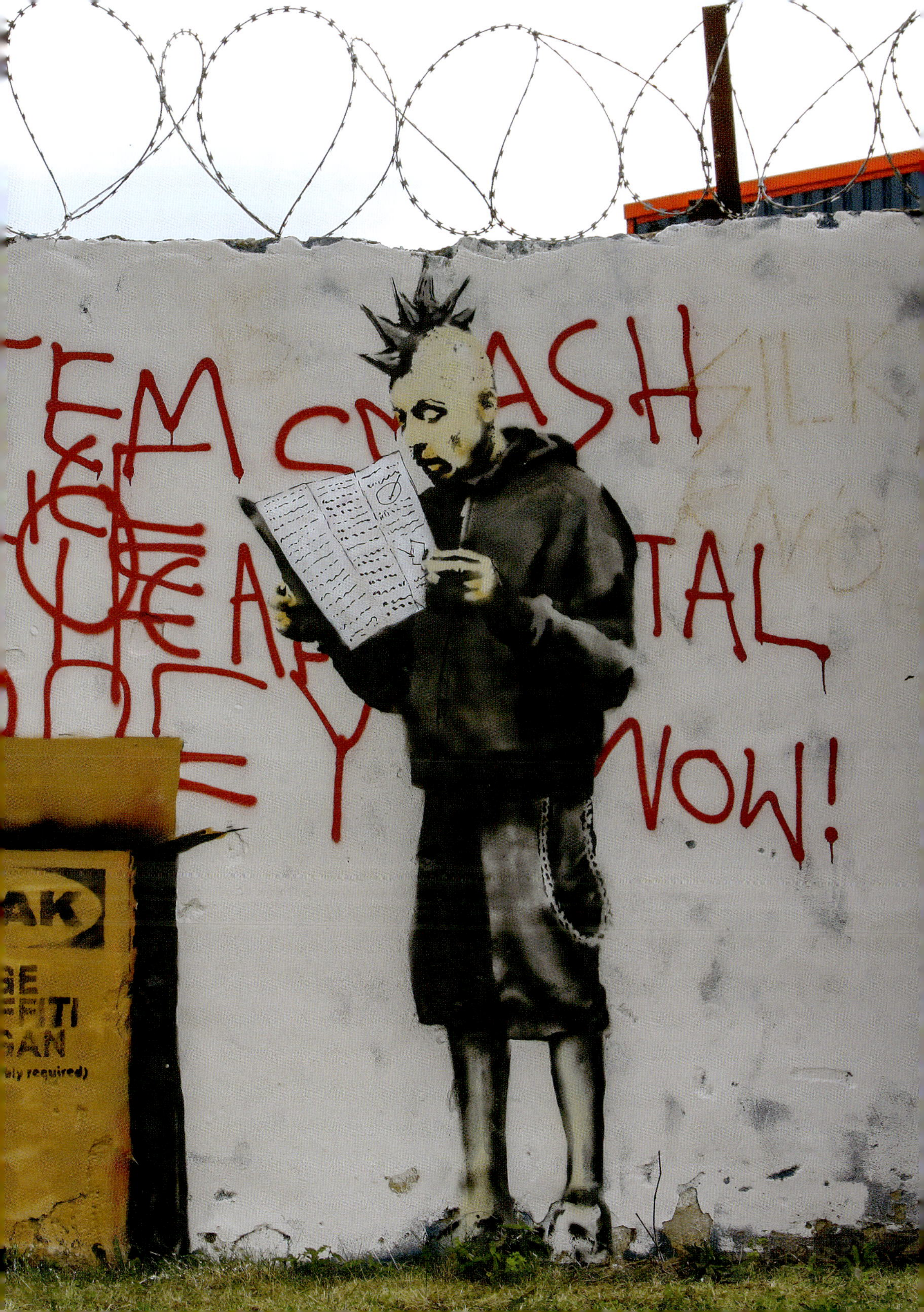

'EM SMASH
TAL
NOW!

lifestyle. Banksy's art grew up in parallel to Reality TV, bohemian gentrification of inner city areas and the phenomenon of social media. Hold up a mirror to Banksy's Street Art and behold it's weird but inevitable reflection - Guerrilla Advertising. Banksy's success paved the way for edgy agencies to sell illegal street art campaigns to their hip entrepreneur clients. Is this stencil art I'm looking at the voice of the voiceless, or is it a paid campaign for a new brand?

Like Brooker's character, Banksy took the money. (Like Brooker, like me, like all of us) And for the most pure and holy of the revolution, he was dead already. But pure revolutionaries don't last long. And do you have to be in poverty to have the right to criticise? Should you have to deny yourself a living in order to have the right to criticise the society in which you live?

Banksy was a starving artist. Now he's rich. So has Banksy changed? He fights on. He continues to snipe. But he's a different animal to the one who wrote those early statements of intent back when Britain was experiencing the dizzy flush of late 1990's self-confidence, the one that passed when the smoking Twin Towers appeared on every TV screen in the world.

Here we attempt to track, in his own words, the development of BANKYISMS from the 1990's to the present day. We try to separate the sincere ideas from the art pranks and provocations. We explain to people who weren't there or maybe grew up in another culture the cultural context from the one in which Banksy was working, his references and influences.

And we ask ourselves, if BANKSYISM was a philosophy for living how would you follow it?

Should you even try?

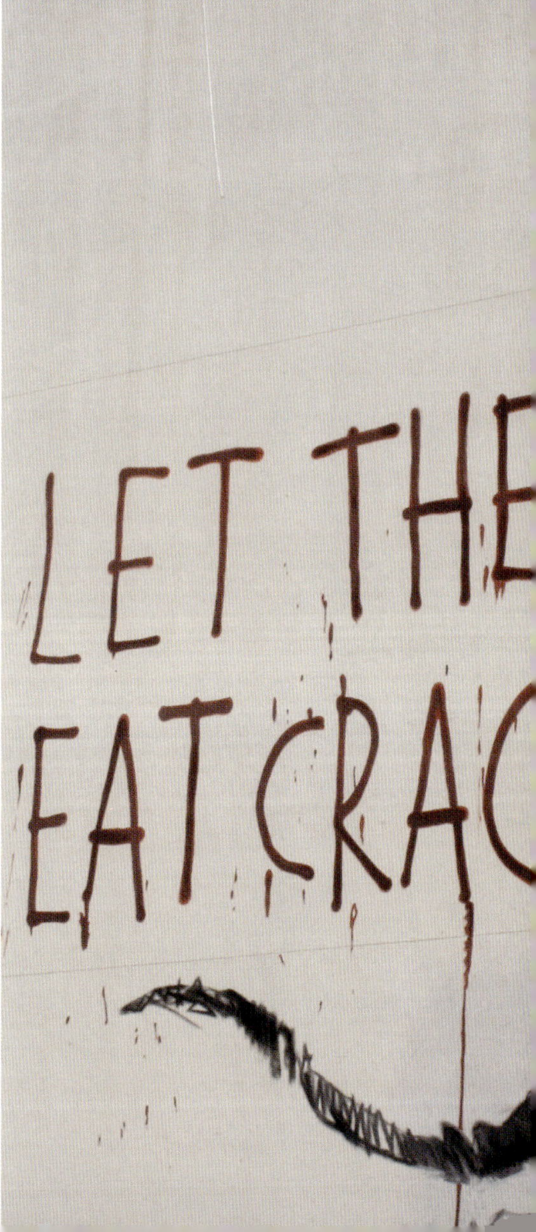

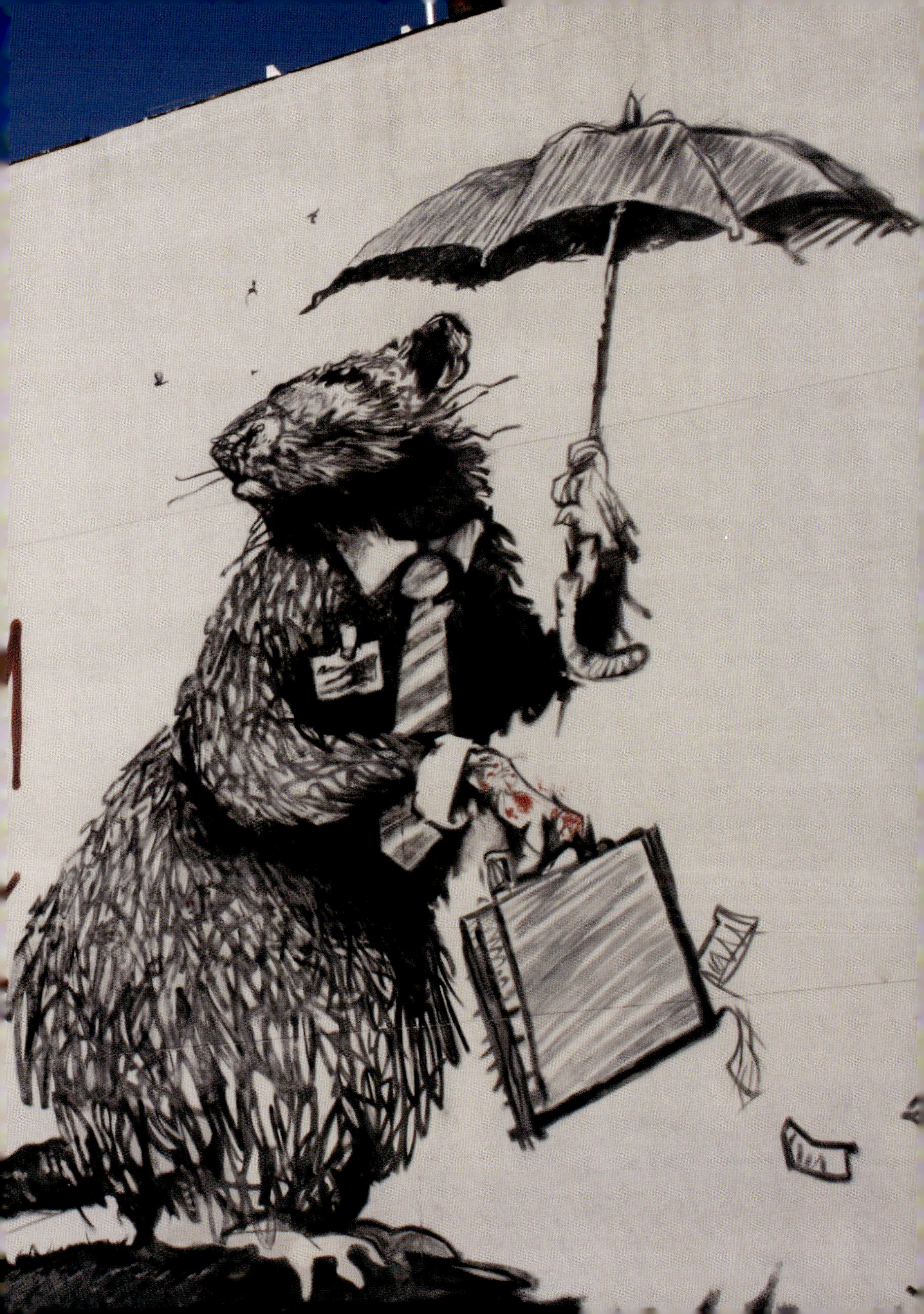

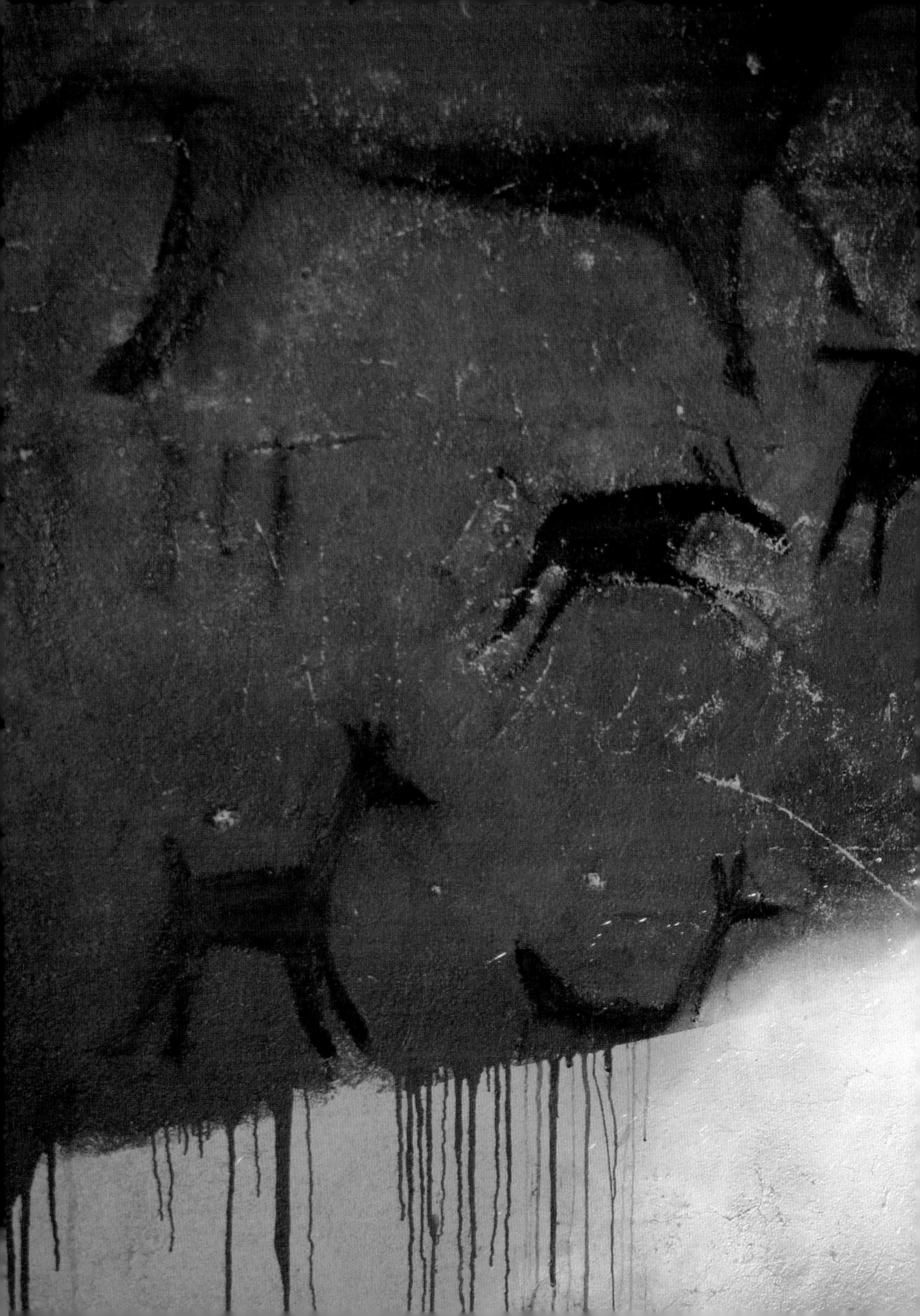

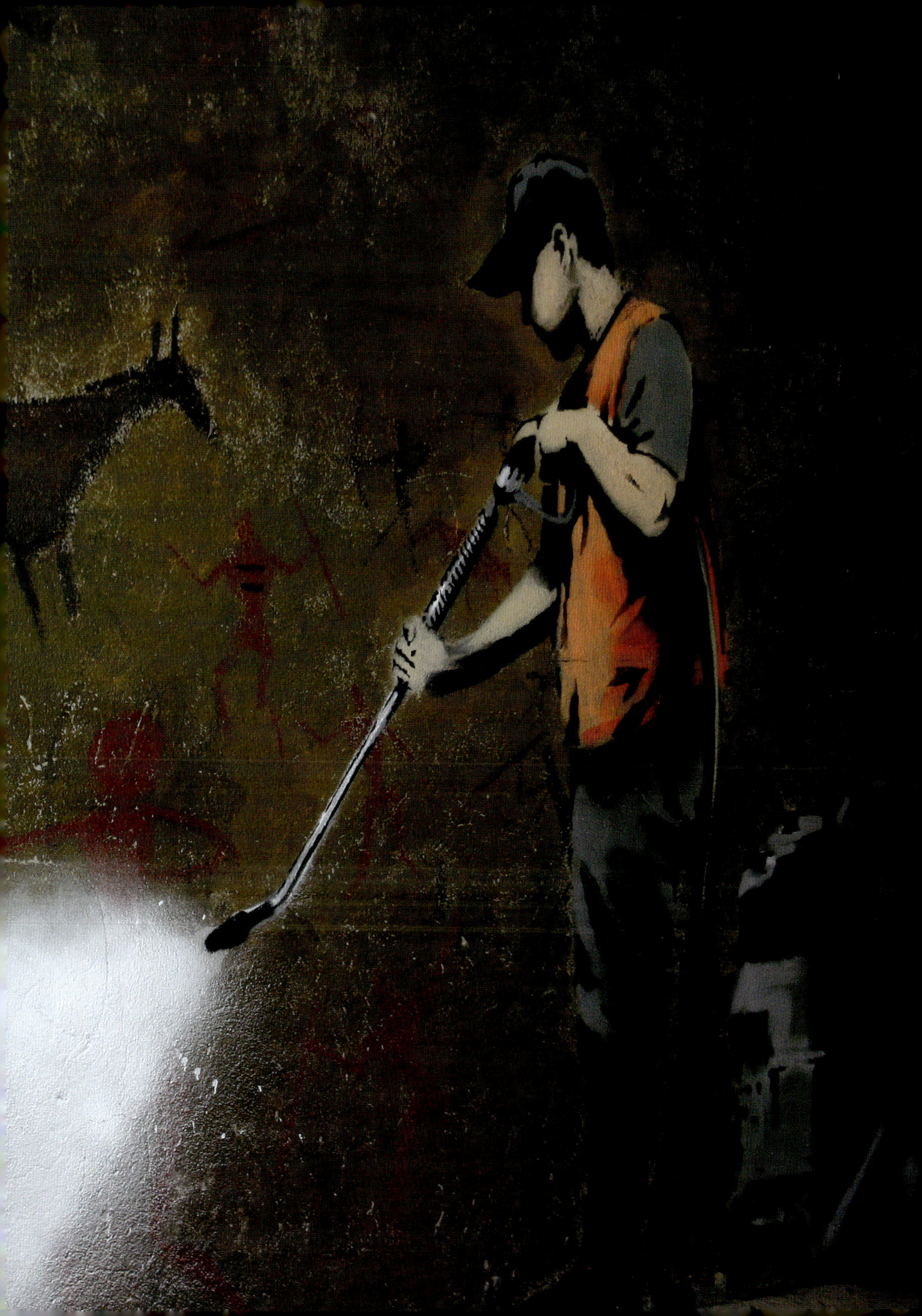

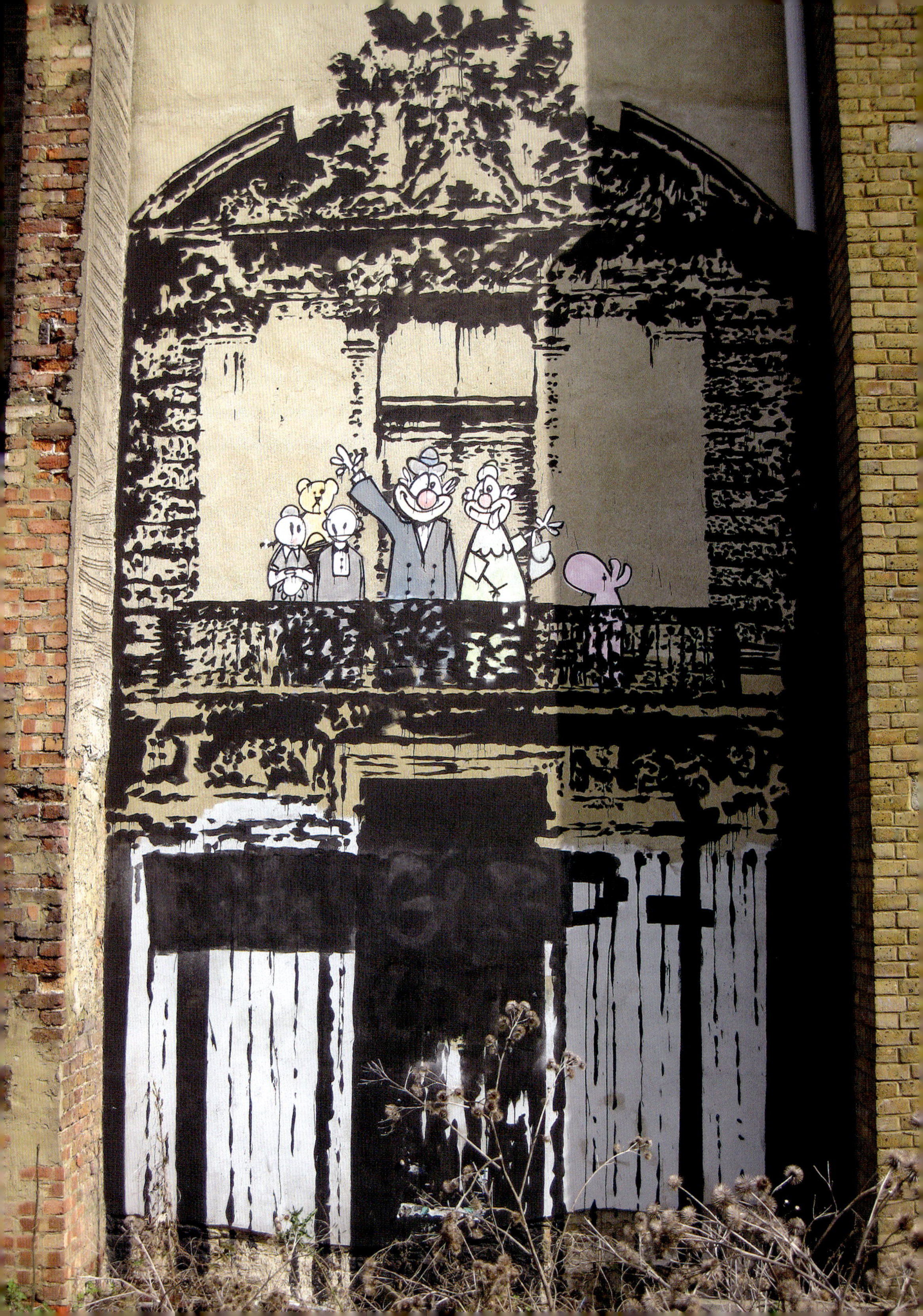

CYNICISM

Cynical is perhaps the most abused word in the English language. It's used to describe anyone who isn't a floppy grinning buffoon, and is widely considered to be the opposite of optimism. It is not. Pessimism is the opposite of optimism.

A cynic is someone who believes that other people are motivated purely by self-interest. Diogenes, one of a small handful of people that Banksy likes to quote, was a Cynic with a capital C. He was part of the original school of Greek Philosophers that invented Cynicism.

A LOT of Banksy's work shows a profound mistrust in the sincerity of people in public life, especially politicians. And this cynicism also extends to self-deprecatory humour. He mocks his own motivations too. So, is Banksy a cynic?

ONE ORIGINAL THOUGHT IS WORTH A THOUSAND MINDLESS QUOTINGS.

DIOGENES

And if you didn't get the joke, the joke is quoting a quote about how dumb it is to quote. And here we have raised the level of meta-quotation by one, in quoting a quotation of a quote that mocks quotation. It's all probably a subtle pop at social media. Banksy loves this kind of house of mirrors shit

"One original thought
is worth a thousand
mindless quotings"
- Diogenes

MORE CRIMES ARE COMMITTED IN THE NAME OF OBEDIENCE THAN DISOBEDIENCE

BANKSY

"Banging Your Head Against a Brick Wall" Banksy

Weapons of Mass Distraction 2001

All British school students study the holocaust. And this is really the most important lesson to learn from the holocaust, people didn't oppose it because MOST PEOPLE JUST DO WHAT EVERYONE ELSE IS DOING. Banksy has obviously thought about the topic, he's indirectly referenced the holocaust in 'The Banality of the Banality of Evil'. (Look up Hannah Arendt). But the problem of obedience extends way beyond any particluar historical event – the Milgram shock experiment in 1961 appeared to prove a worrying tendency for ordinary people to do hideous things when told to by authority figures. Conversely, Banksy advocates small scale acts of disobedience as a kind of vaccination against this tendency. If you've broken small rules, you'll find it easier to break bigger ones if history should require it.

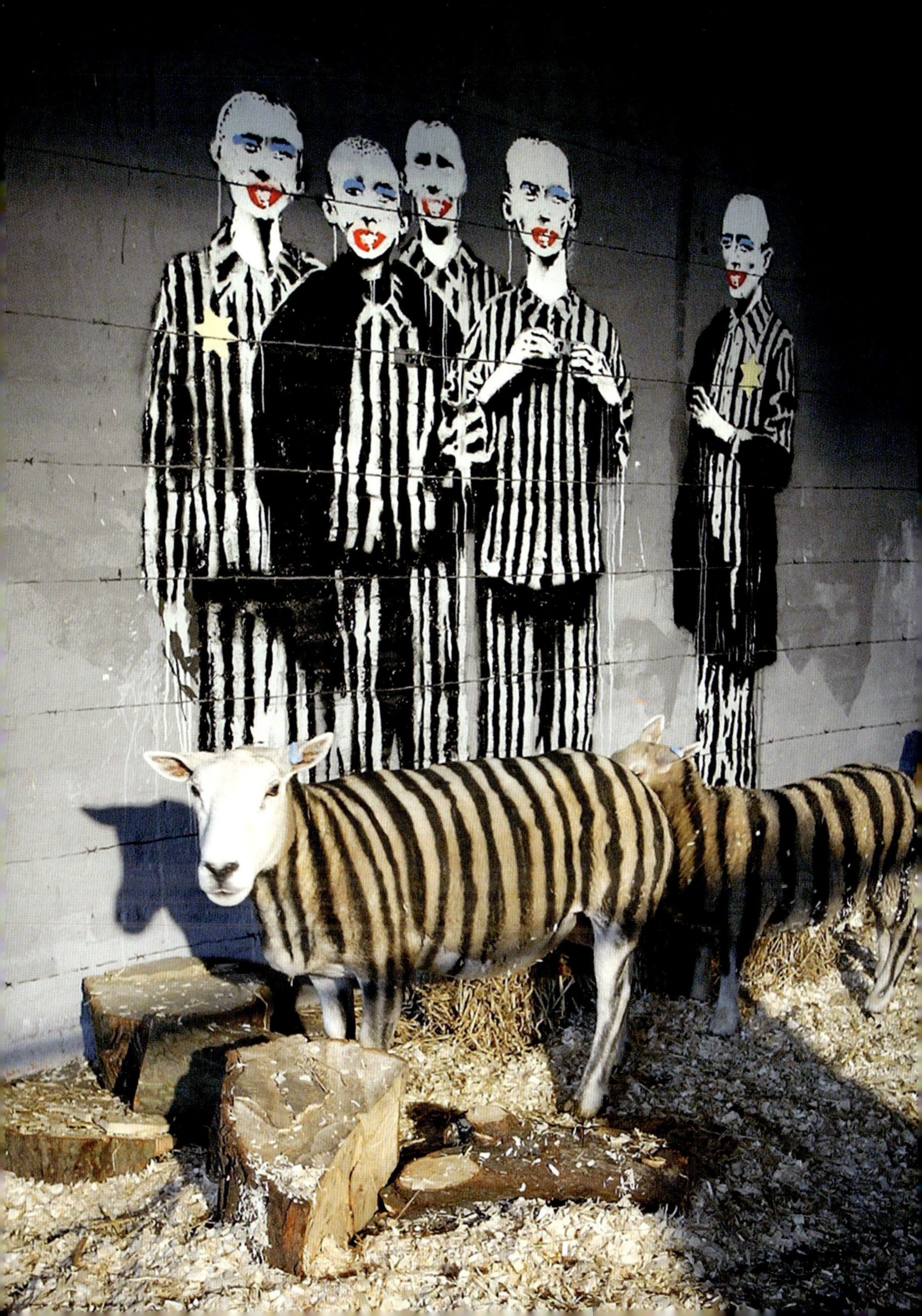

BETTER OUT THAN IN

If you have the good fortune of not being British, you may not know that 'Better Out Than In' is something we limeys say to each other when we burp or fart. The logo of Banksy's 2013 New York 'residency' (haha) was a man **literally,** or even figuratively vomiting art.

"The street is in play."

Better Out Than In, Banksy, NYC 2013

IN play not AT play, meaning it is a contested space, a space that can be played for and won. The street is not a done deal. It's conventions are up for grabs. A recurring theme in Banksy's work, these reminders that you never have to accept a given power structure. Power is often weaker than it appears to be.

"I wanted to make some art without the price tag attached. There's no gallery show or book or film. It's pointless. Which hopefully means something."

Banksy Village Voice Interview, 2013

Who was it that said anything you do for love and not money is a revolutionary act?

"New York calls to graffiti writers like a dirty old lighthouse."

Banksy Village Voice Interview, 2013

Of course, NYC is the Mecca of Modern Graffiti, the 1970's birthplace of the art form. A West Country British boy who grew up cow tipping on cider binges would never be able to resist the call of New York.

"When graffiti isn't criminal, it loses most of its innocence."

Banksy Village Voice Interview, 2013

Nobody is more painfully aware of the irony of his own commercial success than Banksy.

"It doesn't take much to be a successful artist - all you need to do is dedicate your entire life to it."

Banksy Village Voice Interview, 2013

Work life balance is for quitters.

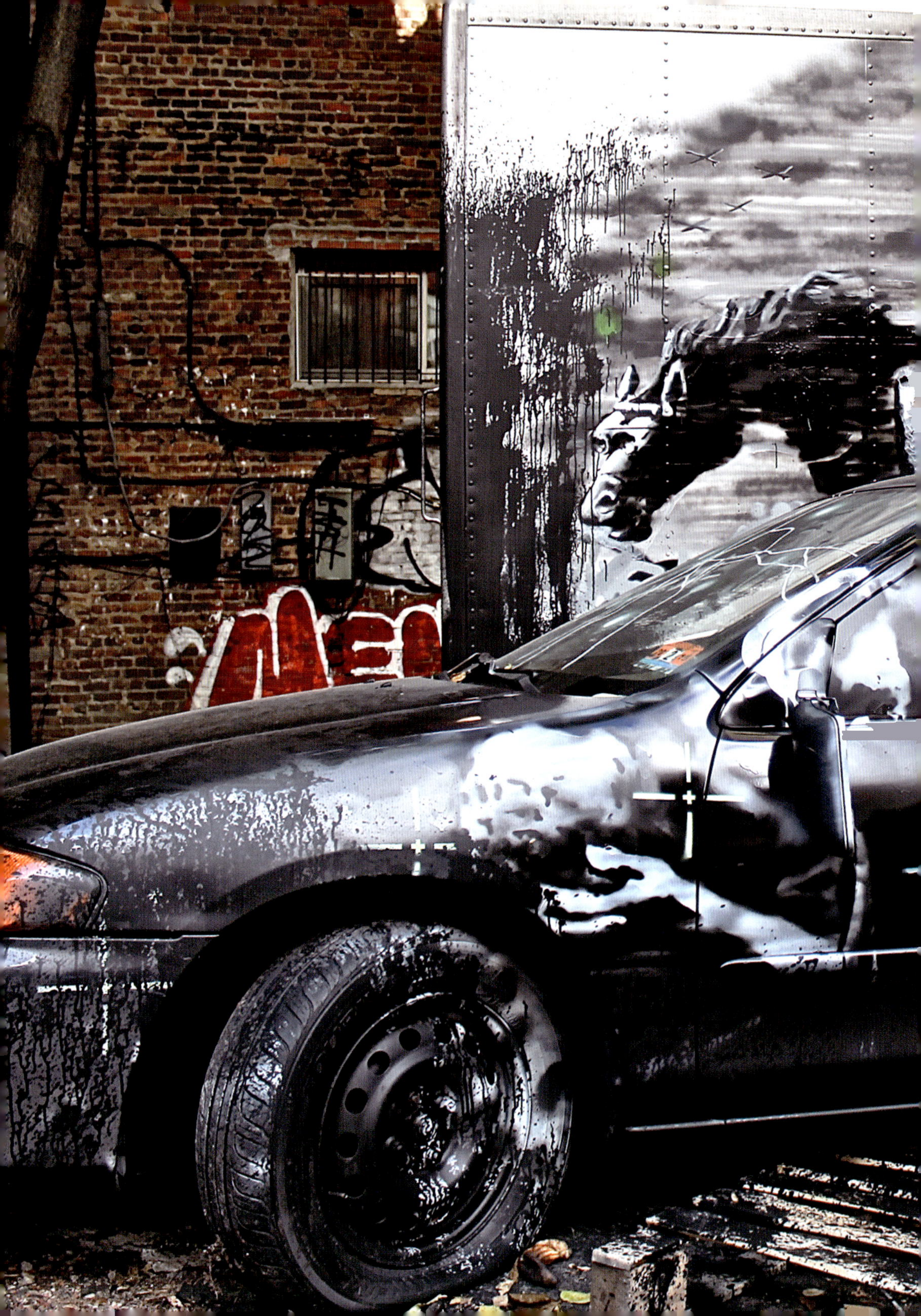

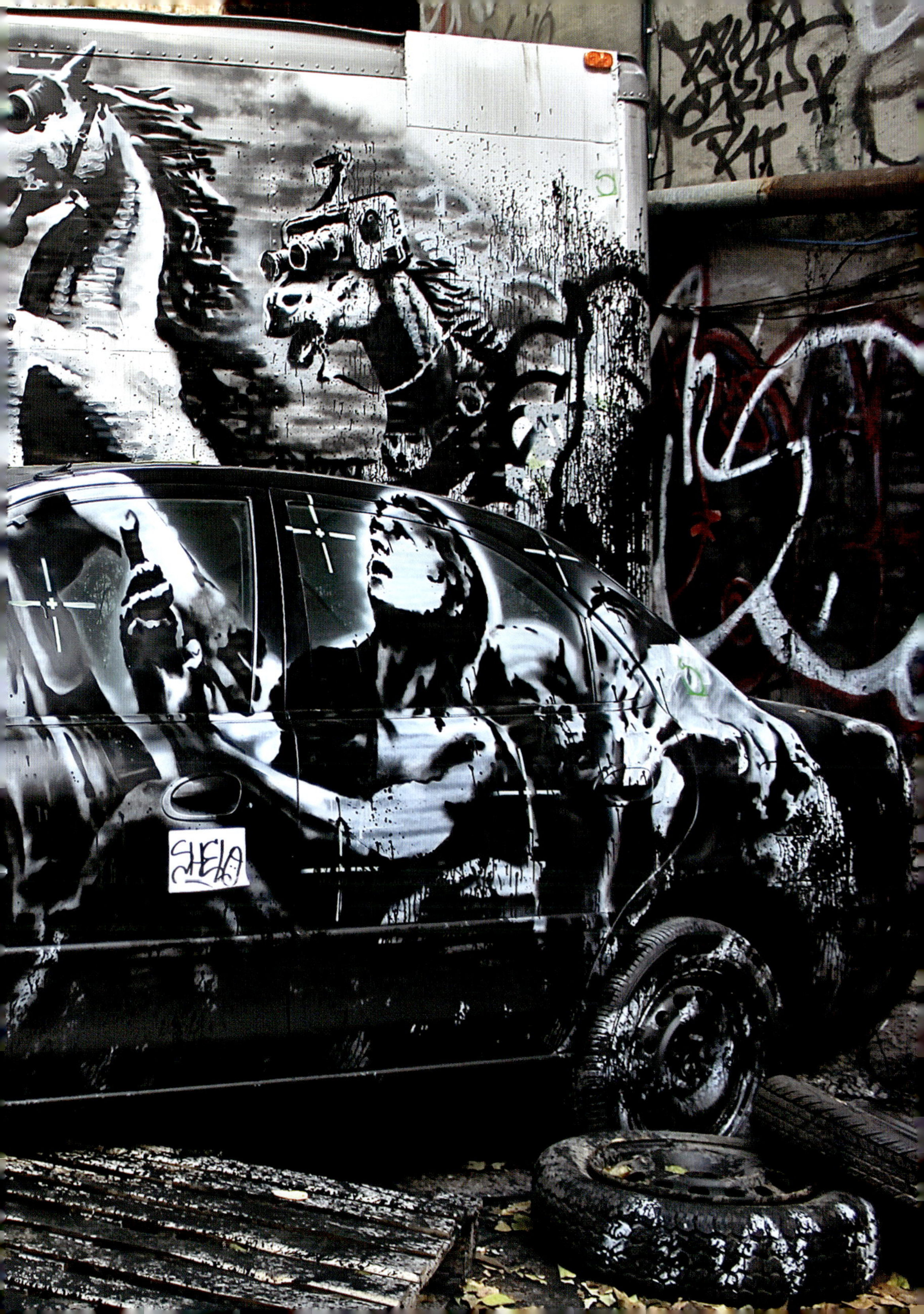

THEY HAVE REARRANGED THE WORLD TO PUT THEMSELVES IN FRONT OF YOU.

THEY NEVER ASKED FOR YOUR PERMISSION, DON'T EVEN START ASKING FOR THEIRS.

BANKSY

"Cut it Out" Banksy

Weapons of Mass Distraction 2004

If you want to know what the future looks like, go to an airport. Being inside an airport is precisely what the whole world would look like if it were designed in the board rooms of global corporations. You drift around a space plastered with gigantic marketing messages from cashpoint to till and back again, a cell in the bloodstream of capital. Everything around you is a brand. As the advertising grows ever more computerised, we drift into the world of Bladerunner. Cyberpunk was supposed to be a warning, not a blueprint!

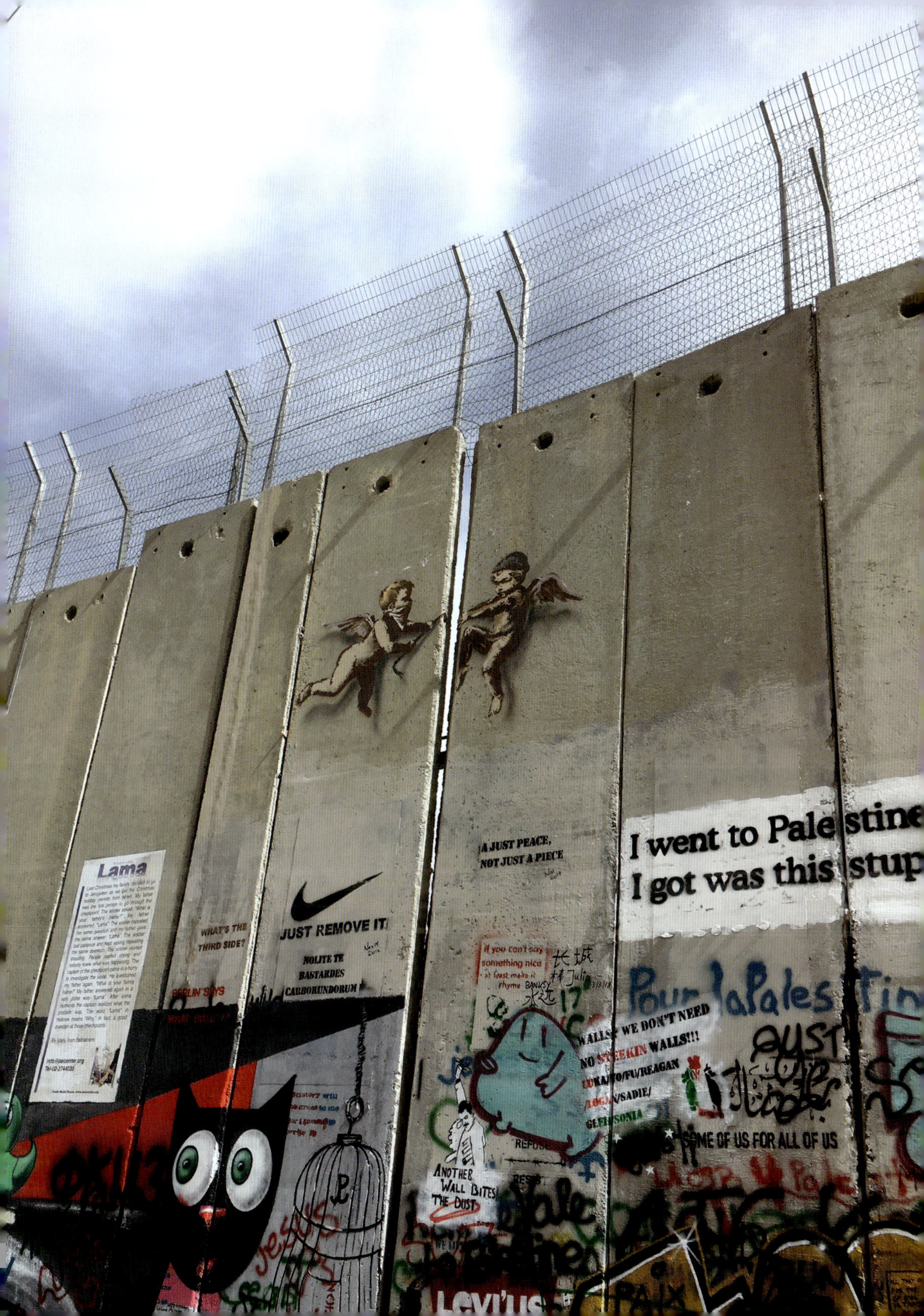

Lama
WHAT'S THE THIRD SIDE?
JUST REMOVE IT
NOLITE TE BASTARDES CARBORUNDORUM
A JUST PEACE, NOT JUST A PIECE
I went to Palestine
I got was this stup
If you can't say something nice at least make it rhyme BANKSY
WALLS WE DON'T NEED
NO STEEKIN WALLS!!!
SOME OF US FOR ALL OF US
Pour la Palestine
ANOTHER WALL BITES THE DUST
LEVI'S

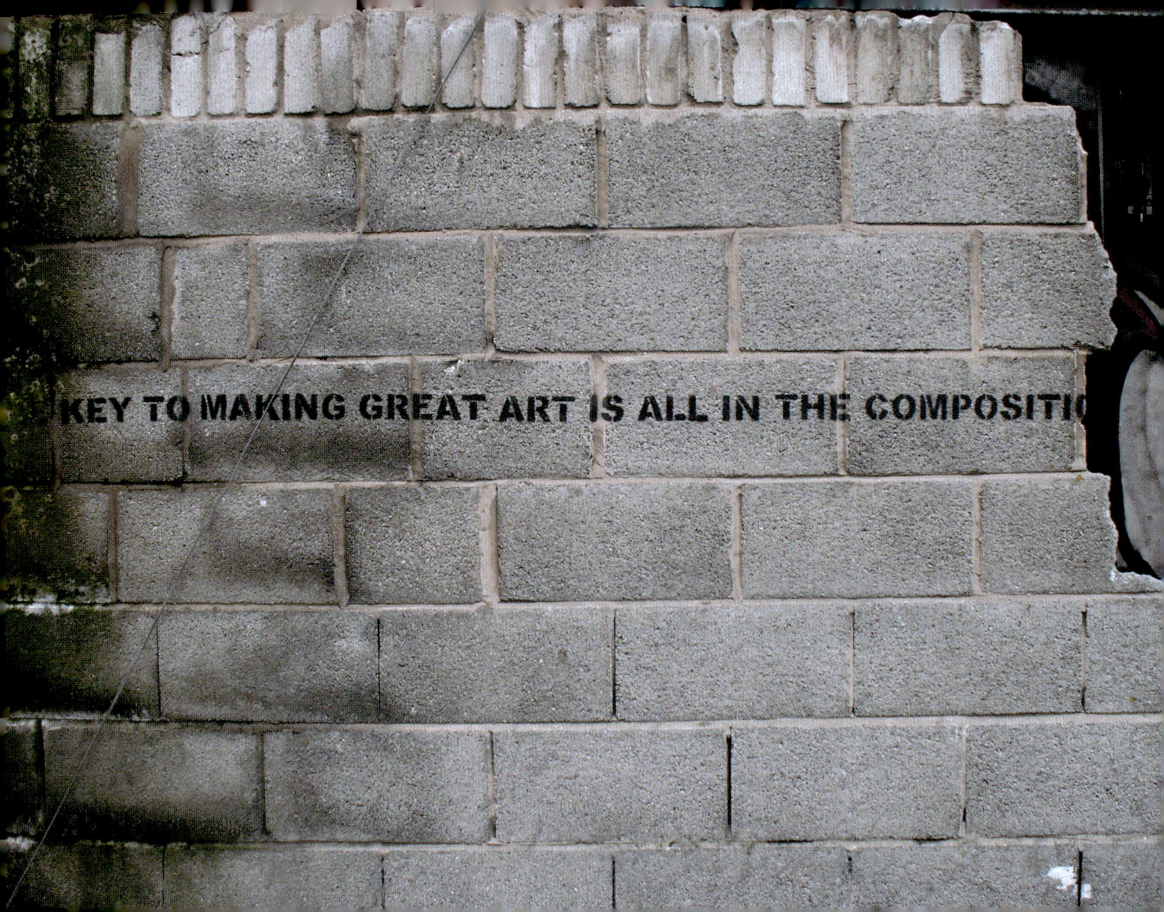

KEY TO MAKING GREAT ART IS ALL IN THE COMPOSITIO

ART'S THE LAST OF THE GREAT CARTELS.

A HANDFUL OF PEOPLE MAKE IT, A HANDFUL BUY IT, AND A HANDFUL SHOW IT. BUT THE MILLIONS OF PEOPLE WHO GO LOOK AT IT DON'T HAVE A SAY.

BANKSY

"Art Attack" Jeff Howe.

Wired Magazine. 2005

Before we all throw the hypocrite stone, on the record Banksy claims to not be the billionaire everyone assumes he is. Much of the headline grabbing auction work sold, is no longer his to sell. Again and again, Banksy makes the point that all other art forms belong to their audiences, living or dying on their popularity alone. Yet he is drawn to the art world like a moth to a flame. In spite of spraying mind the crap on the steps up to the Tate, he's risked his liberty on several occasions to get his work installed in galleries illegally, and then of course came the legal shows. The art world is ripe for a kicking, and much of it is a money laundering scheme for the new rich Russian oligarchs and the various filthy one percenters. However, do we want to live in a world where the only art that gets made is the most popular? Does popular always equal good?

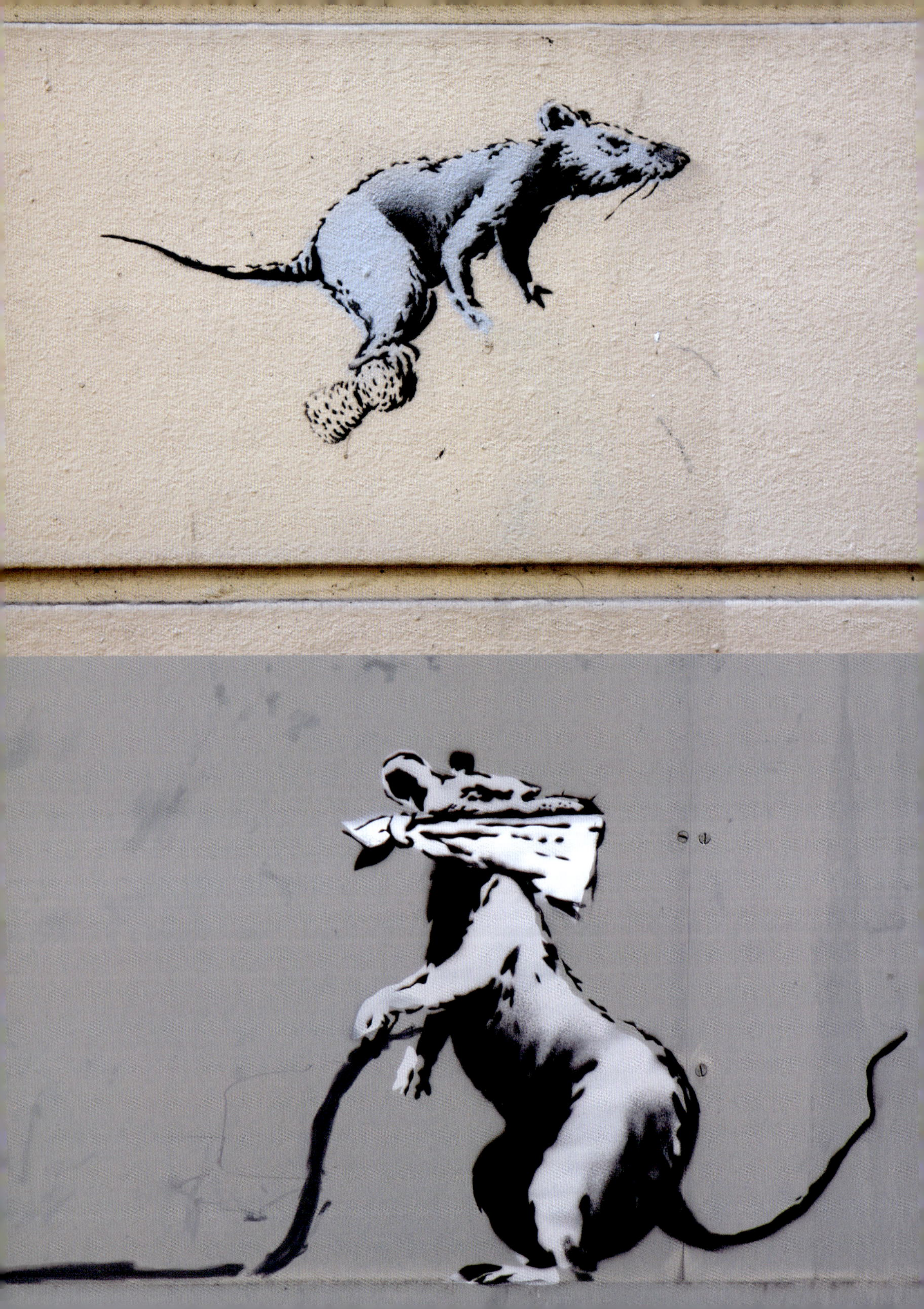

BLEK LE RAT

Now Banksy says he got the idea for stencil graffiti from staring at a stencil painted on a rubbish truck. And maybe that's true. But it's worth mentioning that Blek le Rat was pioneering stencil Graffiti in Paris back in the 1980's when our hero was still scribbling on the back of the seats on the school bus. Banksy is quoted as saying:

"Every time I think I've painted something slightly original, I find out that Blek le Rat has done it as well, only twenty years earller."

Which is a clever way of saying - I don't copy him, I make my work and THEN discover that he already did something similar. Again, possibly true. It's also possible he didn't say it. The 2008 interview with Lee Coan reeks of game playing. The man he interviewed never admitted to being Banksy, and Steve Lazarides claimed to the same journo with a straight face, not to know who Banksy was himself. (Go figure). Coan's tall tales of celebrity japes with an elephant in Los Angeles also sound, well, completely made up. Was Coan in on the joke? (Welcome to the hall of mirrors that is BANKSY).

THEY EXPECT TO BE ABLE TO SHOUT THEIR MESSAGE IN YOUR FACE FROM EVERY AVAILABLE SURFACE BUT YOU'RE NEVER ALLOWED TO ANSWER BACK.

WELL, THEY STARTED THIS FIGHT AND THE WALL IS THE WEAPON OF CHOICE TO HIT THEM BACK.

BANKSY

"Wall & Piece" Banksy

Vintage Publishing 2006

Corporates have been fighting a war to BECOME culture since the 1960's and they've largely won. I wonder how many teenagers today could understand the idea that there might be a culture OUTSIDE of corporate culture, BEYOND the brands. Branding is as natural to them as cleaning their teeth. They have no experience of a NON-COMMERCIAL public space. Public space is the shopping centre. Cultural space is corporate space. Will they understand your call to fight back?

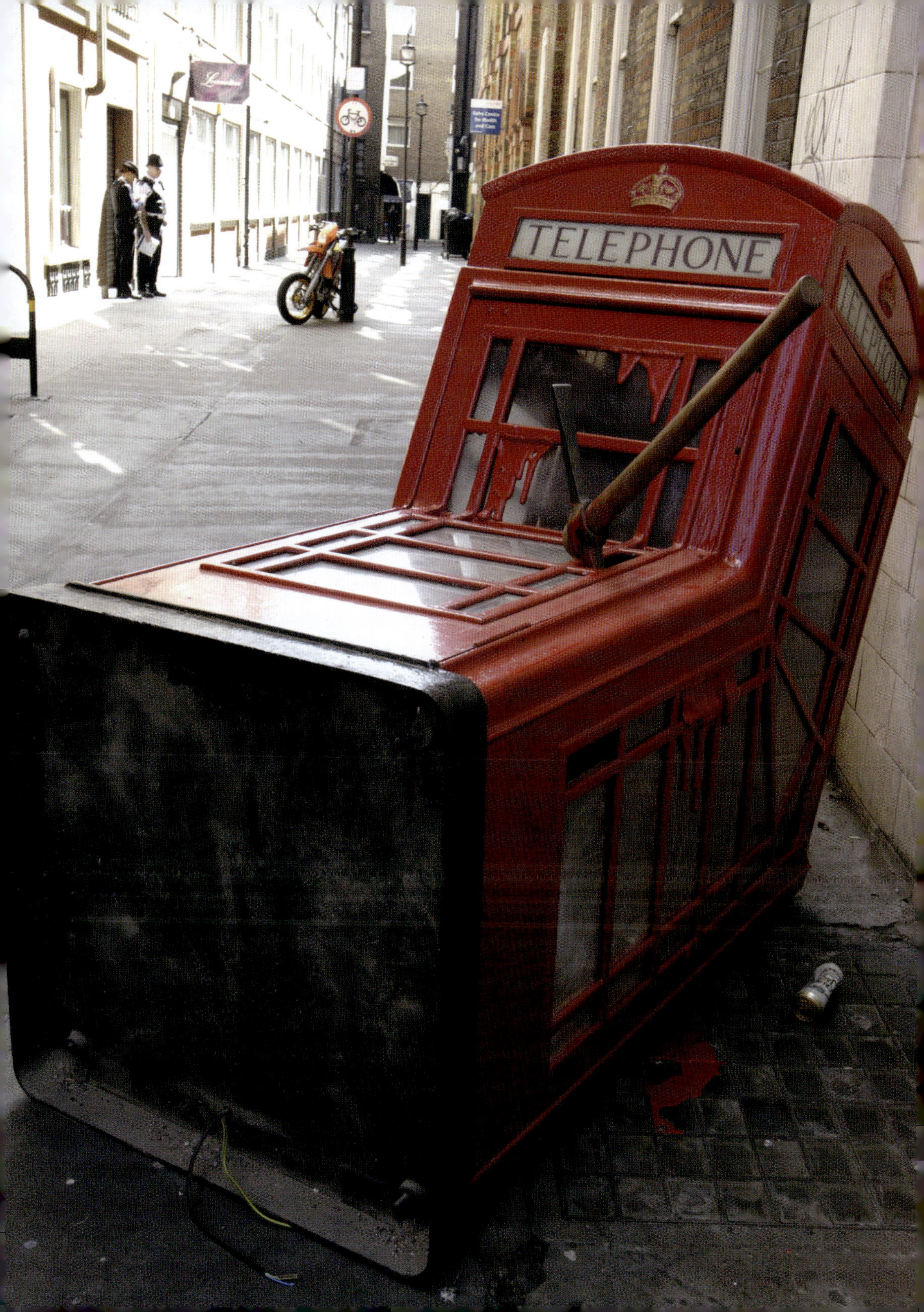

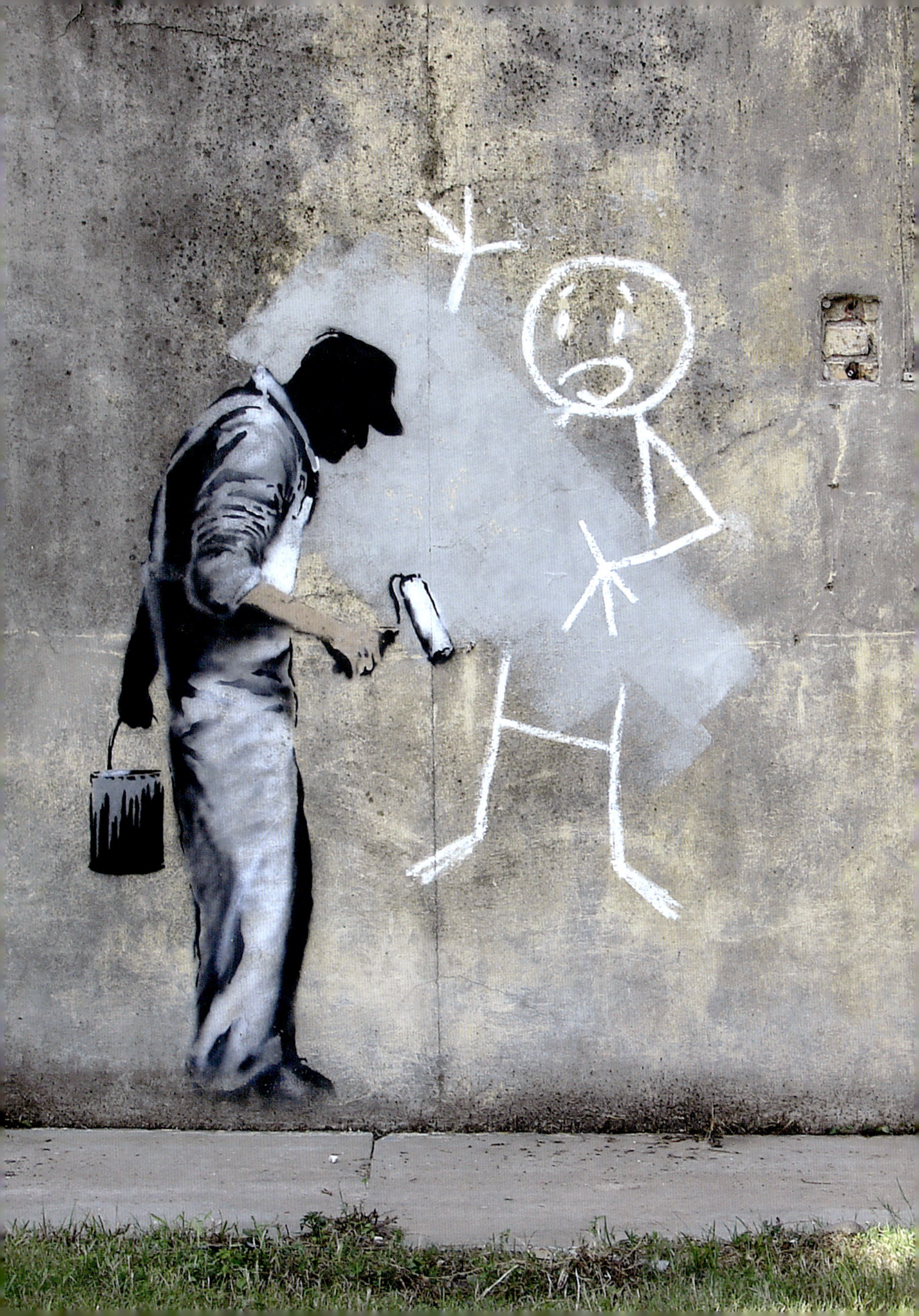

WHEN THE TIME COMES TO LEAVE, JUST WALK AWAY QUIETLY AND DON'T MAKE ANY FUSS.

BANKSY

"Wall & Piece" Banksy

Vintage Publishing 2006

It's good advice for a graffiti artist, but it's always good advice. Who among us knows when to walk away? Isn't that the hardest thing?

AUTHENTICITY

"This is not a photo opportunity."

For someone who likes playing with the truth, Banksy's work has a strong theme of wanting people to live real, authentic experiences. As stand-up Dylan Moran once said to an audience member who was fliming his performance 'Have an unmediated experience for once in your fucking life.'

Banksy's 'This'll look nice when it's framed' parodies his own gallery success, and you could take the same sentiment to its logical conclusion 'This will look nice on instagram'. Which it will. Street Art and Instagram were made for each other. Arguably, Street Art would never have become the darling of the art world without social media.

But Banksy wants people to break out of the hypnotic state of hypermediated life in which we find ourselves. Climbing over the wall of a zoo is one way to take a sledgehammer to this sleepwalking state. Force yourself into the moment though the application of naked fear. Paranoia as a kind of street level mindfulness.

Banksyism: Get off the sofa and be the lead character in your own story for once.

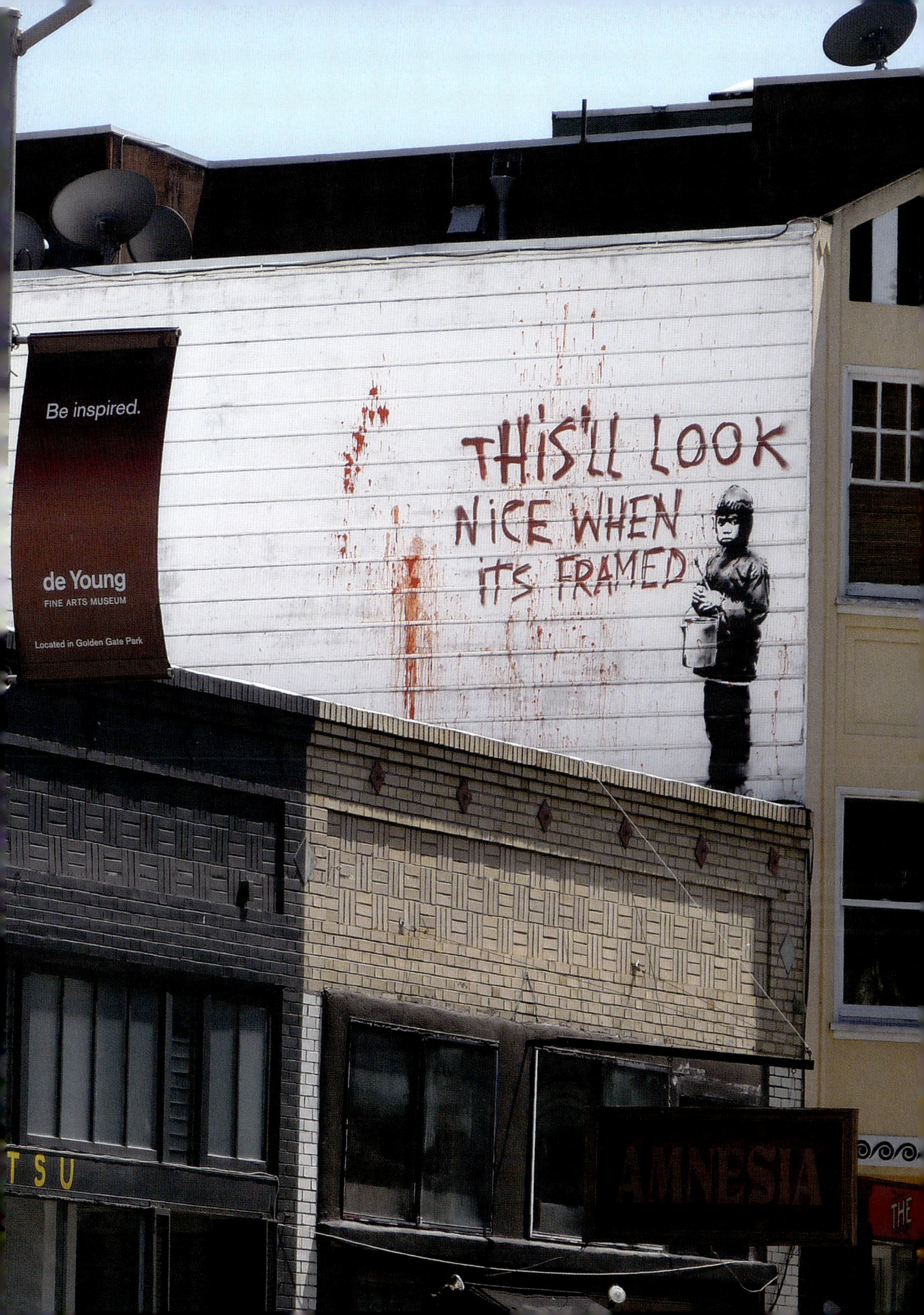

Be inspired.
de Young
FINE ARTS MUSEUM
Located in Golden Gate Park
THIS'll LOOK NICE WHEN ITS FRAMED
TSU
AMNESIA
THE

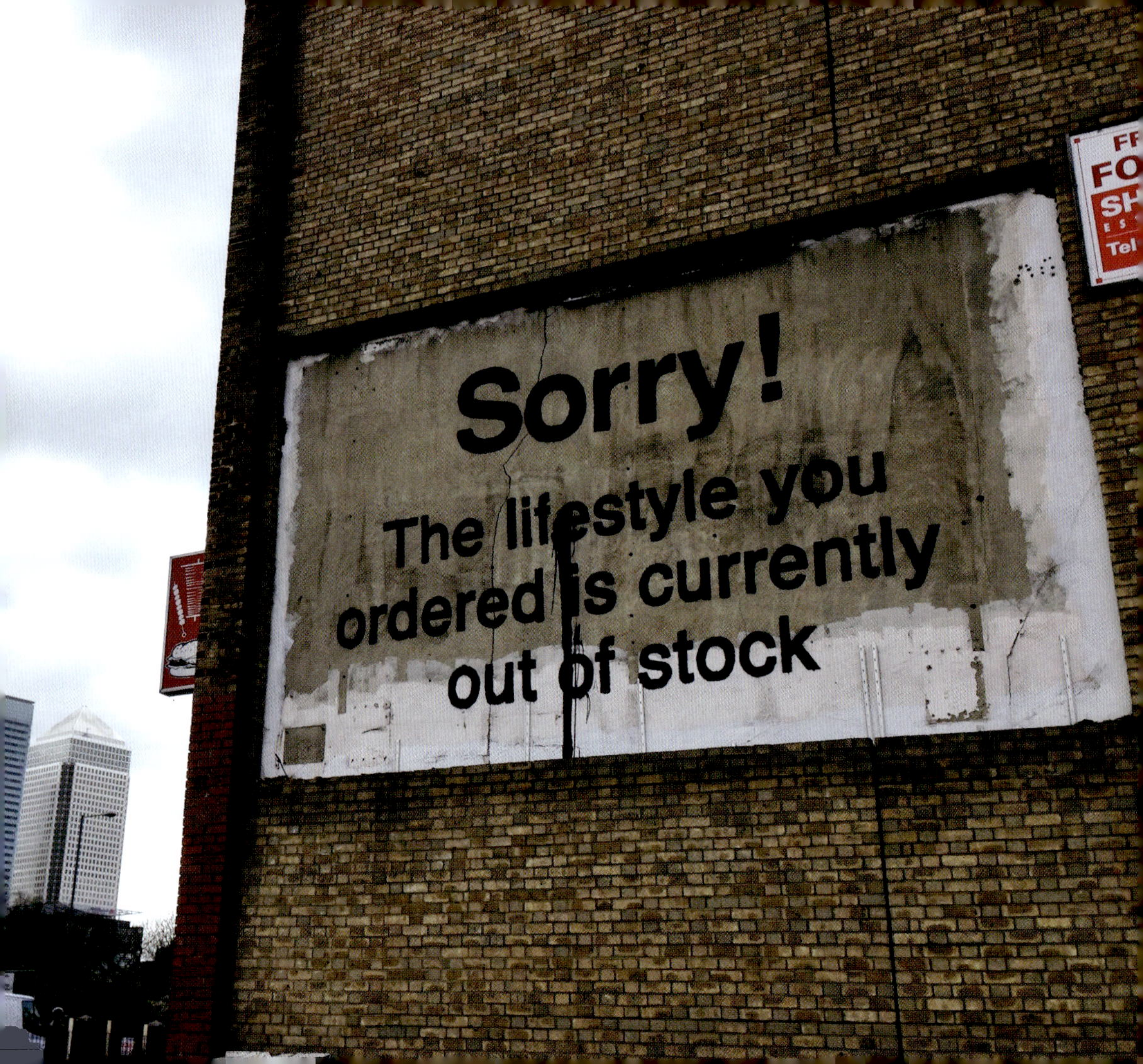
Sorry!
The lifestyle you ordered is currently out of stock

SORRY, THE LIFESTYLE YOU ORDERED IS CURRENTLY OUT OF STOCK

At the beginning of the 20th century people bought stuff because they needed it. Thrift was considered a noble virtue. By the 1990's, people bought stuff because it defined their sense of self. Buying had become an act of self-expression, an identification with a lifestyle. Spending itself had become a noble virtue, a duty to society. When the Twin Towers went down the president of the United States had to urge Americans to go shopping, and even to go back to Disneyworld.

For a fascinating exploration of how this change happened, check out Adam Curtis' documentary series 'Century of Self'.

Lifestyle marketing works because it fits every possible type of person. Whoever you are, you can find a lifestyle that fits. The algorithms have accelerated this process, scouring your email text and social posts to tailor make your marketing messages.

Banksy, again cries out for authenticity by railing against this lifestyle consumerism. But what on earth can it mean, in practical terms, to resist this culture? I ordered the anti-consumerist lifestyle!

NOBODY EVER
LISTENED
TO ME UNTIL
THEY DIDN'T KNOW
WHO I WAS.

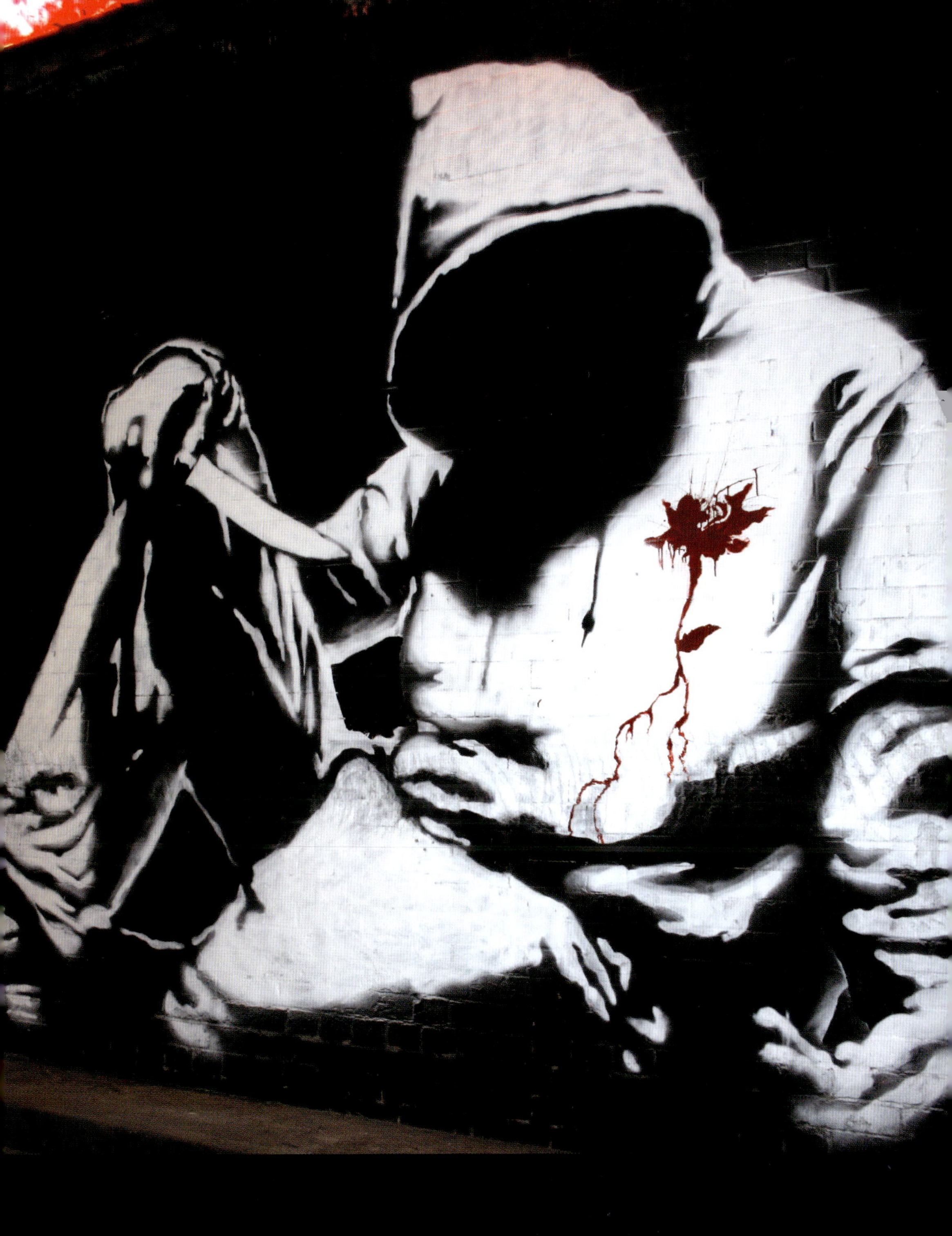

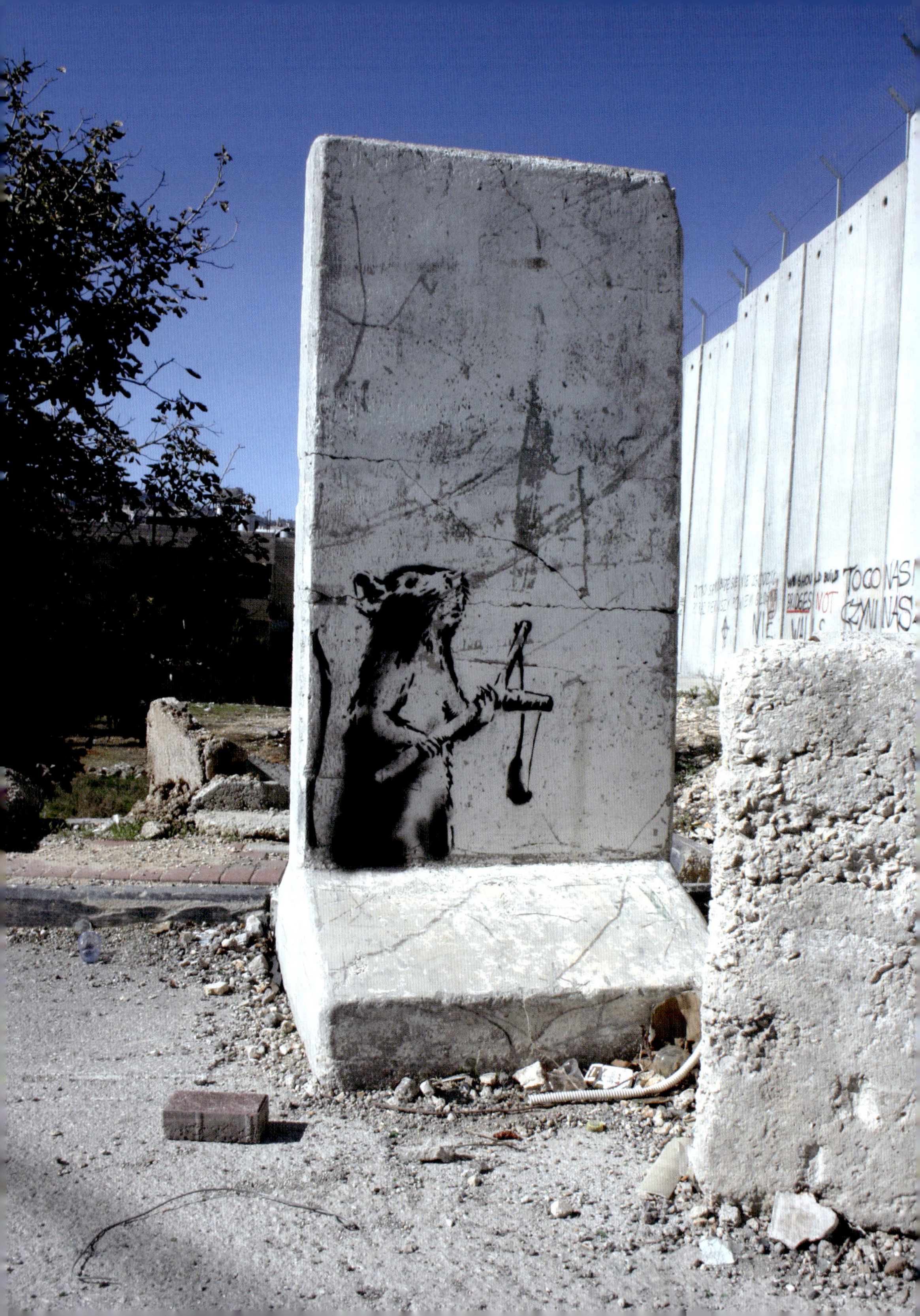
WE SHOULD BUILD
BRIDGES NOT WALLS
NIE
TO CO NAS
CZYNI NAS

IT'S ABOUT
UNDERGROUND
CULTURE...THE THINGS
COME UP FROM THE
SEWERS.

I LIKE THE IDEA OF NICELY
TOOLED UP VERMIN.

THEY'RE NOT QUITE AS STUPID
AS YOU THINK AND THEY HAVE
THE EQUIPMENT TO DEAL
WITH THINGS.

BANKSY

Banksy on Rats

"Creative Vandalism", Jim Carey, Squall Magazine 2002

ANIMAL RIGHTS

Banksy does love animals. Maybe it's something to do with growing up in the rural west country, where cows were the next best thing to New York subway cars for a young graffiti artist. Again and again, he returns to the theme of our schizophrenic attitudes towards animals. He clashes images of cutesy animal characters with the reality of industrial meat production. He juxtaposes our love of pets with our love of chicken nuggets. Is Banksy a vegetarian? PETA apparently asked him to do a campaign for them, something he must have turned down.

In the New York Pet Store and Grill exhibition, featuring a dolphin ride caught up in a tuna fishing net, Banksy seemed equally happy to giggle at the outraged animal rights activist who freed the dolphin from the net.

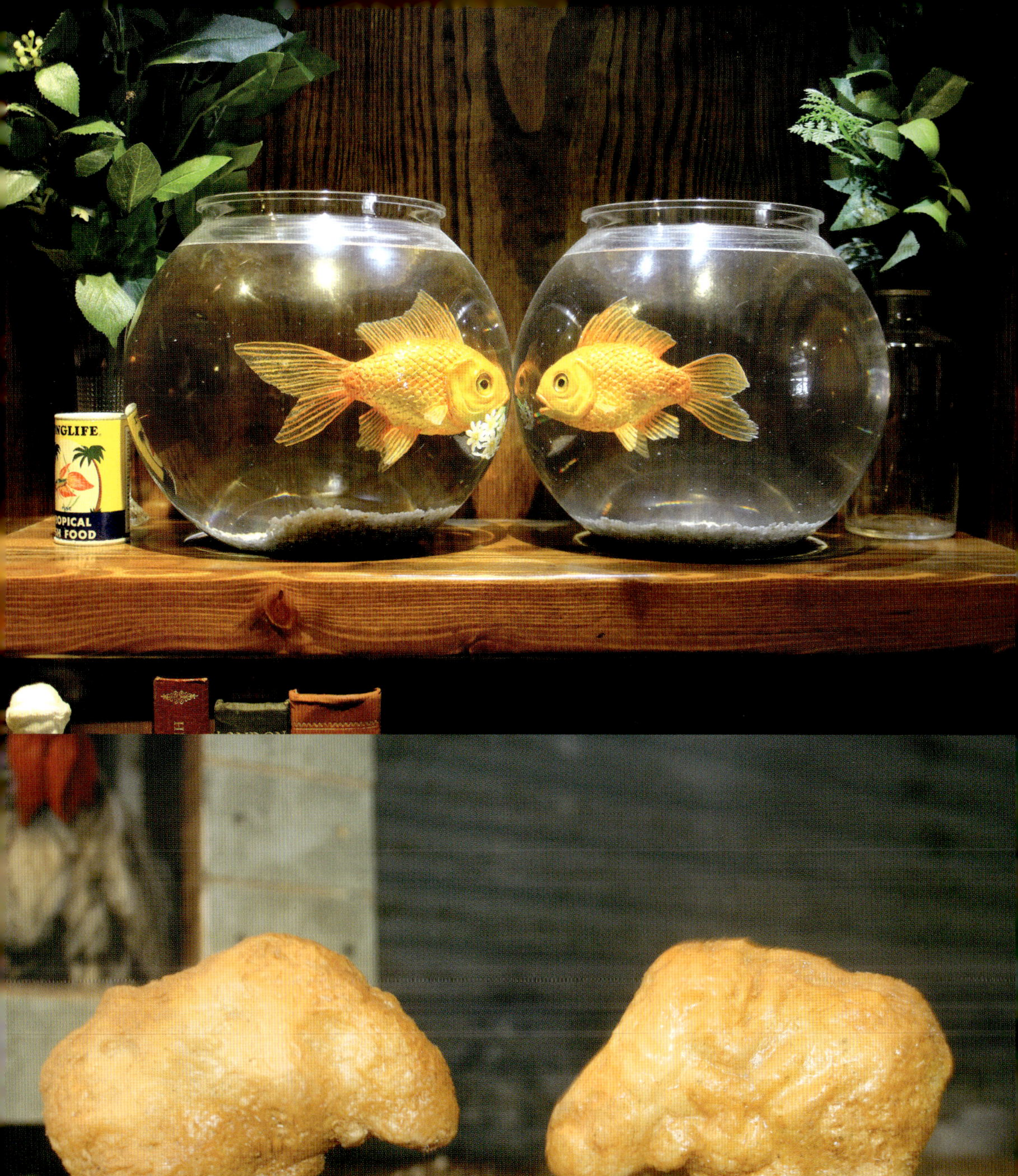

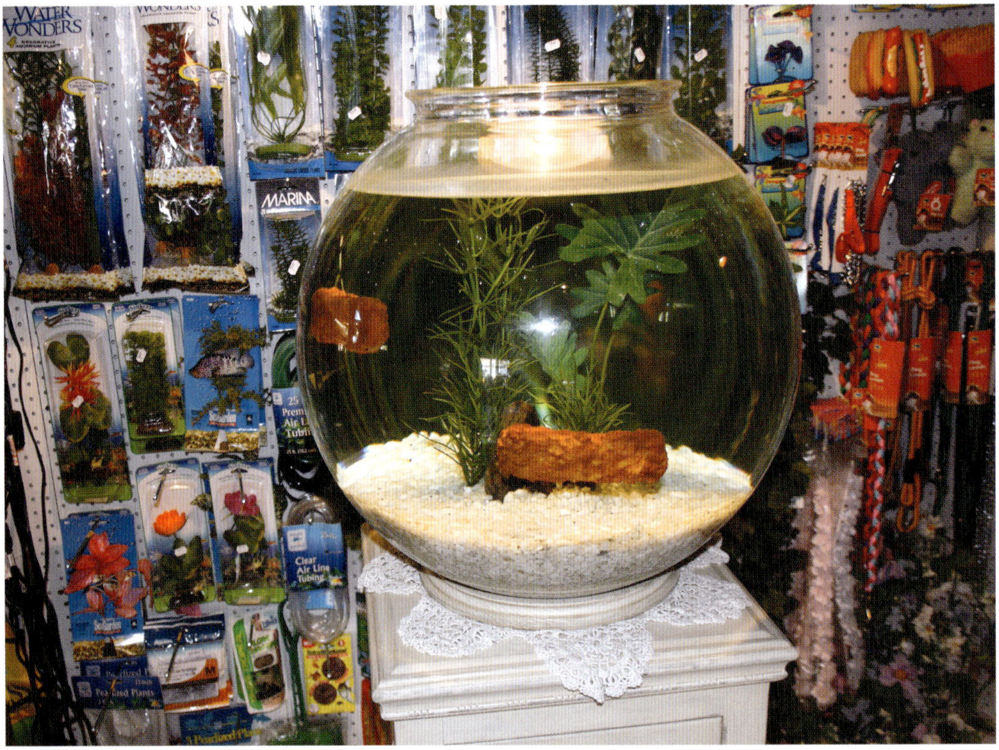

WATER
VONDERS
MARINA

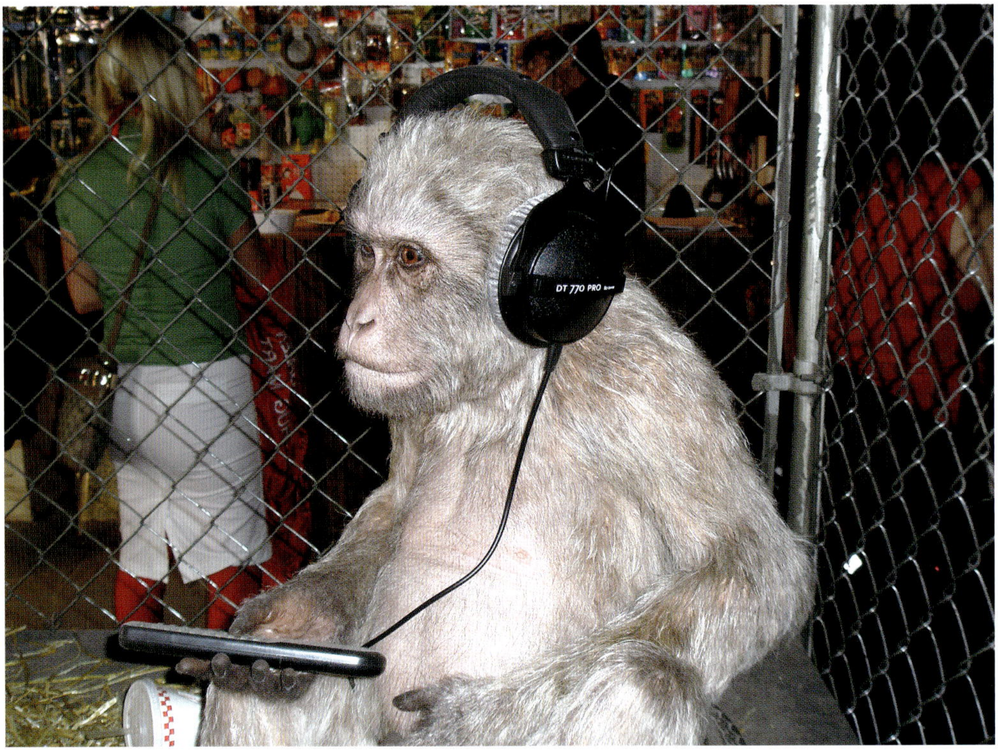

DT 770 PRO

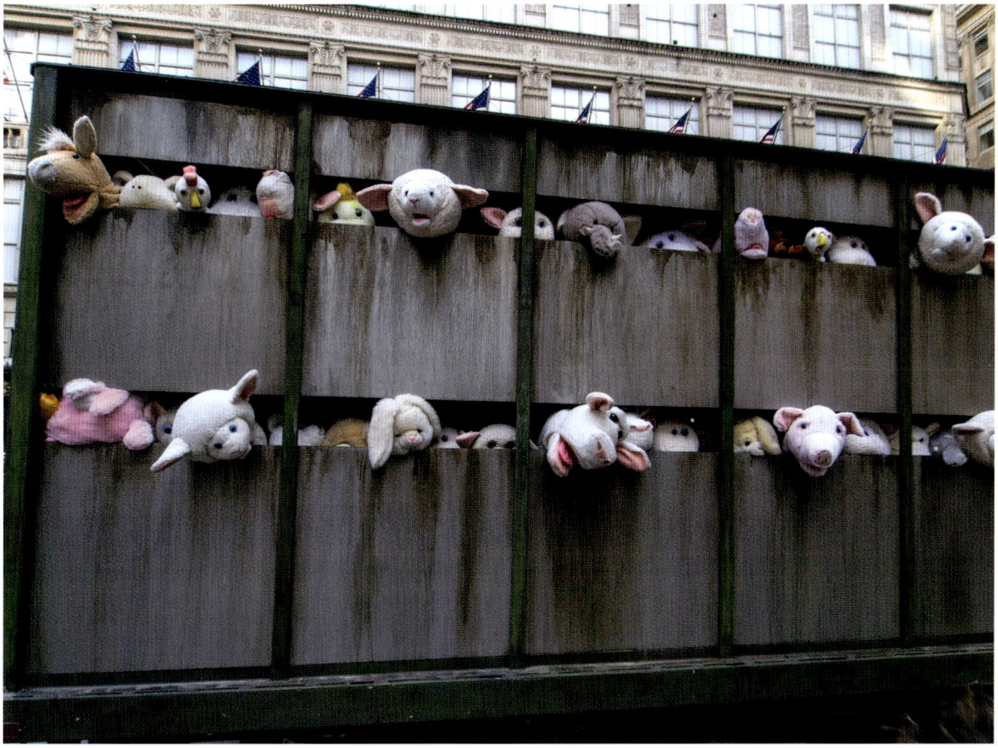

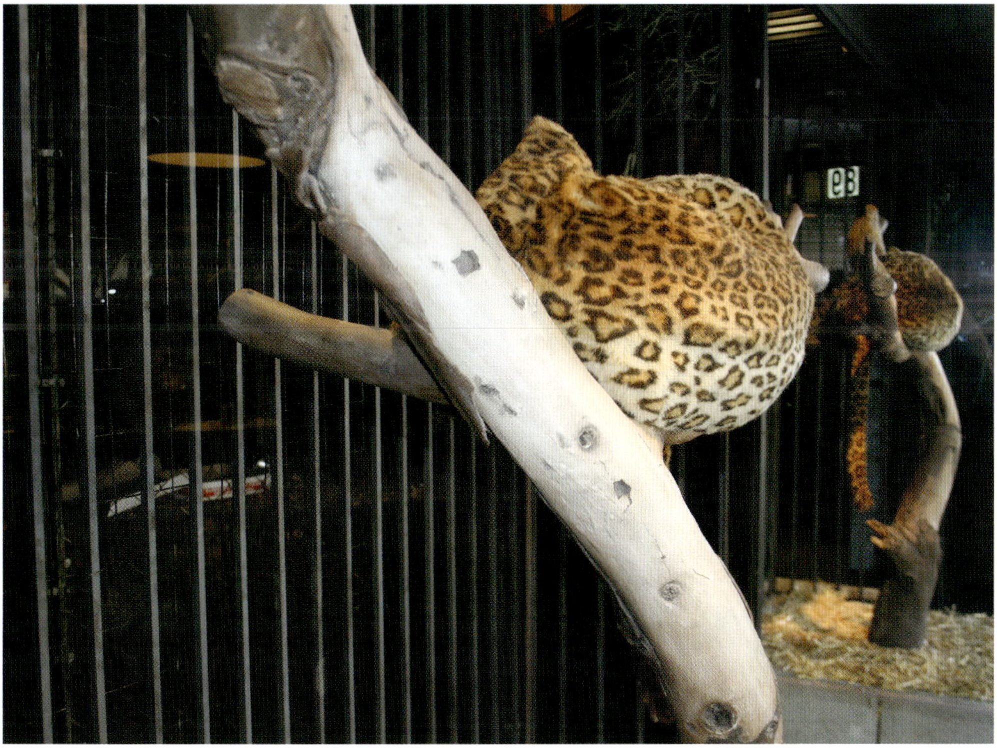

WIN
THE RAT RACE
AND YOU'RE STILL
A RAT.

BANKSY

"Banging Your Head Against a Brick Wall" Banksy
Weapons of Mass Distraction 2001

He who dies with the most toys wins. This is Banksy's original criticism of society and is still the most relevant. We live in an era when people pay to have photos taken on private jets for their instagram accounts. If you want to revel in the full horror of this mindset, look up that documentary on the Fyre festival. Rome is burning. Nero is fiddling. Banksy's rats are looking ever more likely to end up in charge.

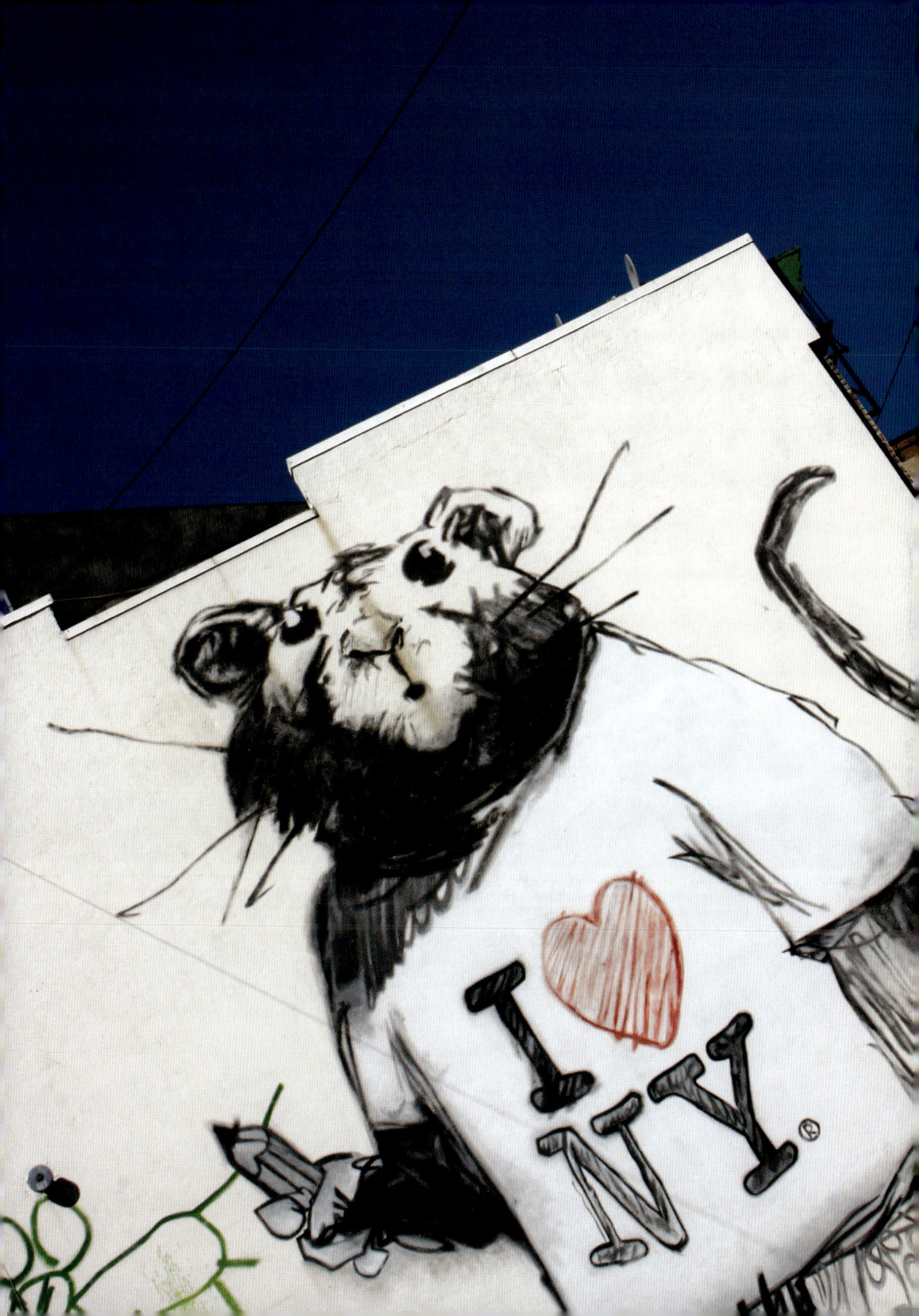

I ♥ NY®

REMEMBER IT'S ALWAYS EASIER TO GET FORGIVENESS THAN PERMISSION

BANKSY

"Wall & Piece" Banksy

Vintage Publishing 2006

It is the unspoken rule. You'll never get anywhere if you play by the rules. However, it is widely taught in expensive educational establishments. You can imagine this being the title of a module at Harvard Business School. It is certainly the Mantra of tech entrepreneurs and their 'disruptive' business models. Nevertheless, it's still valid advice for a young grasshopper embarking on a life. Don't wait for the lights to turn green, they never will. (Top Fact: Originally said by rear Admiral Grace Hopper, the godmother of modern programming languages).

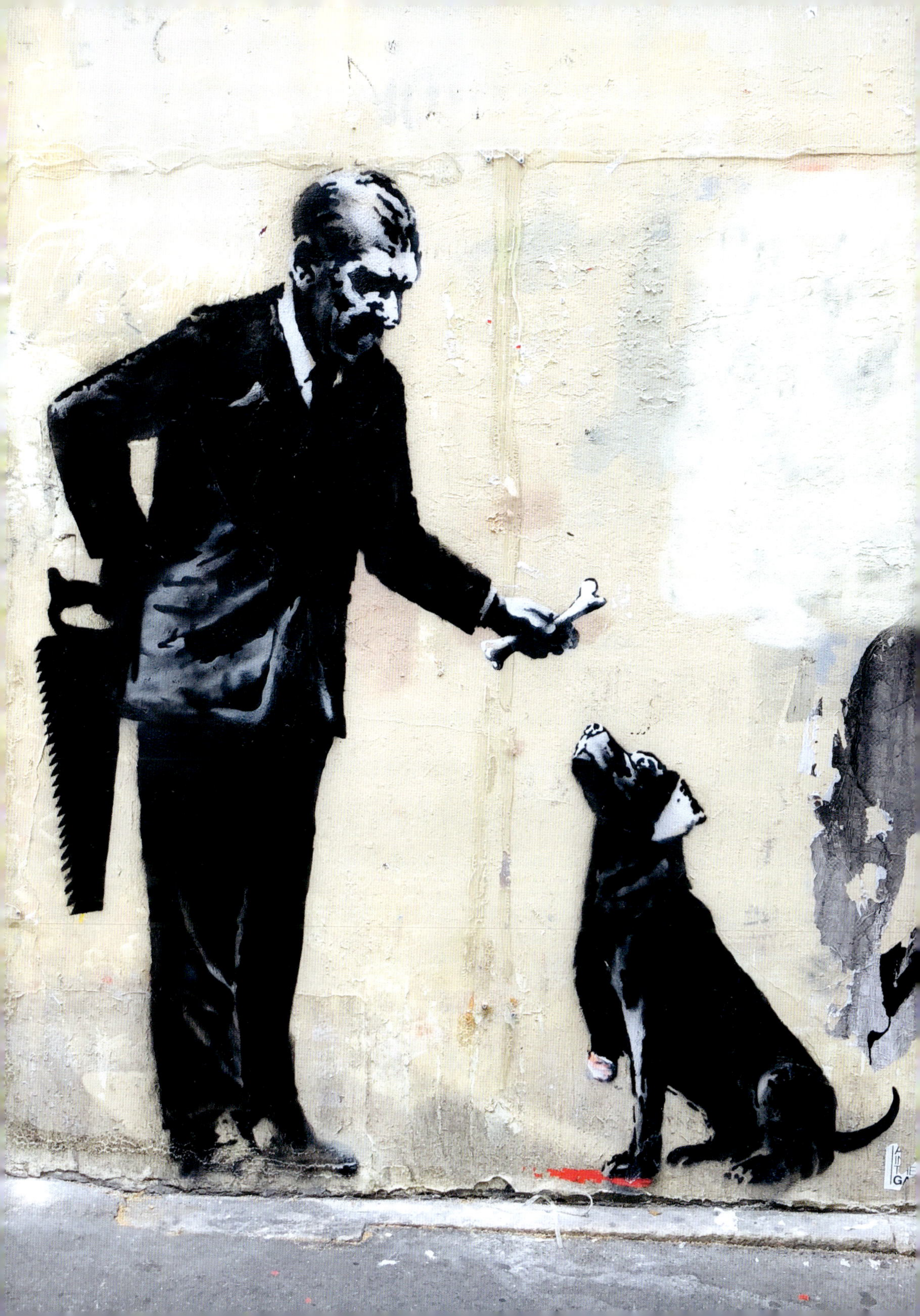

NEW YORK, BIRTHPLACE OF GRAFFITI

Graffiti has always existed. However, Modern Graffiti was born in New York in the 1970's. A young man of Greek origin, a courier, took to writing his tag TAKI 183 all over the city with a marker pen. In 1971 the New York Times did a feature on TAKI 183, spawning a slew of imitators. In 1972 he was a founder member of a group called United Graffiti Artists - modern graffiti culture was born and soon spread around the world. Not long after, characters were introduced and then pieces got bigger and bigger in the war for attention. Banksy references this original culture in several of his pieces, including his pilgrimages to NYC itself.

At times Banksy has been critical or even hostile towards the old school, notoriously painting over a King Robbo masterpiece by Camden Lock, starting a Graffiti war with Team Robbo (2012). But in the end, it's clear he loves his old school heritage. His balloon Banksy, the last piece of his Inside Out NYC 'Residency' in 2013, was a homage to the original bubble lettering style of the 1970's. And his calls to protect 5Pointz showed his desire to preserve some of that NYC graffiti heritage.

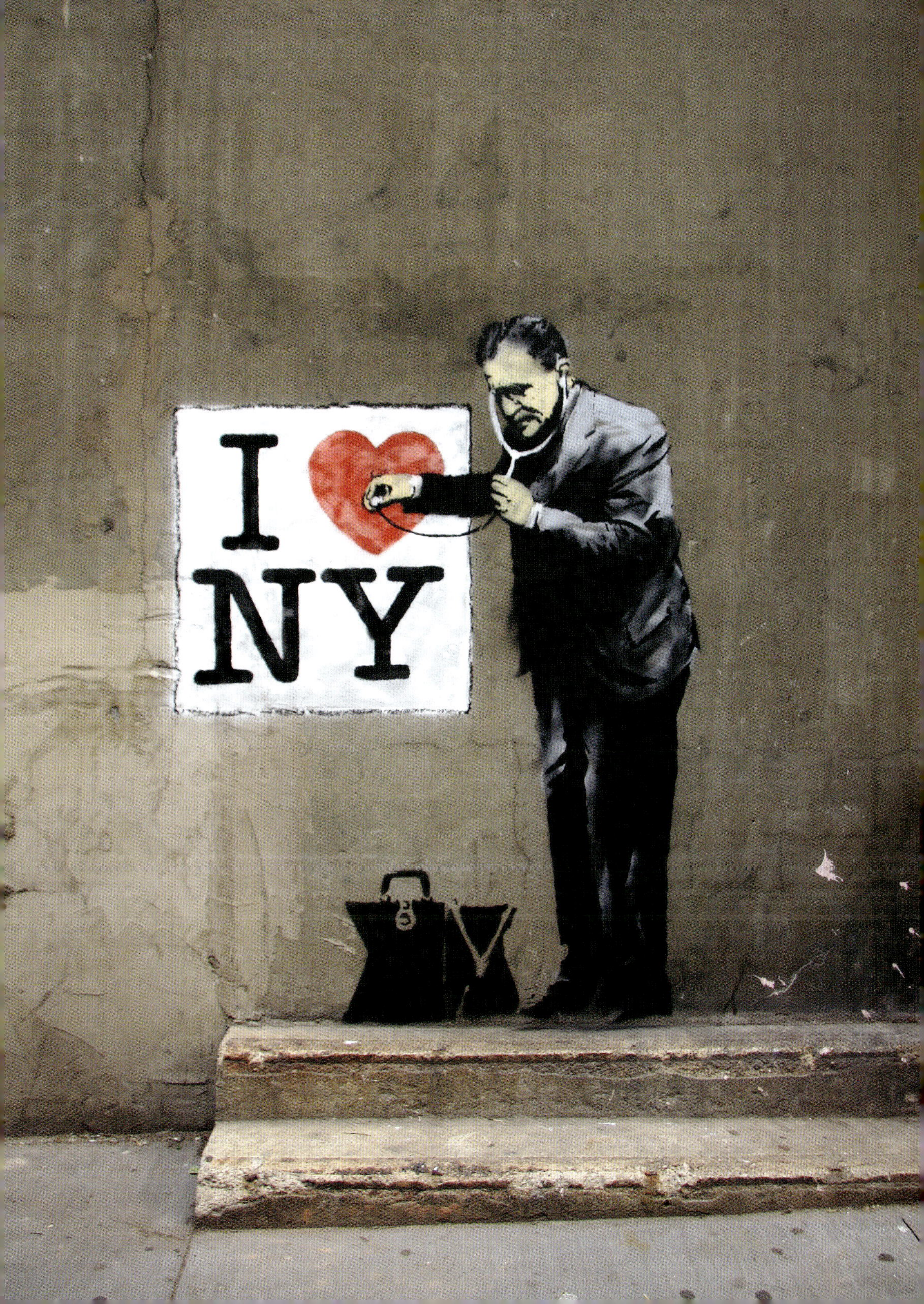

I ♥
NY

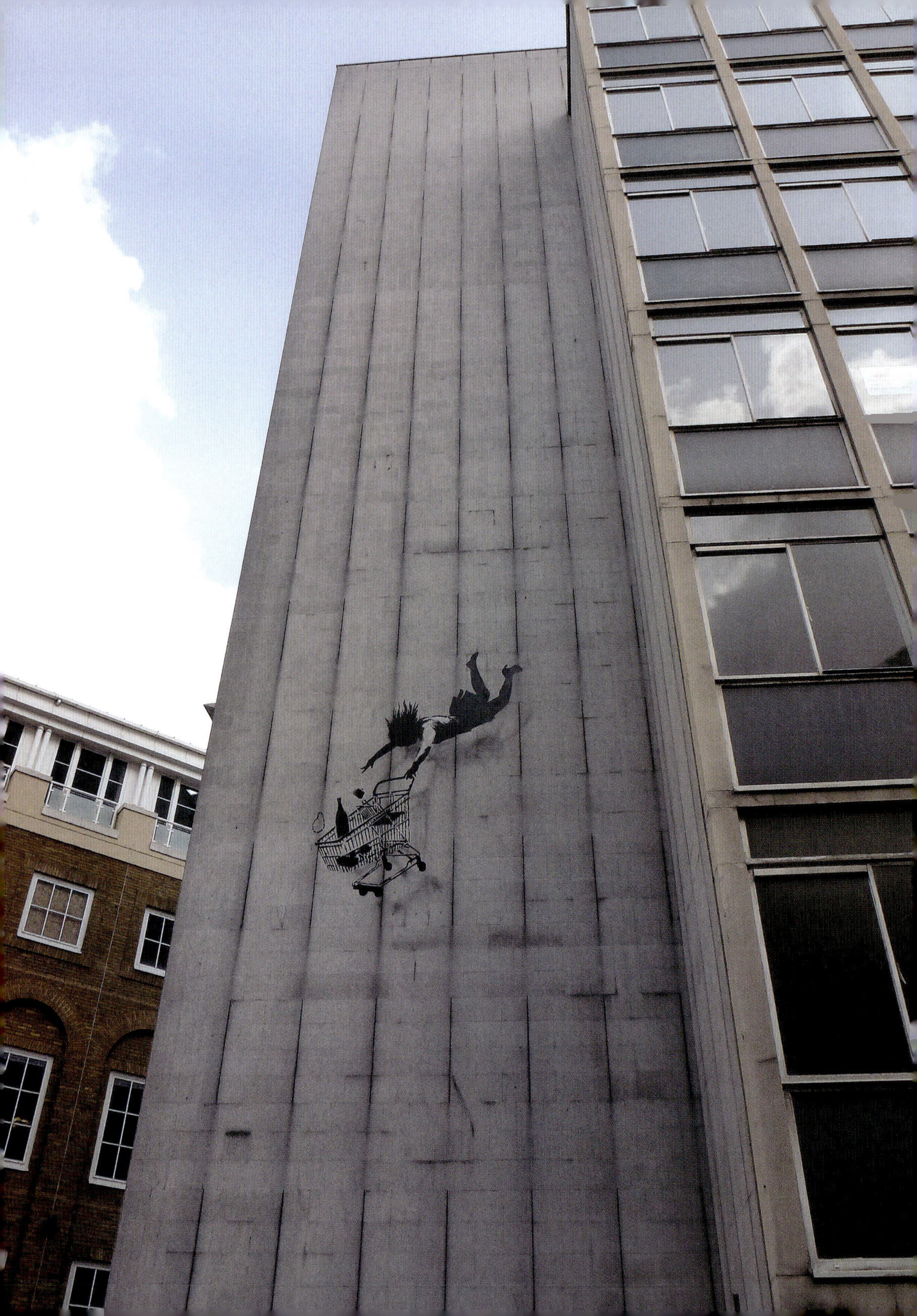

CRIME
AGAINST PROPERTY
IS NOT REAL CRIME.

BANKSY

"Wall & Piece" Banksy

Vintage Publishing 2006

La propriété, c'est le vol! Proudhon, 1840. 'Property is theft!'
Which even Marx though was a bit confusing. More clearly,
all property starts out as theft. Society starts when people
fence off land and say 'this is mine', which is historically and
currently achieved by brute force. Coming into the modern
city, you encounter everything around you as somebody
elses's property, even the so called public spaces. The claim
to ownership is not in any sense concretely real. Therefore
crime against it cannot be real. This is Banksy at his most
(perhaps accidentally) Marxist, shock! horror!

I THINK ANDY WARHOL GOT IT WRONG:

IN THE FUTURE, SO MANY PEOPLE ARE GOING TO BECOME FAMOUS THAT ONE DAY EVERYBODY WILL END UP BEING ANONYMOUS FOR 15 MINUTES.

BANKSY

"Banksy: The Naked Truth" Banksy interviewed by Shepard Fairey

Swindle Magazine 2006

For a vandal Banksy sure is a cultured old sod. He's not shy
of name dropping the odd icon

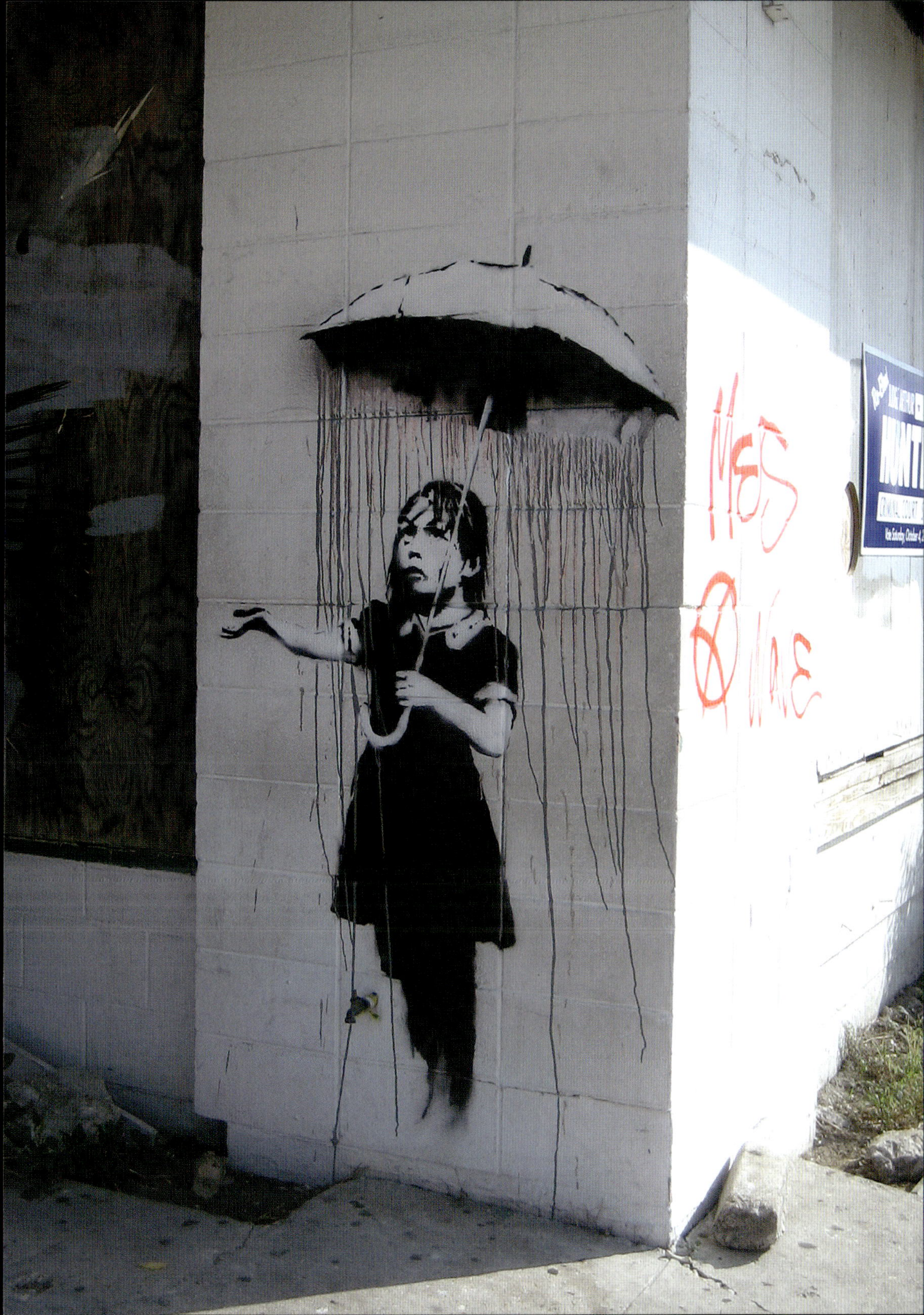
MES
DUAE

DREAMS OF A NEW CITY

Imagine a city where graffiti was legal. Imagine the world as if it were a beautiful place. Imagine a world after capitalism. Banksy dreams of a utopia where art remakes the world, popular art made by the people for the people. This is the same old dream the avant garde artists had, the situationists had and maybe every teenager since teenagers were invented. Still, it's a beautiful dream.

"And you, forgotten, your memories ravaged by all the consternations of two hemispheres, stranded in the Red Cellars of Pali-Kao, without music and without geography, no longer setting out for the hacienda where the roots think of the child and where the wine is finished off with fables from an old almanac. That's all over. You'll never see the hacienda. It doesn't exist. The hacienda must be built."

Gilles Ivain (Ivan Chtcheglov), October 1953. Printed in Internationale Situationniste #1

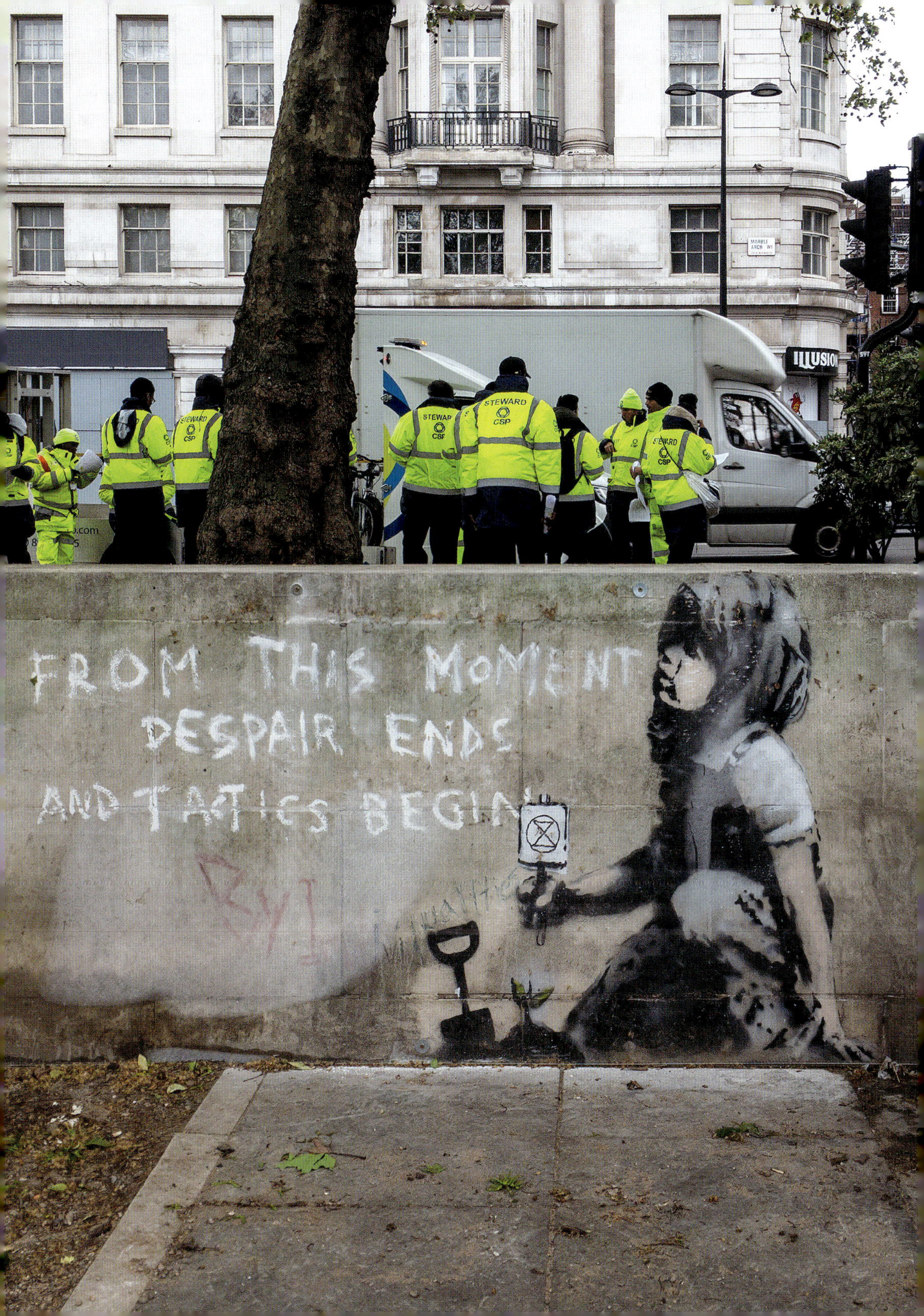

FROM THIS MOMENT
DESPAIR ENDS
AND TACTICS BEGIN

ONE NATION UNDER CCTV

BANKSY

"Wall & Piece" Banksy
Vintage Publishing 2006

The proliferation of Closed Circuit Television in the UK took place in paralell to Banksy's career. In the early 1990's it was unusual to see a CCTV camera outside of urban centres. By the time of writing there are an estimated 6 million cameras in use. The normalisation of being filmed is now so complete that the next generation will wonder what this piece was on about. Especially as CCTV is widely used to monitor behaviour in British Secondary Schools. Studies from 2003 showed roughly two thirds of the public were broadly supportive of the installation of more CCTV. A 2013 study found that CCTV does nothing to reduce violent crime, but can reduce vehicle crime. The development of facial recognition technology is the new frontier of this debate.

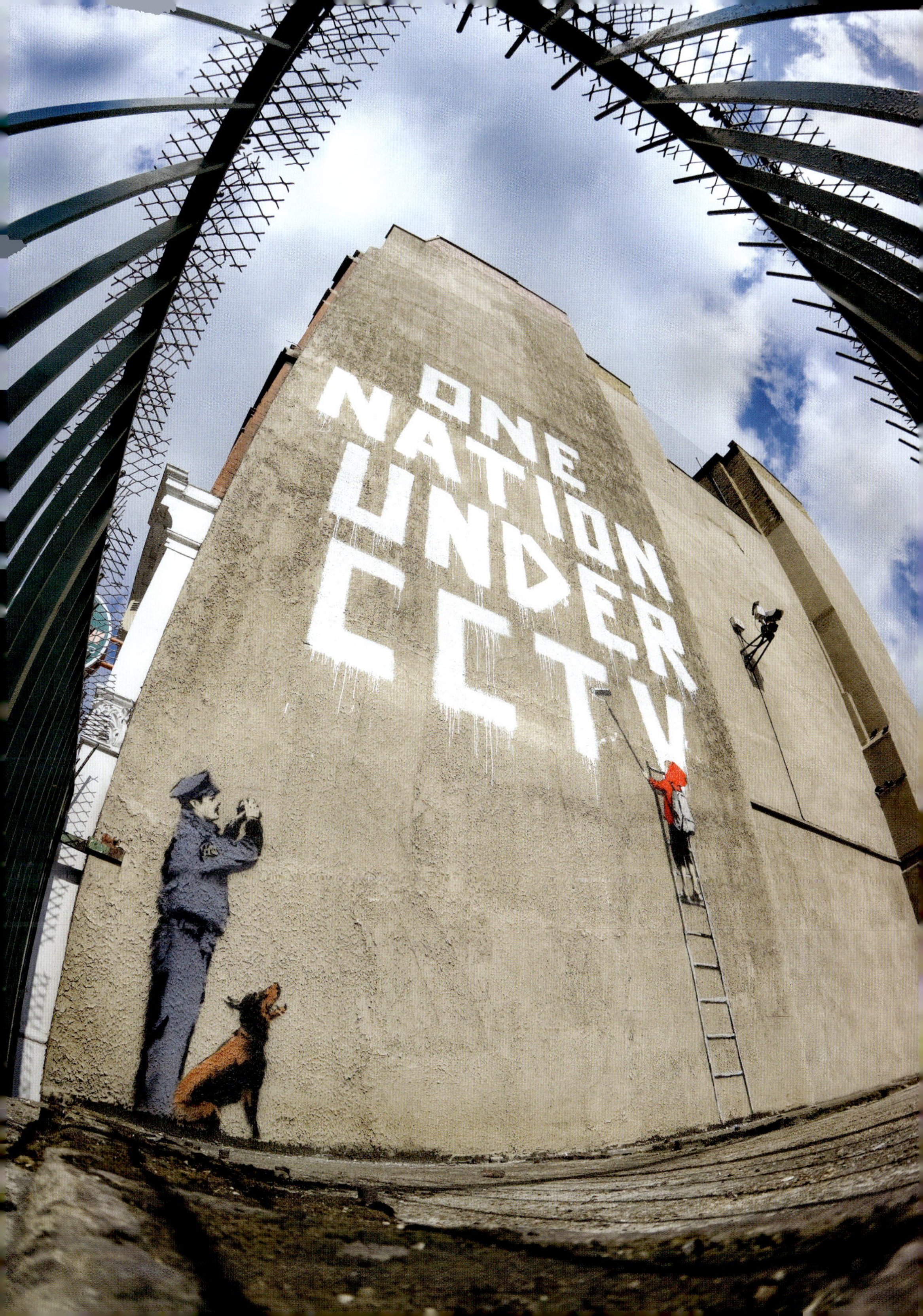
ONE
NATION
UNDER
CCTV

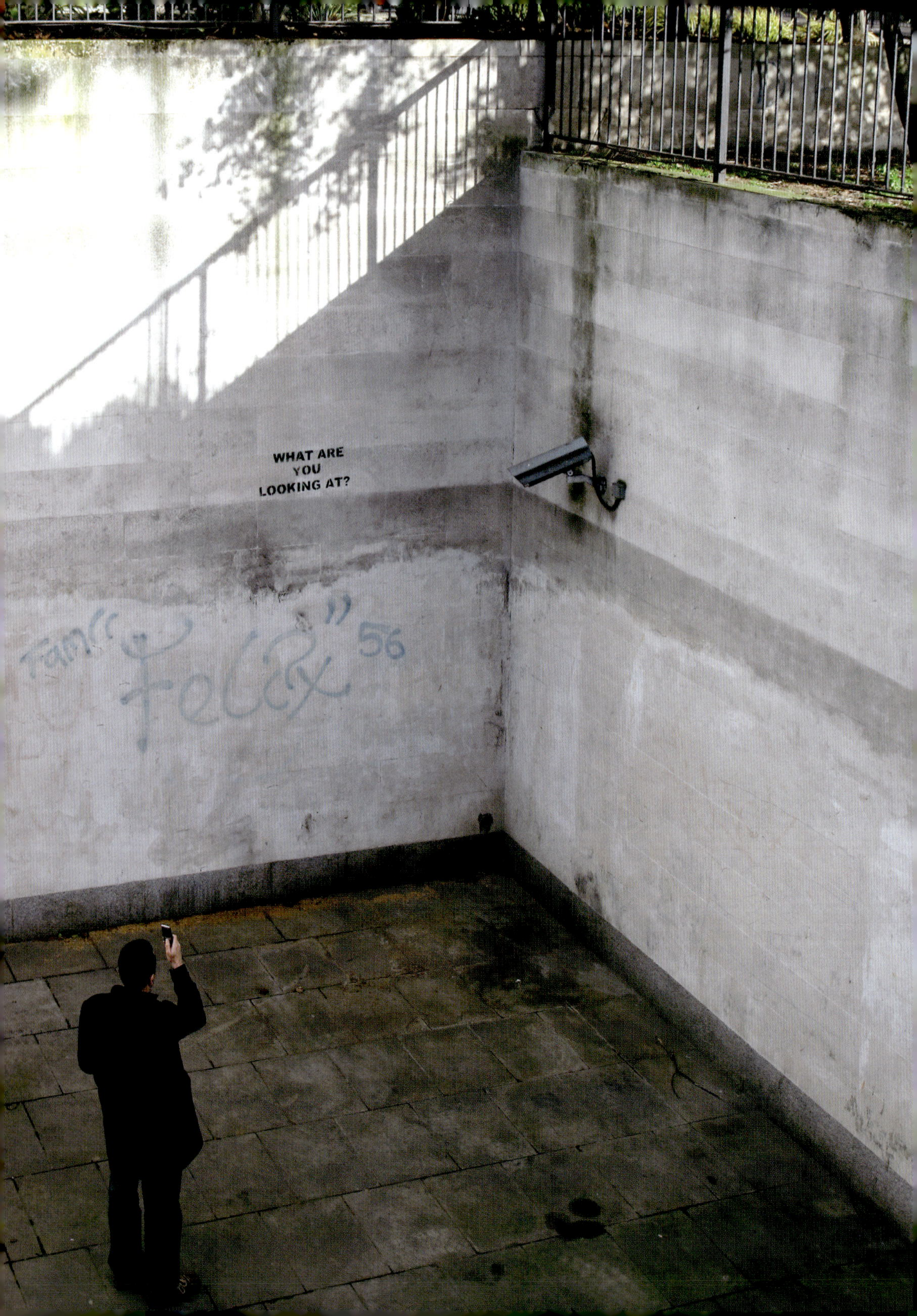

WHAT ARE
YOU
LOOKING AT?

ANY ADVERT IN PUBLIC
SPACE THAT GIVES YOU
NO CHOICE WHETHER YOU
SEE IT OR NOT IS YOURS.

IT'S YOURS TO TAKE, REARRANGE
AND RE-USE. YOU CAN DO
WHATEVER YOU LIKE WITH IT.

ASKING FOR PERMISSION IS LIKE
ASKING TO KEEP A ROCK SOMEONE
JUST THREW AT YOUR HEAD.

BANKSY

"Cut it Out" Banksy

Weapons of Mass Distraction 2004

This raises an interesting question, does this mean that you
can take the chuggers and the marketers who stand on the
high street trying to buttonhole you? Do they also belong to
you? Could we paint stencils on them? Of course, that would
just be a fight in the prison yard between the prisoners

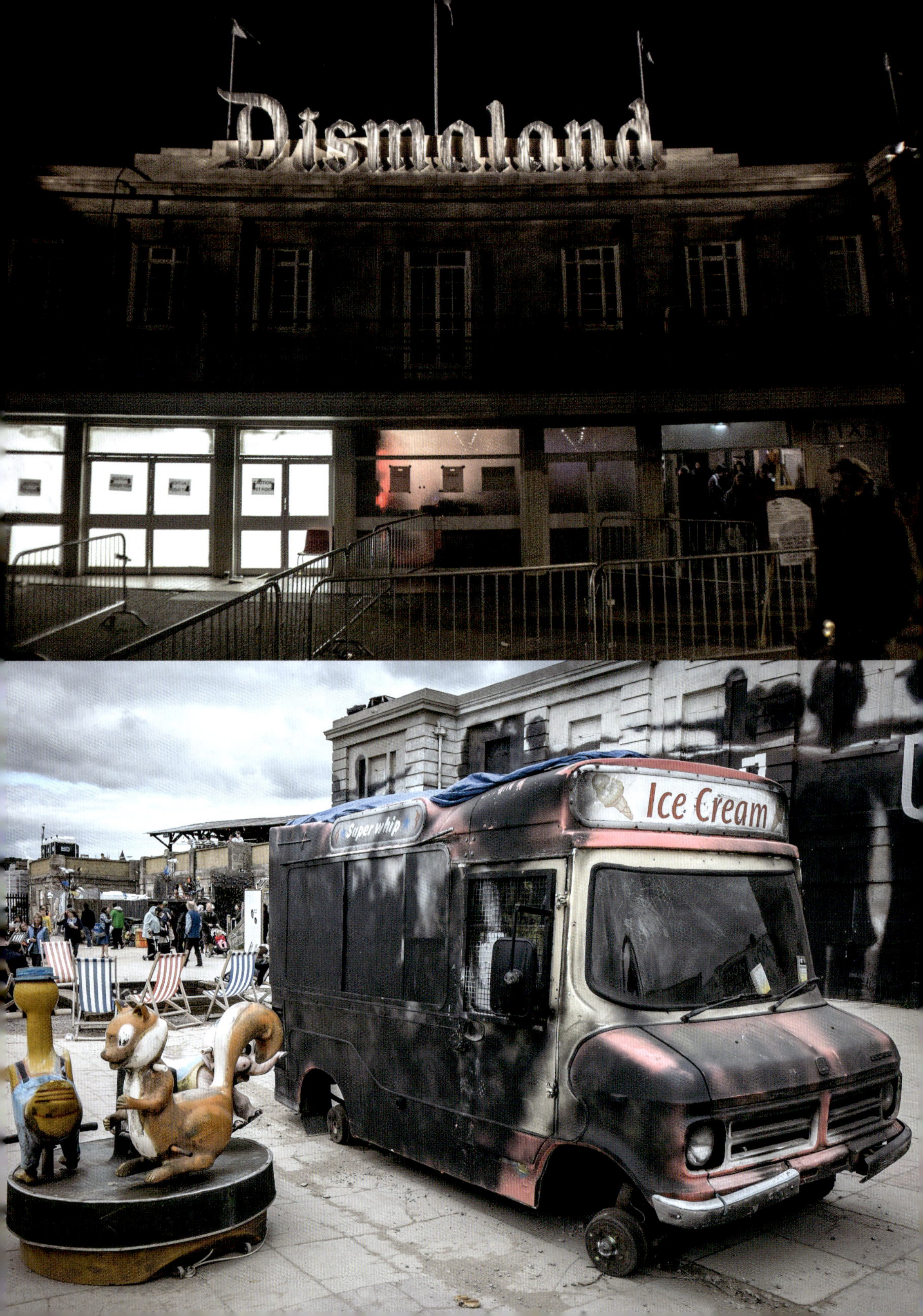
Dismaland
Ice Cream
Super whip

DISMALAND

Weston-super-Mare, Somerset, England

August-September 2015

"Essentially, the big theme is that
theme parks should have bigger themes."

- Banksy Interview, Juxtapoz Magazine, October 2015

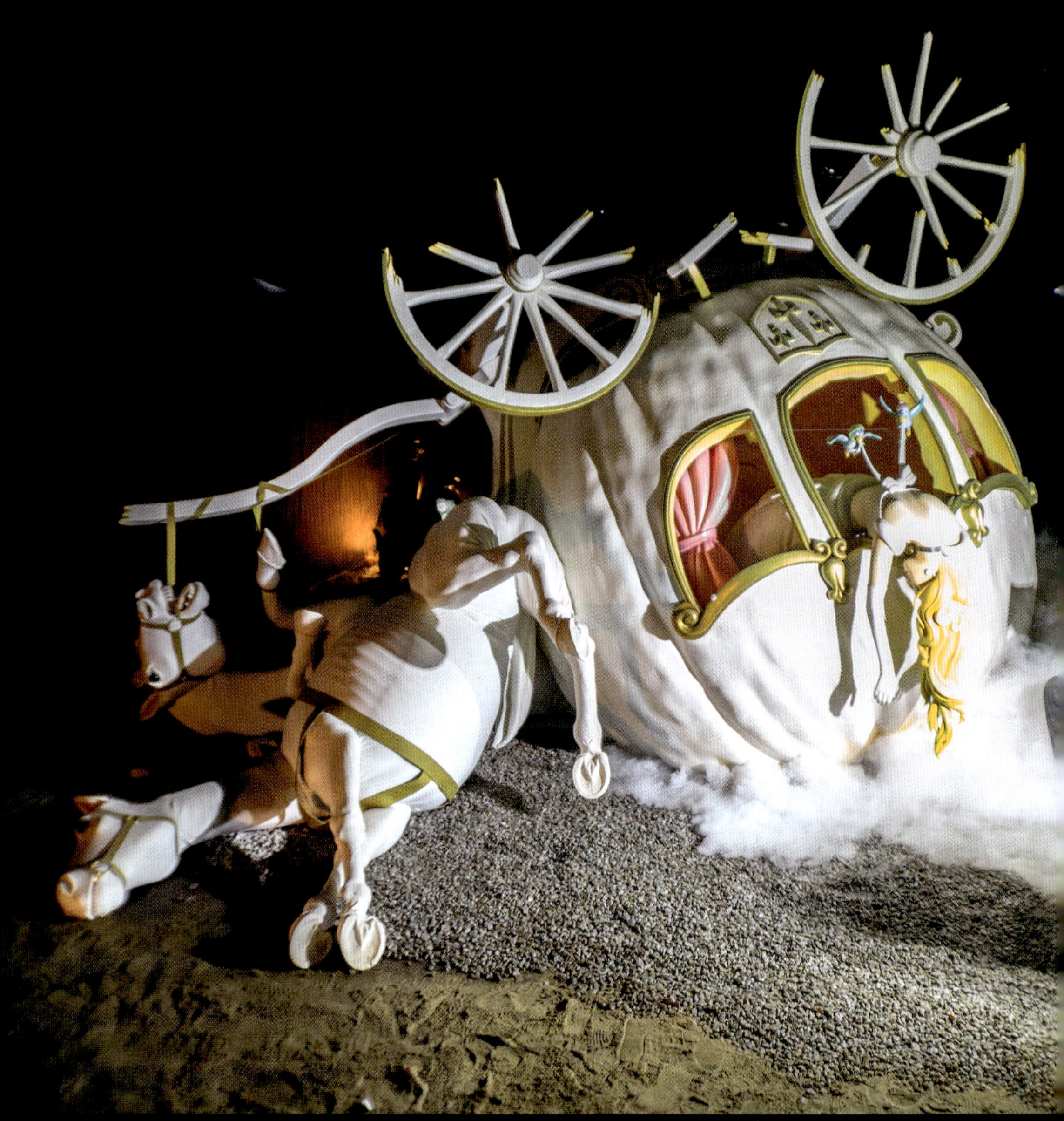

We have this idea in modern society that leisure time exists, and leisure time has certain special properties, the main one being that we should not have to consider the horror of our reality very much when we are at leisure, we should be allowed mindless escapism. But where do you go to escape from all the escapism? Dismaland was a way of posing this question.

"No amount of PR or hype can sell the world something if it's not exciting you."

Banksy Interview, Juxtapoz Magazine, October 2015

The placement of the event was poignant to Brits, but possibly lost on the international audience. Crap seaside resorts like Weston-super-Mare are still popular with working class families who would never have the cash to take the kids to Florida for the full Disney experience.

"My satisfaction level is independent of your opinion."

Banksy Interview, Juxtapoz Magazine, October 2015

And Banksy wasn't very satisfied. He reflected that creating the expectation of a theme park left the visitors unsatisfied with experiencing just an art show.

"The Cinderella sculpture is only complete when surrounded by a gawping crowd snapping photos. The audience is the punchline."

Banksy Interview, Juxtapoz Magazine, October 2015

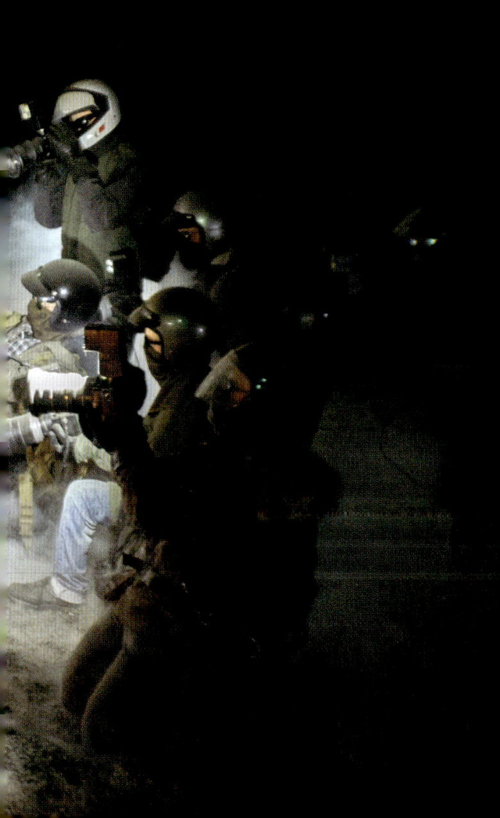

Sometimes Robin Hood wondered if the peasants were just idiots and maybe King John was right after all.

"We just built a family attraction that acknowledges inequality. "

Banksy Interview, Sunday Times, October 2015

Sadly, people generally prefer not to be reminded that they are losing a rat race they never volunteered to take part in - which is why escapism still sells rather well.

Broke people in the USA vote against universal health care because they believe they're only one crap shoot away from being the next millionaire, they're voting against paying higher taxes on their fantasy future income.

Brits generally prefer a kind of stoic reverse snobbery. We don't need all that glitzy nonsense that rich people like. Life doesn't get any better than Weston-super-Mare.

"[Dismaland is] ambitious, but it's also crap. I think there's something very poetic and British about all that."

Banksy Interview, Sunday Times, October 2015

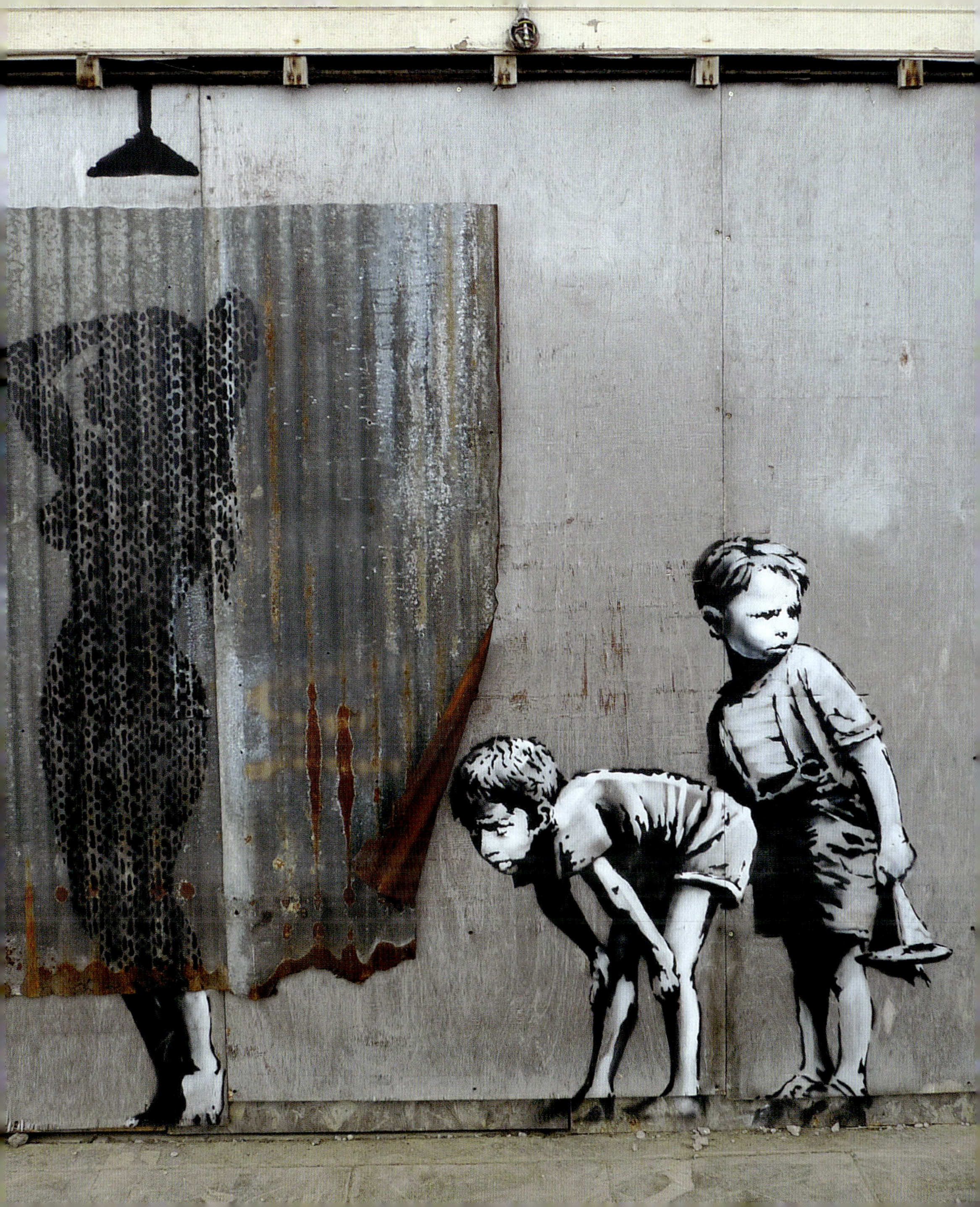

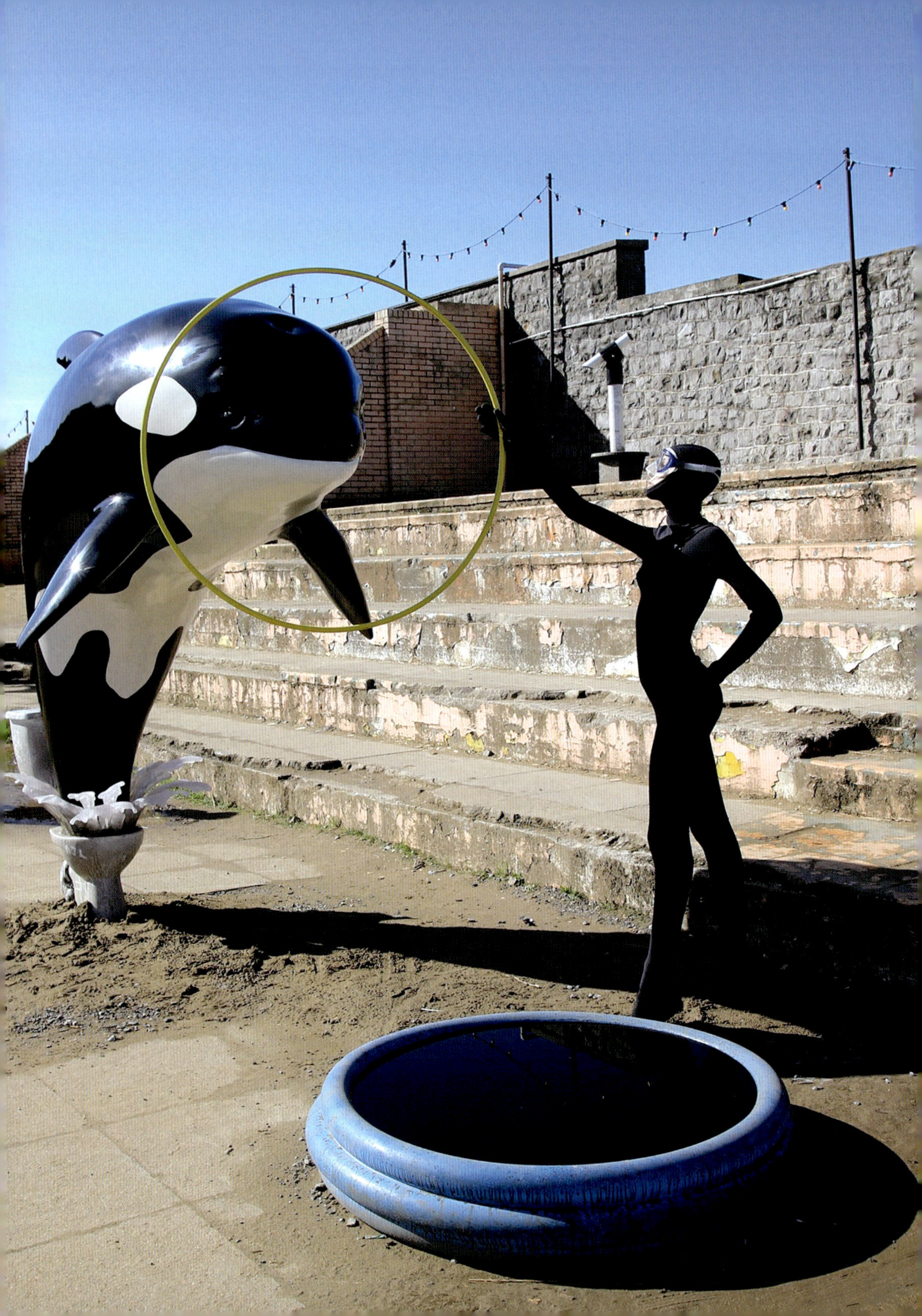

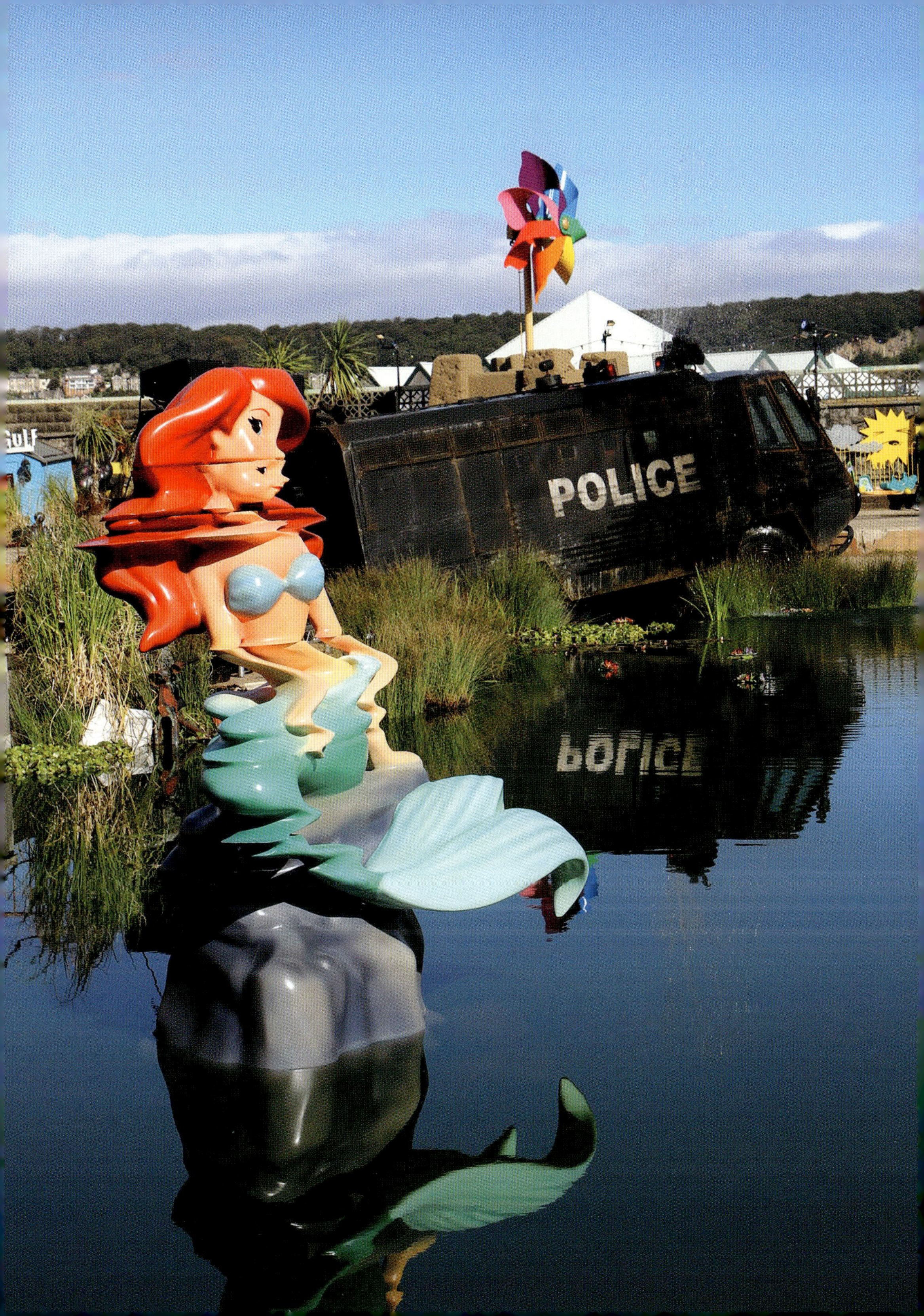

POLICE

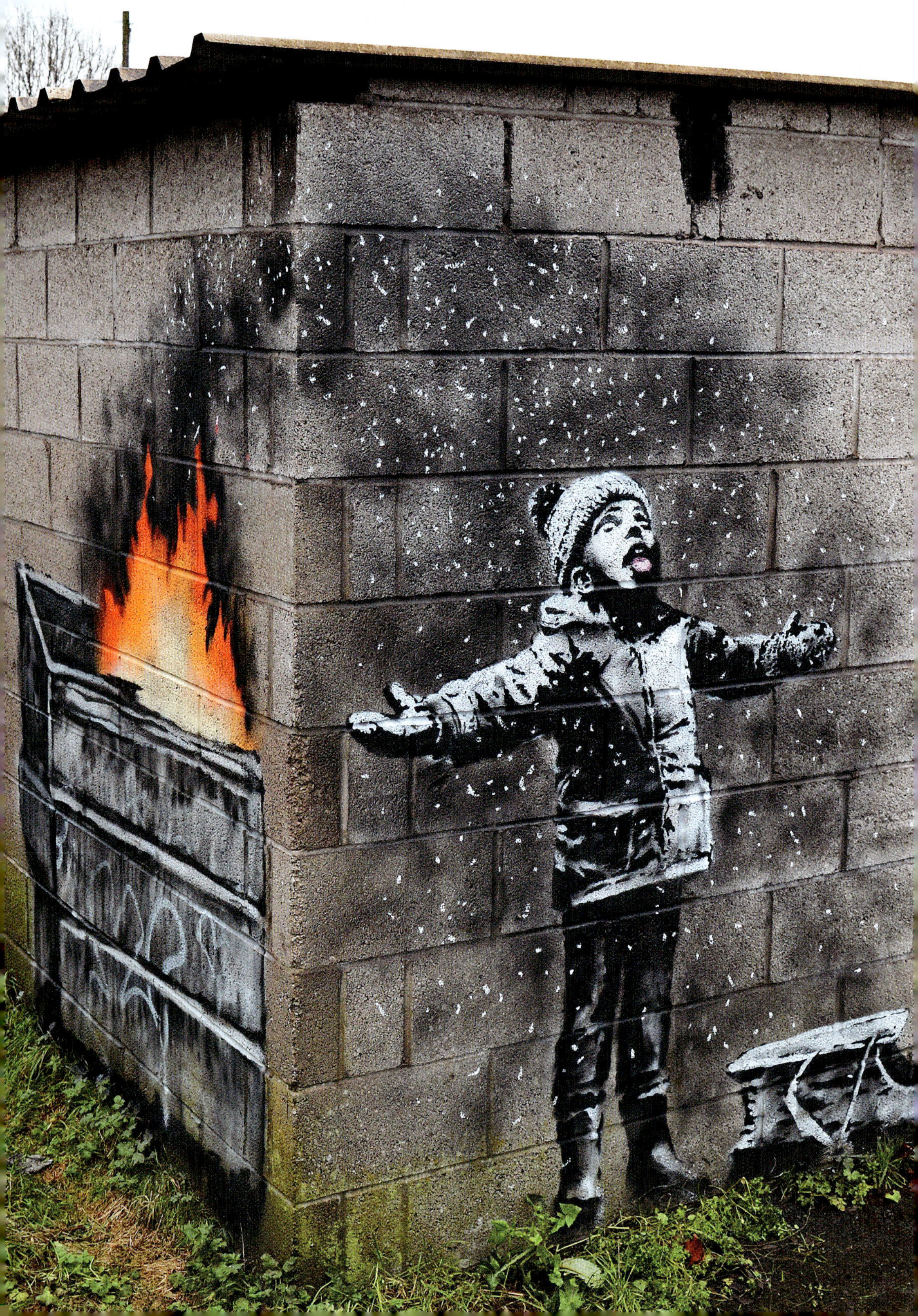

PEOPLE EITHER LOVE ME OR HATE ME, OR THEY DON'T REALLY CARE.

BANKSY

"Wall & Piece" Banksy

Vintage Publishing 2006

Possibly inspired by the British delicacy 'Marmite', a tar black gunk made of fermented vegetables that half the nation loves to spread on toast and the other half the nation thinks is demon vomit. Marmite cleverly turned this 'you either love it or hate it' feature into an advertising campaign in 1996, a campaign so effective that Brits often refer to something divisive as a Marmite Issue. Here Banksy, who openly admires the creativity of advertising even as he despises the practice, parodies the Marmite slogan to his own sardonic ends.

THERE ARE FOUR BASIC HUMAN NEEDS; FOOD, SLEEP, SEX AND REVENGE

BANKSY

"Wall & Piece" Banksy

Vintage Publishing 2006

Revenge is an interesting choice. Because most people can't be arsed with it. But perhaps revenge is a driver in Banksy's work. He's getting revenge on the world, revenge on the corporate culture that takes the piss out of us all the time, revenge on the art world that makes us believe that rich people can control what is and is not art, revenge on the people who told him his pictures would never be in the Louvre. Maybe John Lydon was right 'anger is an energy.'

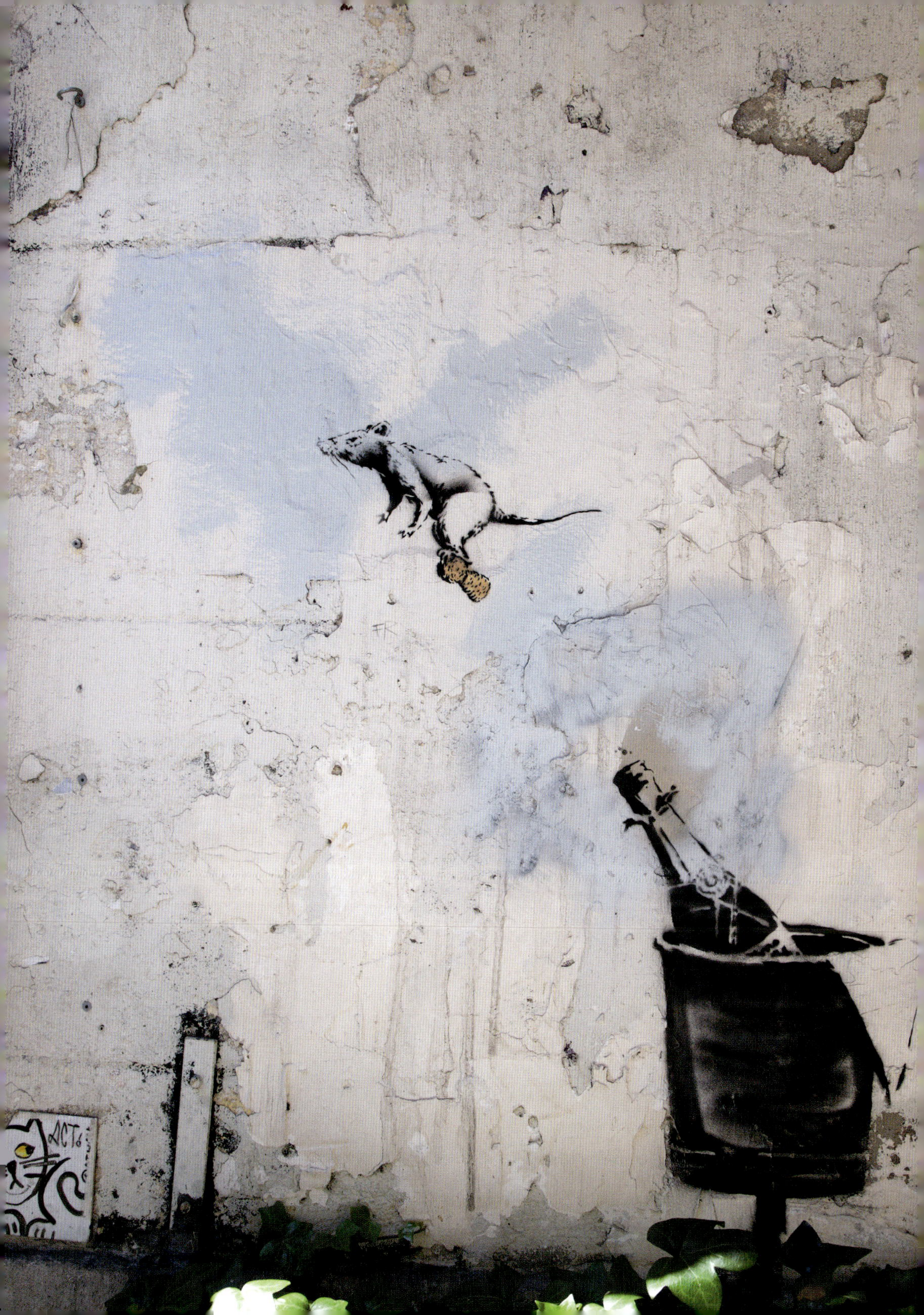

THE REFUGEE CRISIS

The world is experiencing a migrant crisis. And if you want to know what that means in concrete terms, there's few better places to start than the Vice Documentary series 'Europe or Die'. Banksy has been one of very few voices in our culture to persistently draw attention to the crisis. And as the effects of the environmental crisis grow more frequent and more violent, the number of migrants in the world is set to grow.

Most recently, Banksy used his Croydon shop 'Gross Domestic Product', to release work highlighting the incredible risks that people take to get into refugee boats crossing the Mediterranean. Alongside the work itself, a welcome mat was cleverly designed to benefit migrants stuck in camps, who sewed the products out of old lifejackets. You can find the product at lovewelcomes.org.

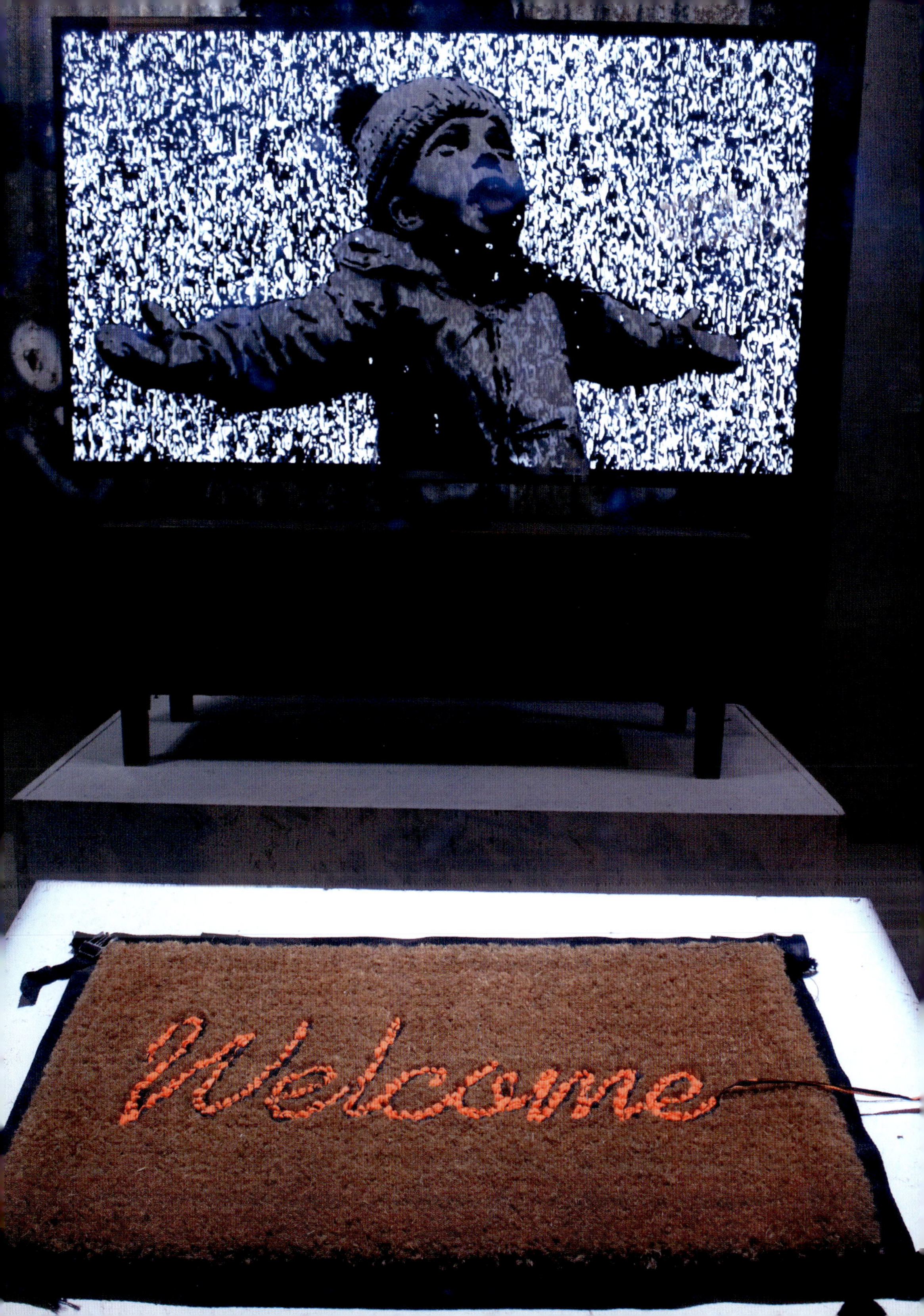
Welcome

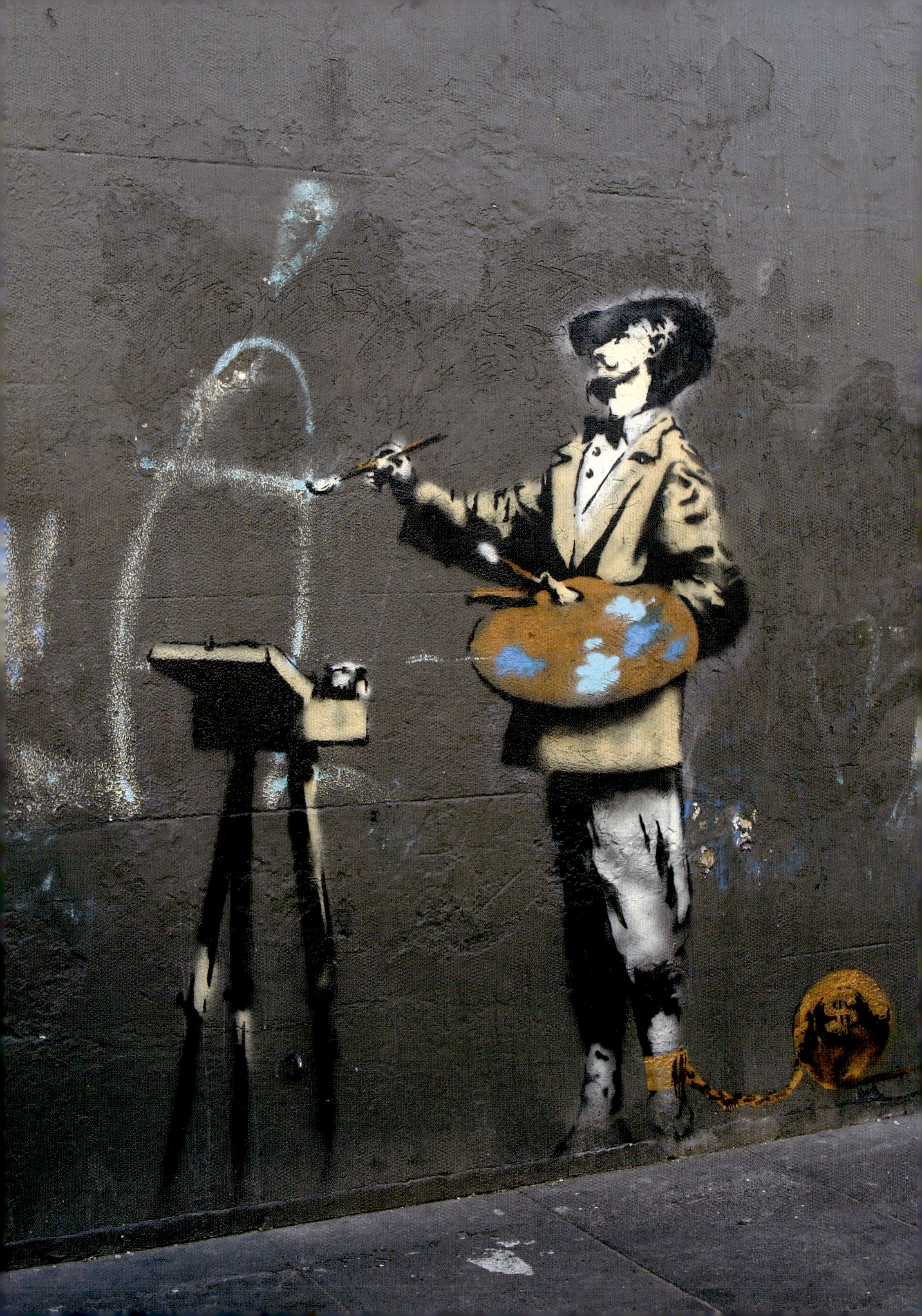

THE ART WORLD IS THE BIGGEST JOKE GOING.

IT'S A REST HOME FOR THE OVERPRIVILEGED, THE PRETENTIOUS, AND THE WEAK.

BANKSY

"Banksy: The Naked Truth" Banksy interviewed by Shepard Fairey

Swindle Magazine 2006

Banksy is never angrier than when he's talking about the art world. But who is the art world? Who exactly is it that makes him so angry? Is everyone involved in art a target to this rage?

I NEED SOMEONE TO PROTECT ME FROM ALL THE MEASURES THEY TAKE IN ORDER TO PROTECT ME.

BANKSY

"Wall & Piece" Banksy

Vintage Publishing 2006

Reminiscent of 'Who watches the watchmen?' from Alan Moore's disturbing masterpiece 'The Watchmen'. Throughout the noughties civil liberties were eroded as public fear of terrorism justified anti terror laws allowing the government unprecedented powers of surveillance. As the government in Hungary has just given themselves absolute power to protect the people from the coronavirus pandemic, we are reminded that dictatorships often start out 'protecting' the people from a national emergency of some kind.

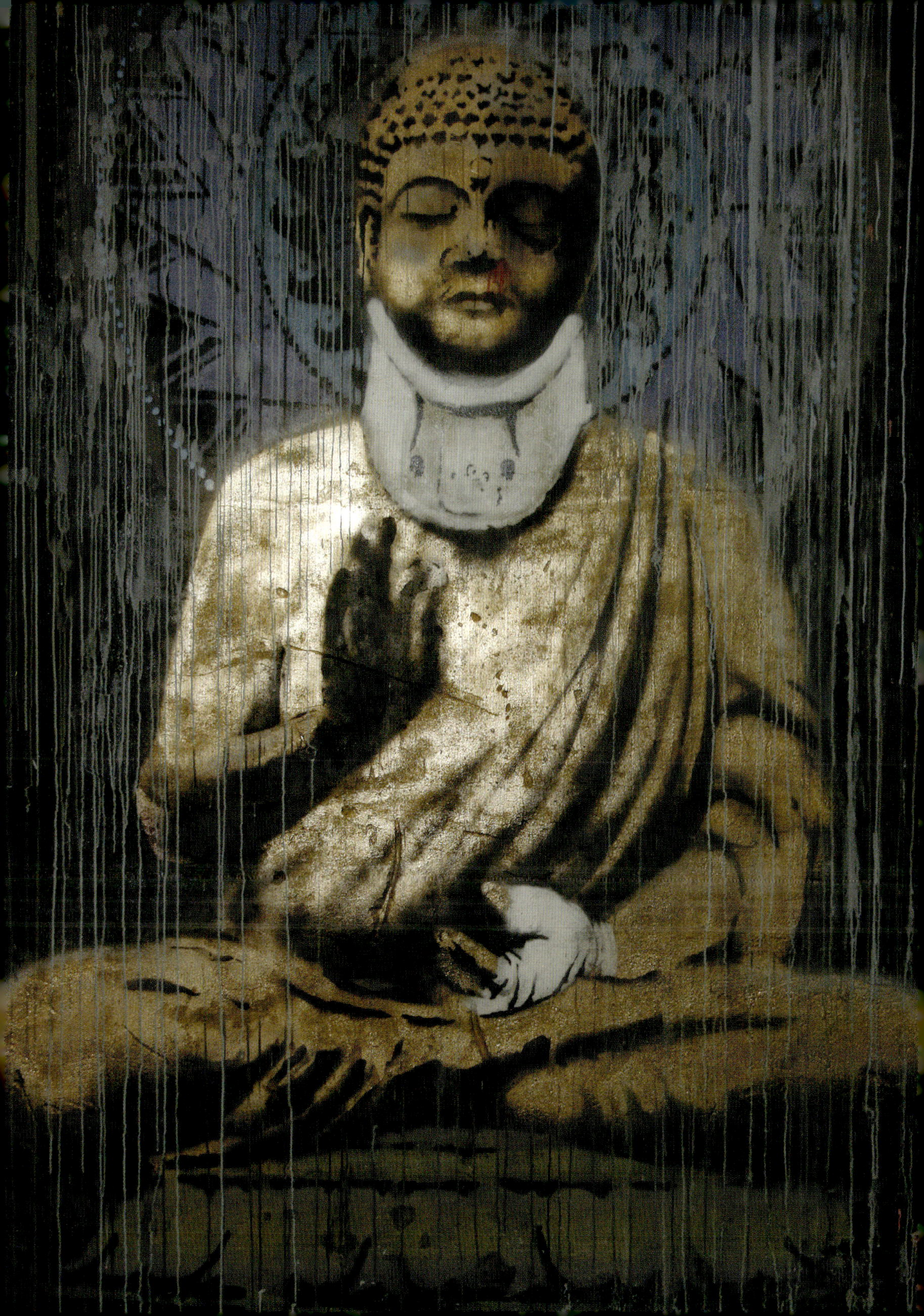

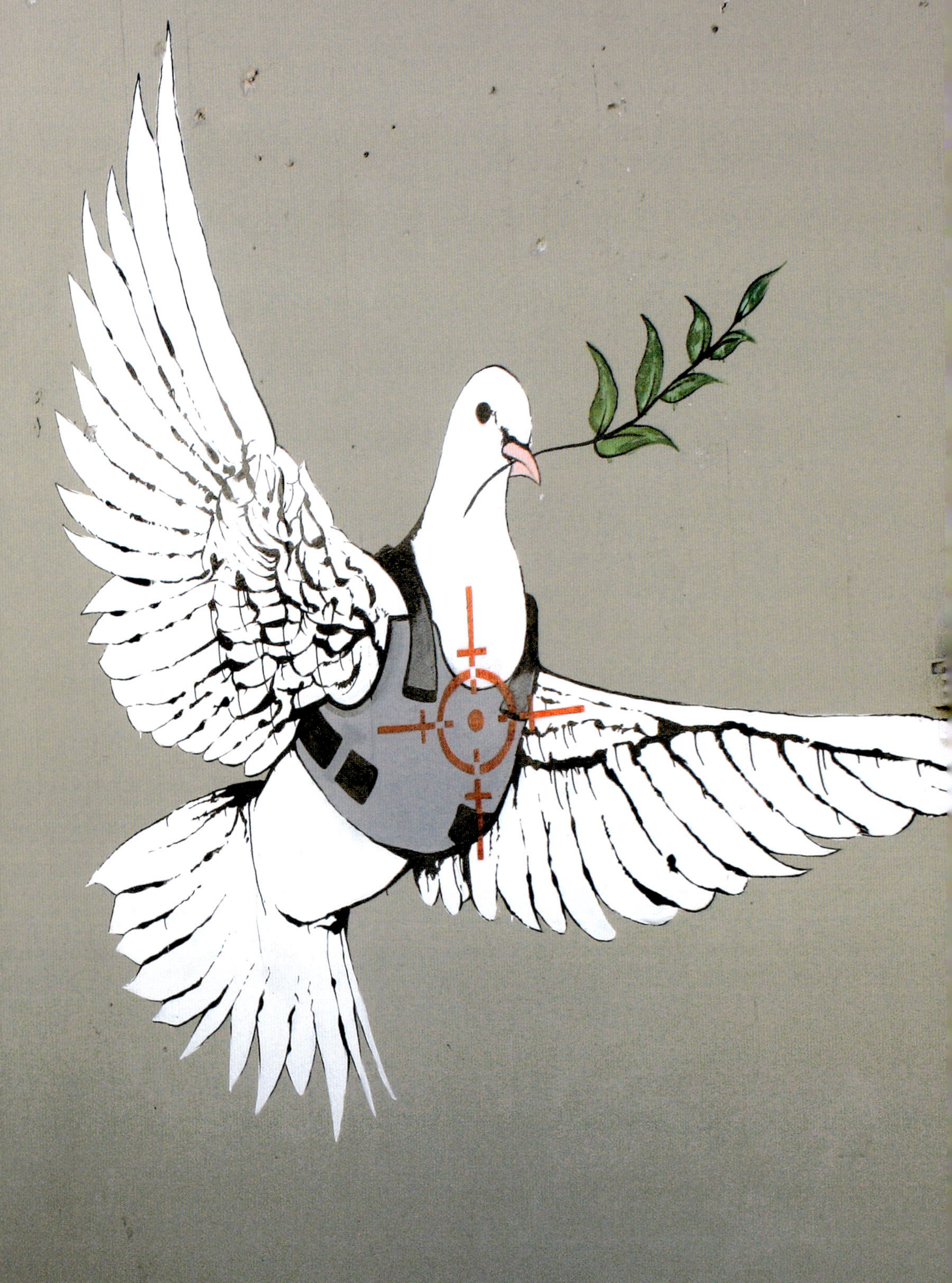

EAT, SPRAY, LOVE.

If Banksy wrote a self-help book, what might it say?

1. Don't wait for permission - in every single sense that this makes sense, yes.

2. Don't overthink it - Imagine your audience is drunk, they probably are.

3. Make it for everybody - if everyone doesn't get it, don't do it.

4. Make it mean something - the world is completely fucked. You should at least acknowledge this in your work.

5. Take great big hairy balled risks - Would anyone know who Banksy was if he hadn't climbed over the wall of Barcelona zoo like a lunatic?

6. Be consistent, be tenacious - Creative people are easily distracted. You only get known if you do the same things over and over again for ever.

7. It's not about you, it's about your work - You don't need to bare your soul on social media, or 'start the conversation'. The work is the conversation.

8. Find freedom in low-status - If you have zero expectations of your living standards you can work without worrying about money

9. Choose your gigs wisely - It's the jobs you turn down that define you.

10. Hustle up - whatever you have to do to buy the time to work, do it.

11. Collaborate - Ask for Help. Banksy used teams from very early on

12. Give help - give the next generation a leg up when you can

13. When money comes, use it, don't let it use you. - Make bigger things. And repeat until culturally irrelevant.

IN LOS ANGELES, YOU CAN RISE WITHOUT A TRACE.

BANKSY

"Banksy revealed?"

Banksy interviewed by Shelley Leopold for the LA Weekly, 2010

In the flurry of promotional interviews he did for his big film release, Banksy maintained absolute sincerity - he swore the whole thing was a truthful documentary, and he sounded as astonished by the rise of Mr Brainwash as all of us. Moreover he seemed fascinated in both a positive and negative way with the LA Art Scene, it's absolute lack of guile and it's endless hunger for the next big thing. A hunger that can catapult completely empty gestures up into the stratosphere of high value art auctions, everyone involved terrified to be the boy who shouts out that the emperor isn't wearing any clothes.

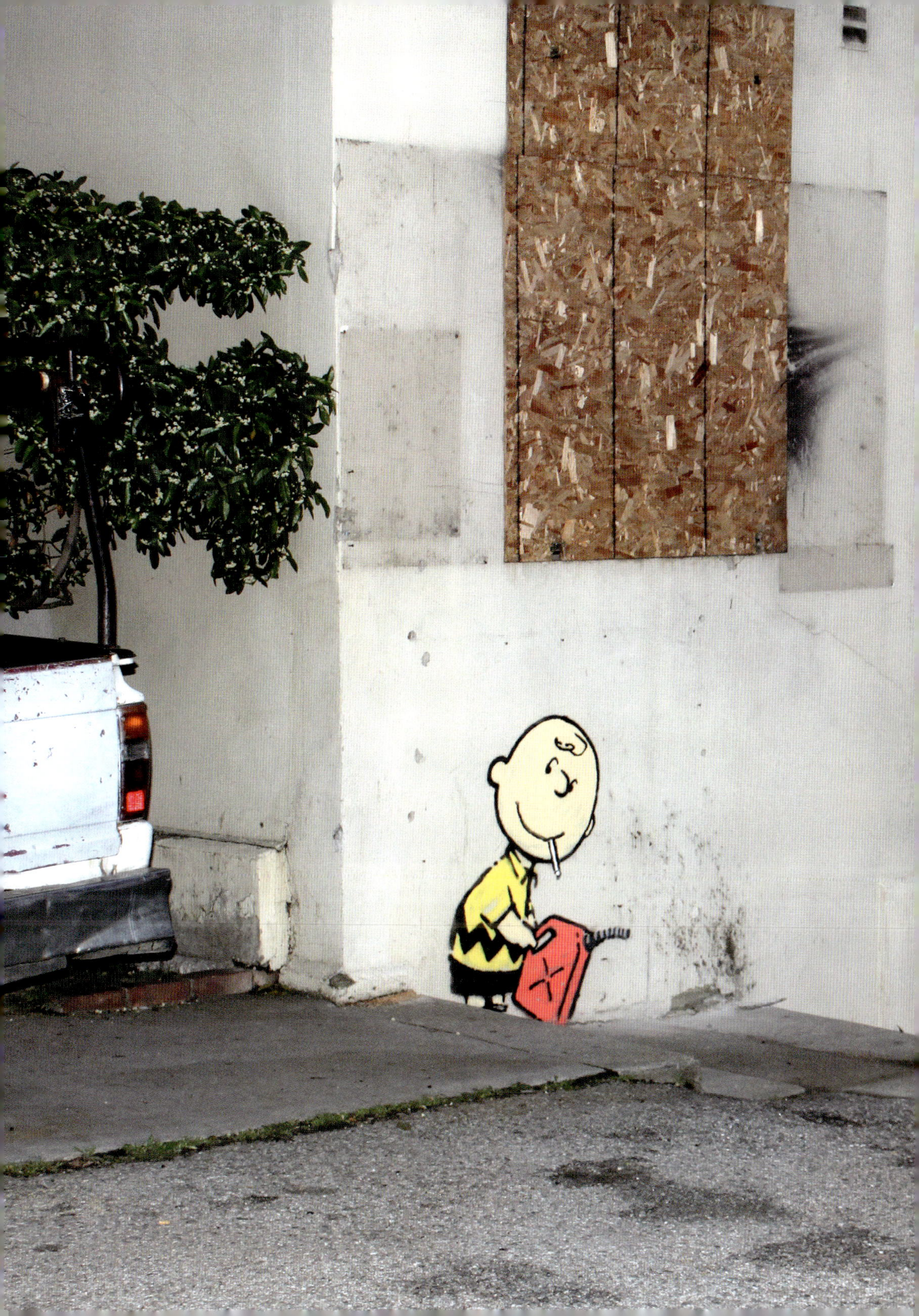

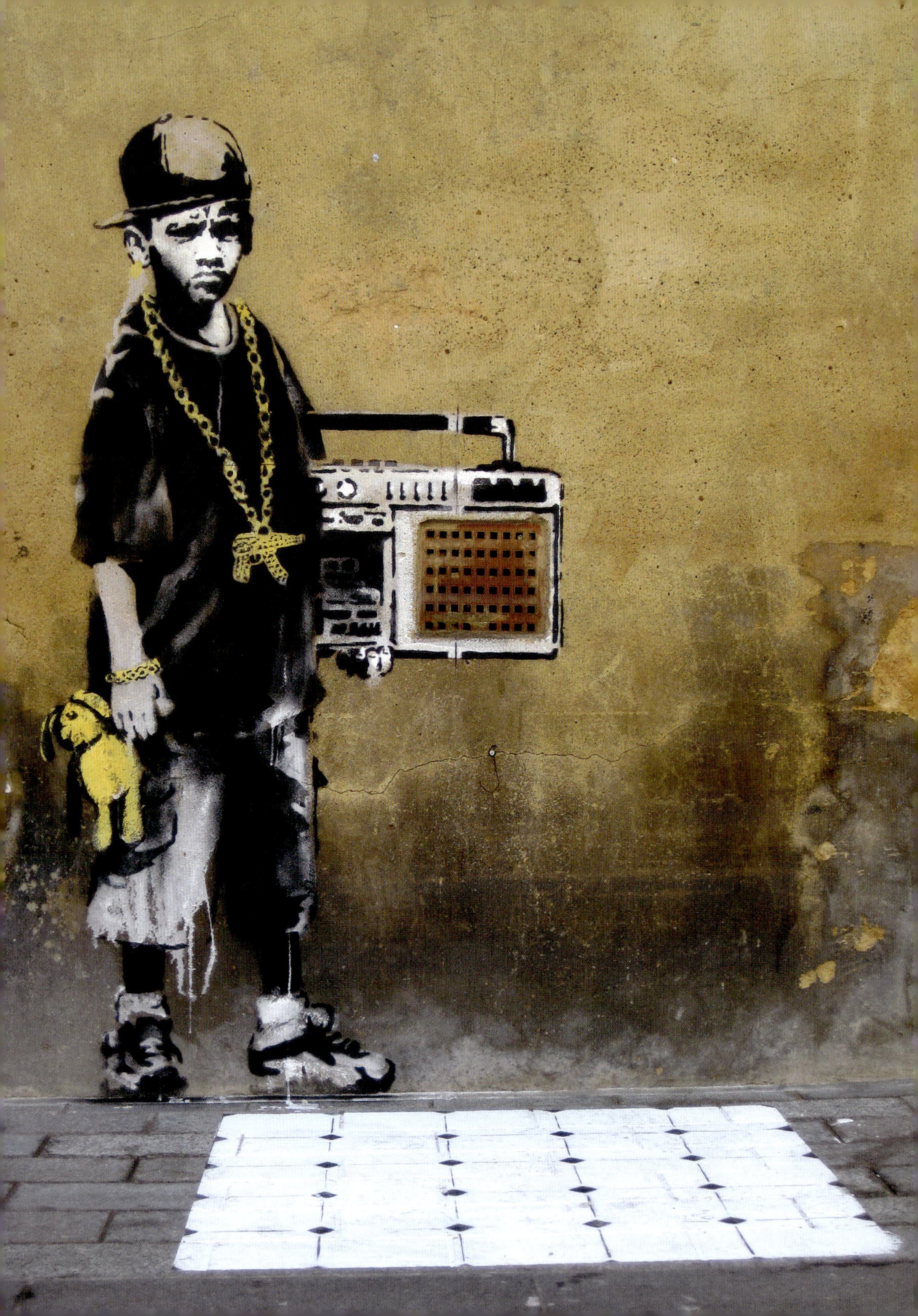

ULTIMATELY, I JUST WANT TO MAKE THE RIGHT PIECE AT THE RIGHT TIME IN THE RIGHT PLACE.

ANYTHING THAT STANDS IN THE WAY OF ACHIEVING THAT PIECE IS THE ENEMY, WHETHER IT'S YOUR MUM, THE COPS, SOMEONE TELLING YOU THAT YOU SOLD OUT, OR SOMEONE SAYING, "LET'S JUST STAY IN TONIGHT AND GET PIZZA."

BANKSY

"Banksy: The Naked Truth" Banksy interviewed by Shepard Fairey

Swindle Magazine 2006

Radical simplification is a friend to all. What is the one thing you'd rather die than fail to achieve today? Everything else is the enemy.

SUB-VERTISING & CULTURE JAMMING

Subvertising is the art of changing an advert to subvert it's message. It's been around a while. In the 1990's and the 2000's subvertising went through a bit of a golden age as it was the cultural weapon of choice for a number of anti-capitalist groups. Culture Jamming, coined in 1984, was promoted by a Canadian magazine called Adbusters who organised the International Buy Nothing Day event.

Many street artists in the 1990's were coming from a spirit of Culture Jamming, Shepard Fairey for example used Obey to draw attention to the way in which powerful things make themselves look powerful, mimicking the detailed iconography you might see on a dollar bill, subvertising a kind of American legal document aesthetic.

Banksy was operating very much as a big carrot in this cultural soup. (Witness classic subvertising like 'Because I'm Worthless' a subversion of the l'oreal slogan 'Because I'm worth it'.) Keep an eye out for other examples of Banksy playing the subvertising game...

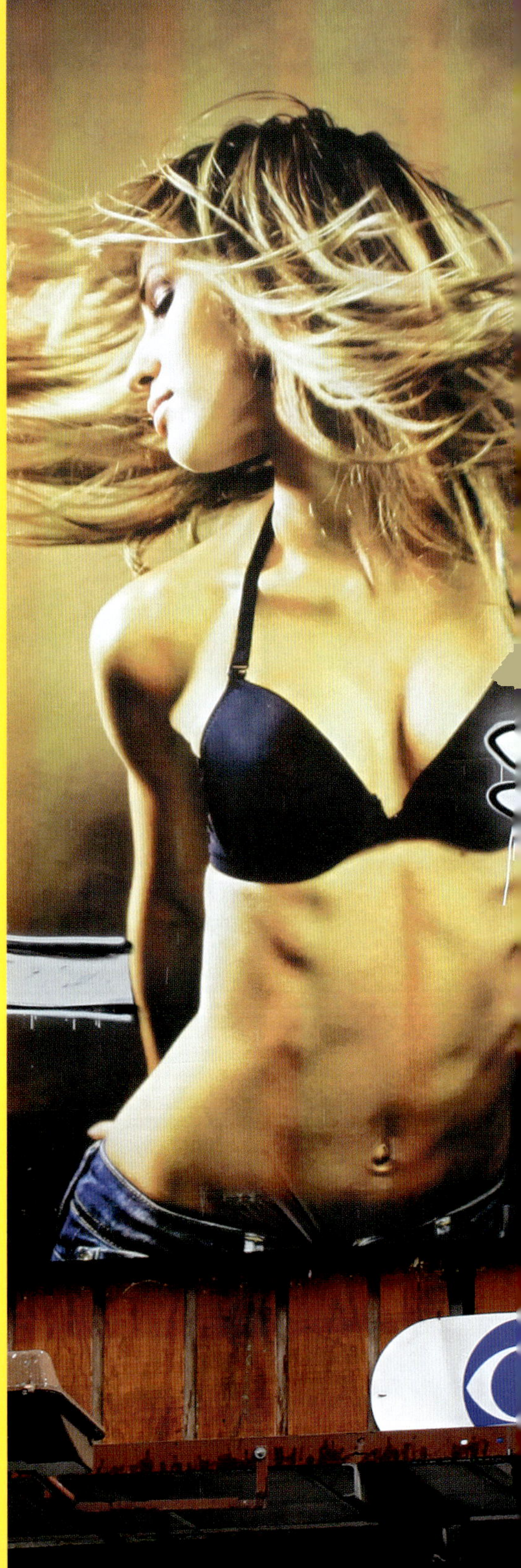

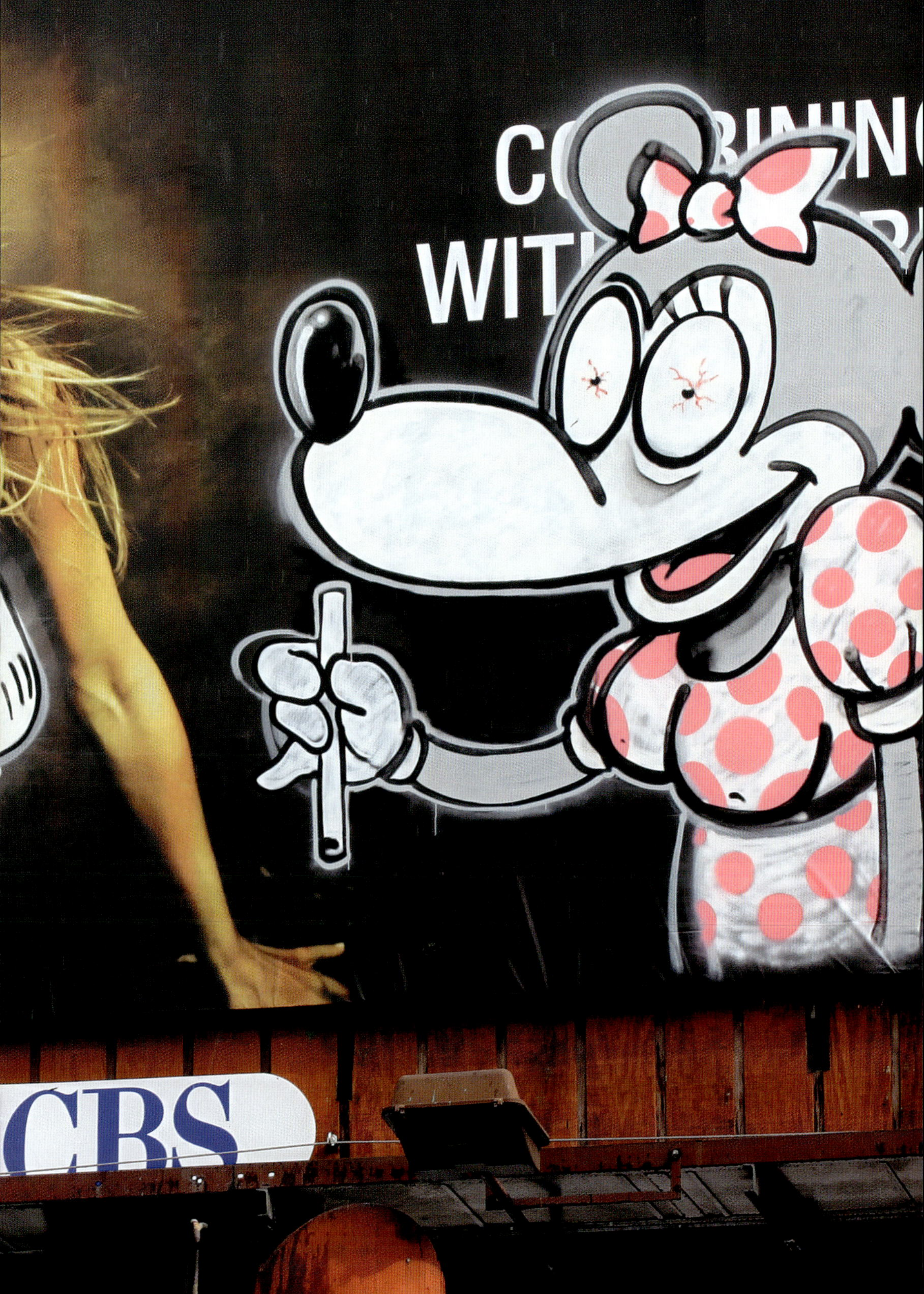

COMBINING
WITH
CBS

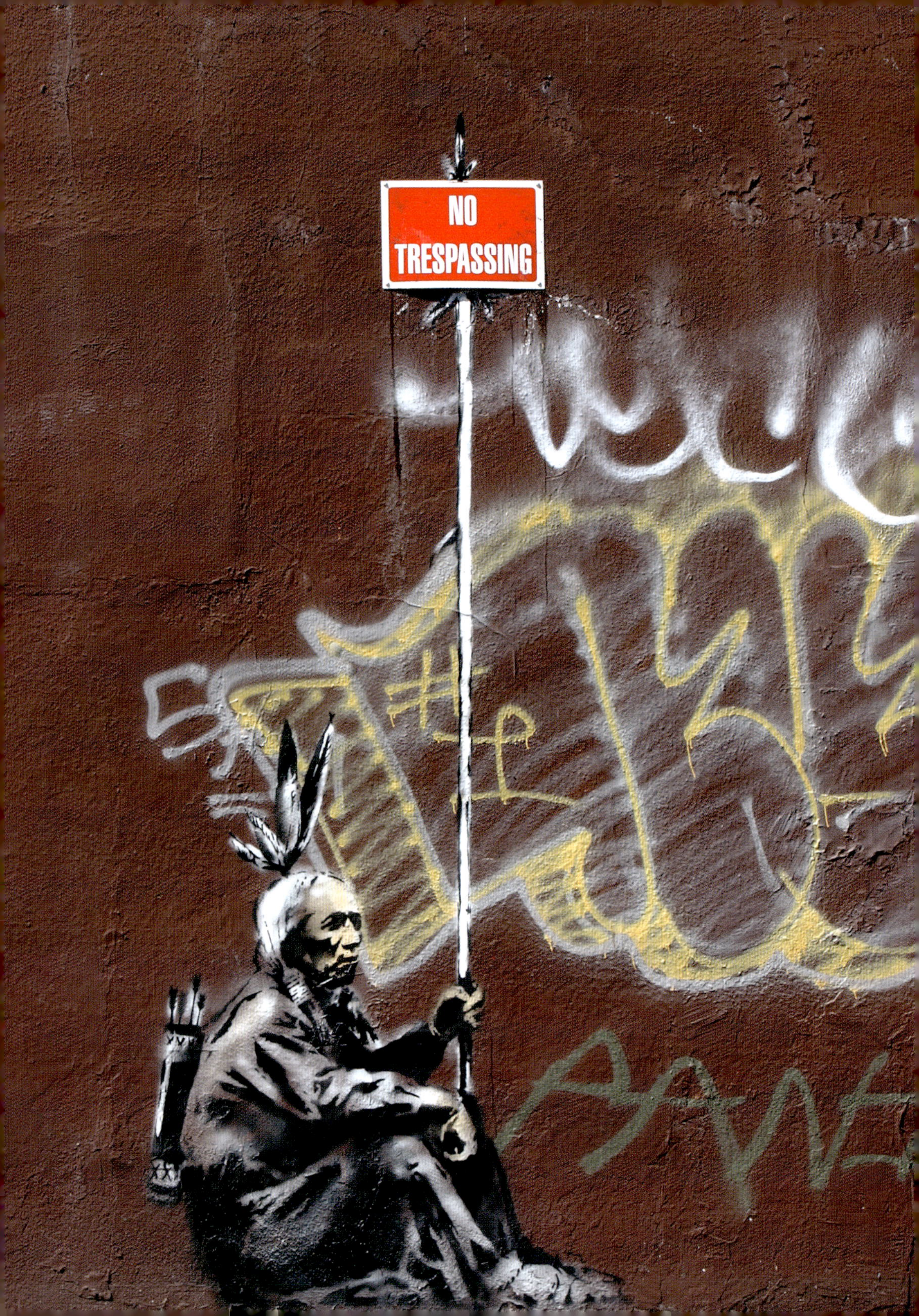

NO
TRESPASSING

AMERICA'S CAPACITY TO BE INFURIATING IS MATCHED ONLY BY ITS CAPACITY TO REINVENT ITSELF INTO SOMETHING BRILLIANT.

BANKSY

"Banksy revealed?"

Banksy interviewed by Shelley Leopold for the LA Weekly, 2010

We Brits have a tendency to distract ourselves from our own sinking cultural ship by sniggering at the foolishness in the colonies. Banksy distances himself from this easy position, admitting to his own love hate relationship with American culture. After all, it all comes from Hip Hop and Hip Hop comes from over there...

I'D LIKE TO SAY I'M
POLITICALLY MOTIVATED,
BUT THE REALITY IS
I'M JUST FAR TOO LAZY
FOR CAPITALISM.

IF BANKSY HAS BECOME A BRAND,
THEN IT'S A BRAND THAT DOESN'T
BELIEVE IN ITSELF.

BANKSY

Banksy's first Australian interview, Kylie Northover

Sydney Morning Herald 2010

The curse of the ambitious anti-capitalist

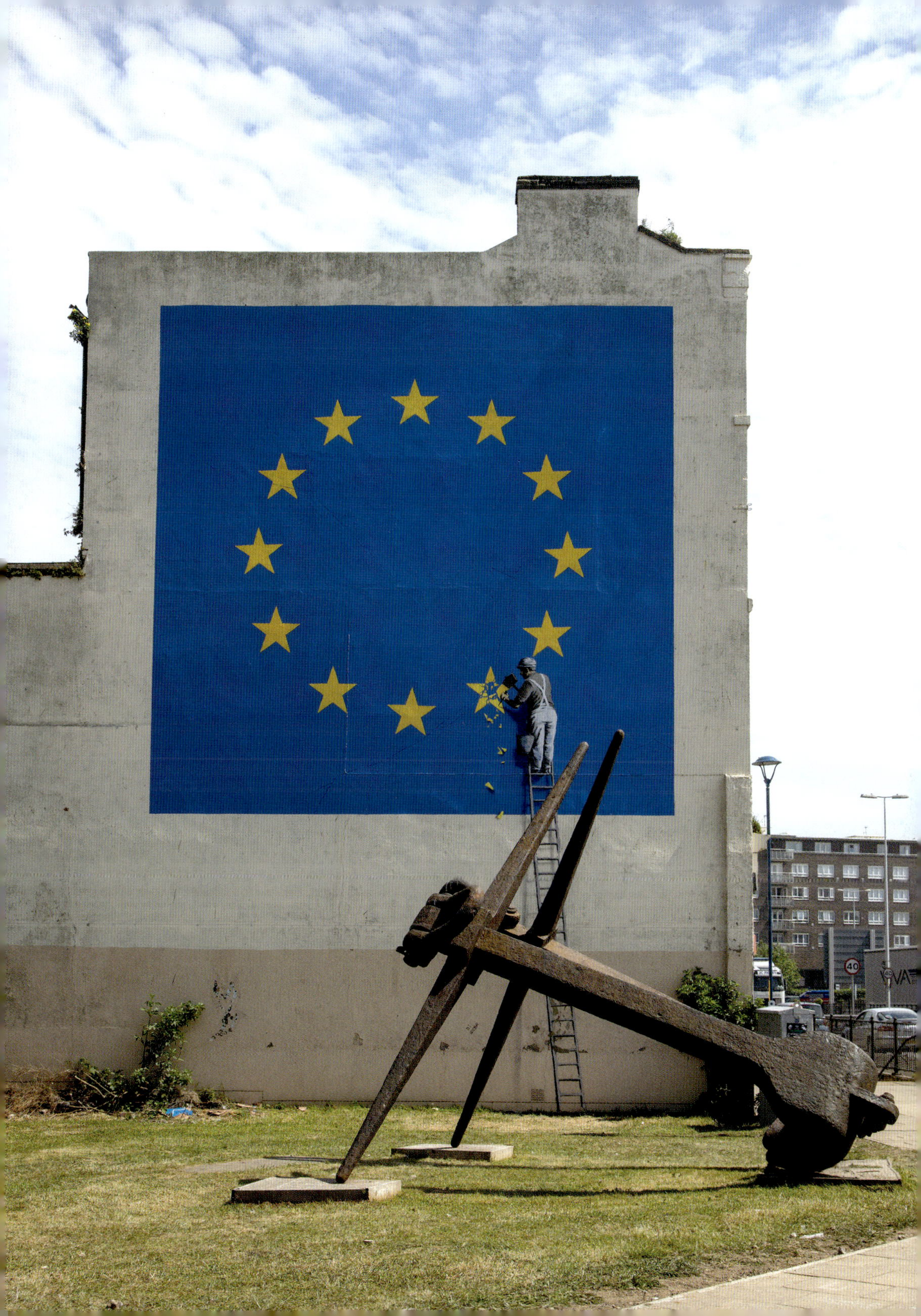

LOW-BROW
IN LOS ANGELES

Banksy deliberately targeted the Los Angeles art scene in his early efforts to break into indoor exhibition work. Why LA? Possibly because of the established Lowbrow Art Scene, something that has a long history of mutual respect with Graffiti culture.

Lowbrow AKA Pop Surrealism came out of the 1970's counterculture on the West Coast and was influenced by punk and underground comix among many other colourful street cultural elements like hot rod culture and tiki. The earliest graffiti characters were taken straight from underground comix, full of psychedelic weirdness and hippy erotica like the work of Vaughn Bode.

By the 1990's Lowbrow was (and still is) a thriving art scene in LA, creating the perfect space for Banksy to appear with his sensational live elephant stunt in Barely Legal, 2005.

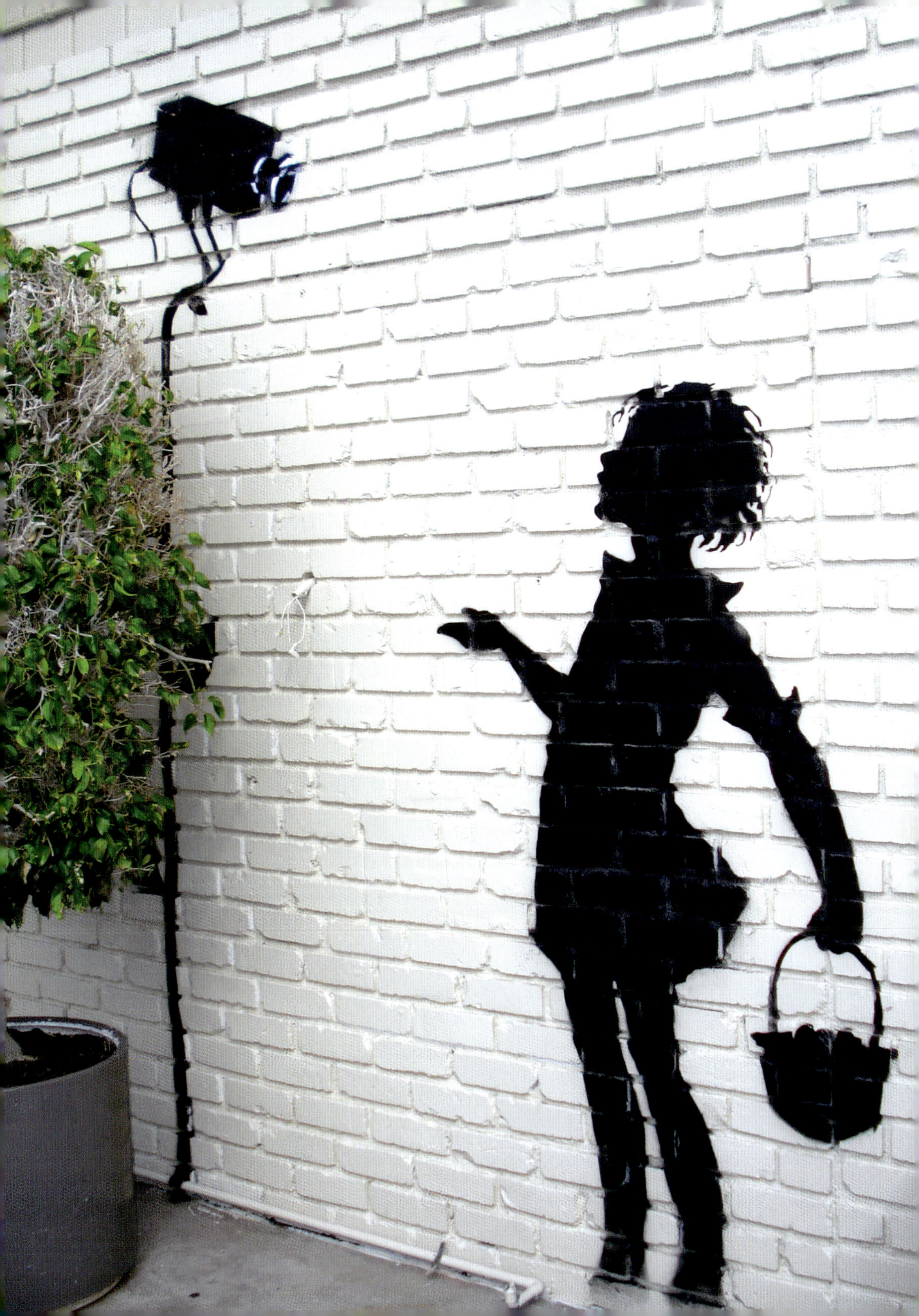

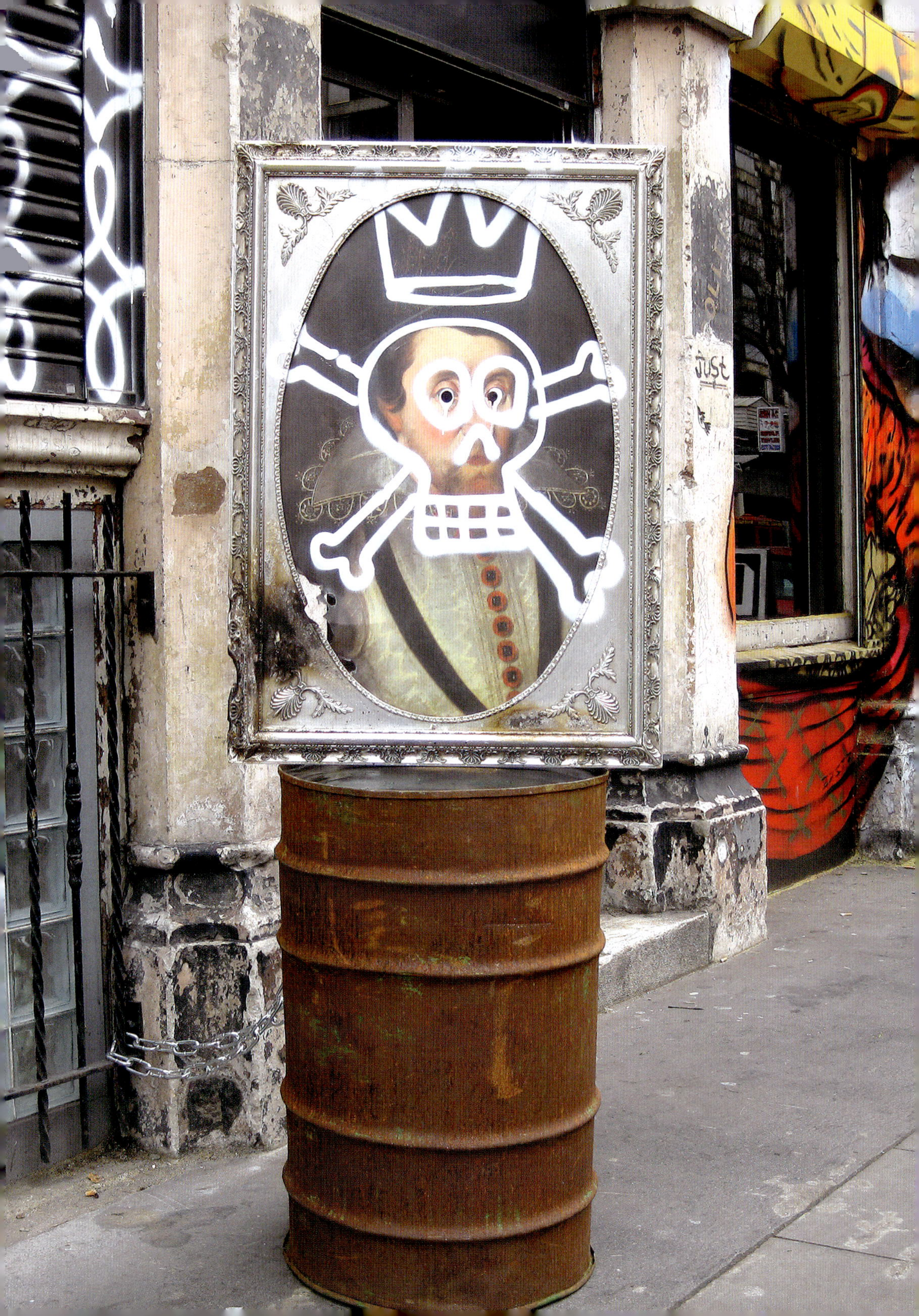

JUST

MODERN ART IS A DISASTER AREA.

NEVER IN THE FIELD OF HUMAN HISTORY HAS SO MUCH BEEN USED BY SO MANY TO SAY SO LITTLE.

BANKSY

"Wall & Piece" Banksy

Vintage Publishing 2006

The point of art, then, is to say something. This is a principle of Banksyism that he has never shifted on. Art, on it's own, is pointless - it's job is to pass on a message of some kind. Banksy's art is symbolic. In other words, it isn't just an image - it's more like a piece of graphic design. It says something, and it is not entirely up to you to choose what it means - there is an intentional meaning whether you agree with it or not. Some of his art is more lyrical, the message is a feeling, and some of it is more symbolic - the message is literally a message. But there is always a message.

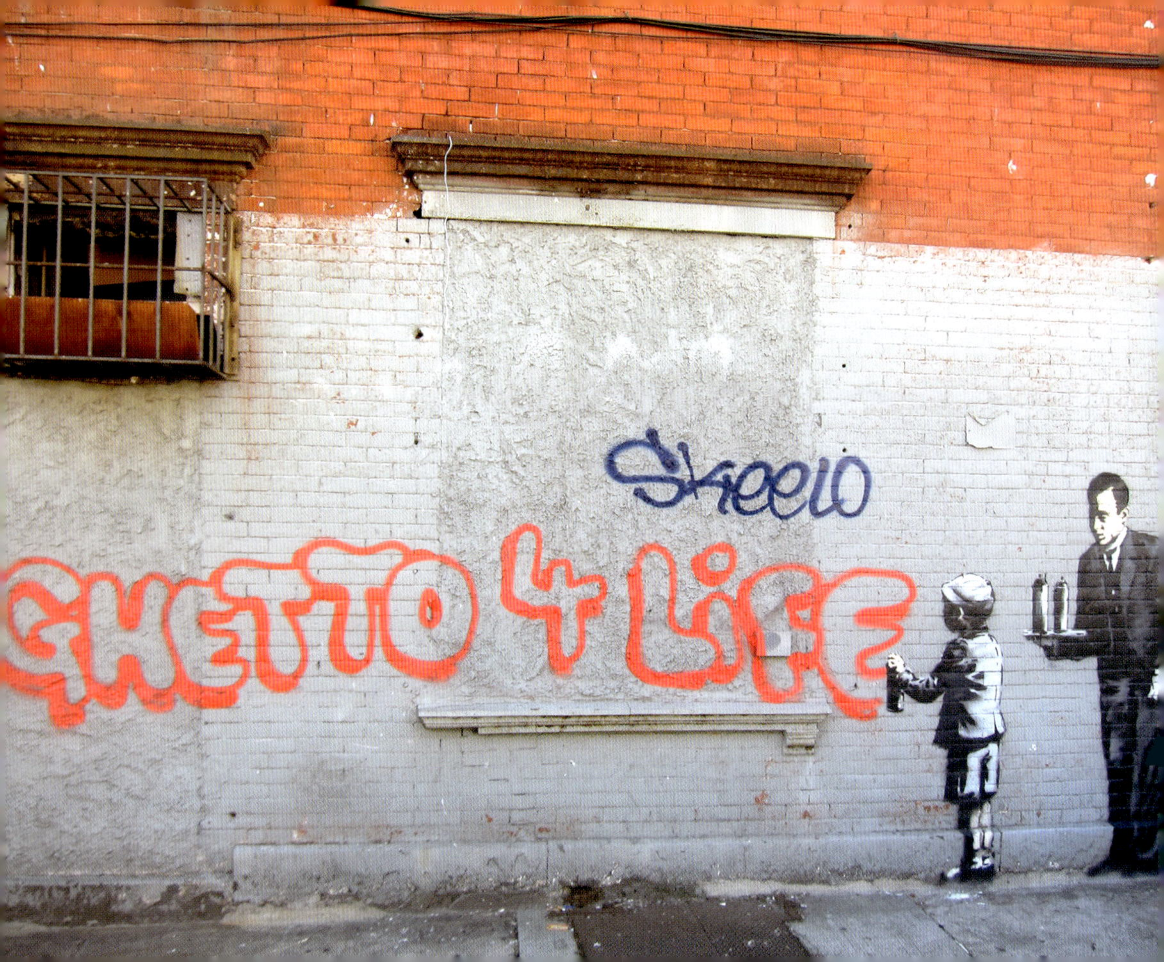
Skeelo
GHETTO 4 LiFE

I TELL MYSELF I USE ART TO PROMOTE DISSENT, BUT MAYBE I AM JUST USING DISSENT TO PROMOTE MY ART.

I PLEAD NOT GUILTY TO SELLING OUT. BUT I PLEAD IT FROM A BIGGER HOUSE THAN I USED TO LIVE IN.

BANKSY

"Banksy interview" Ossian Ward

Time Out London 2010

Captured within the web of capital, each of us struggles to make space for a little freedom and as we do we pull the ropes that bind the others a little tighter. How can we burn the web away without losing our skin?

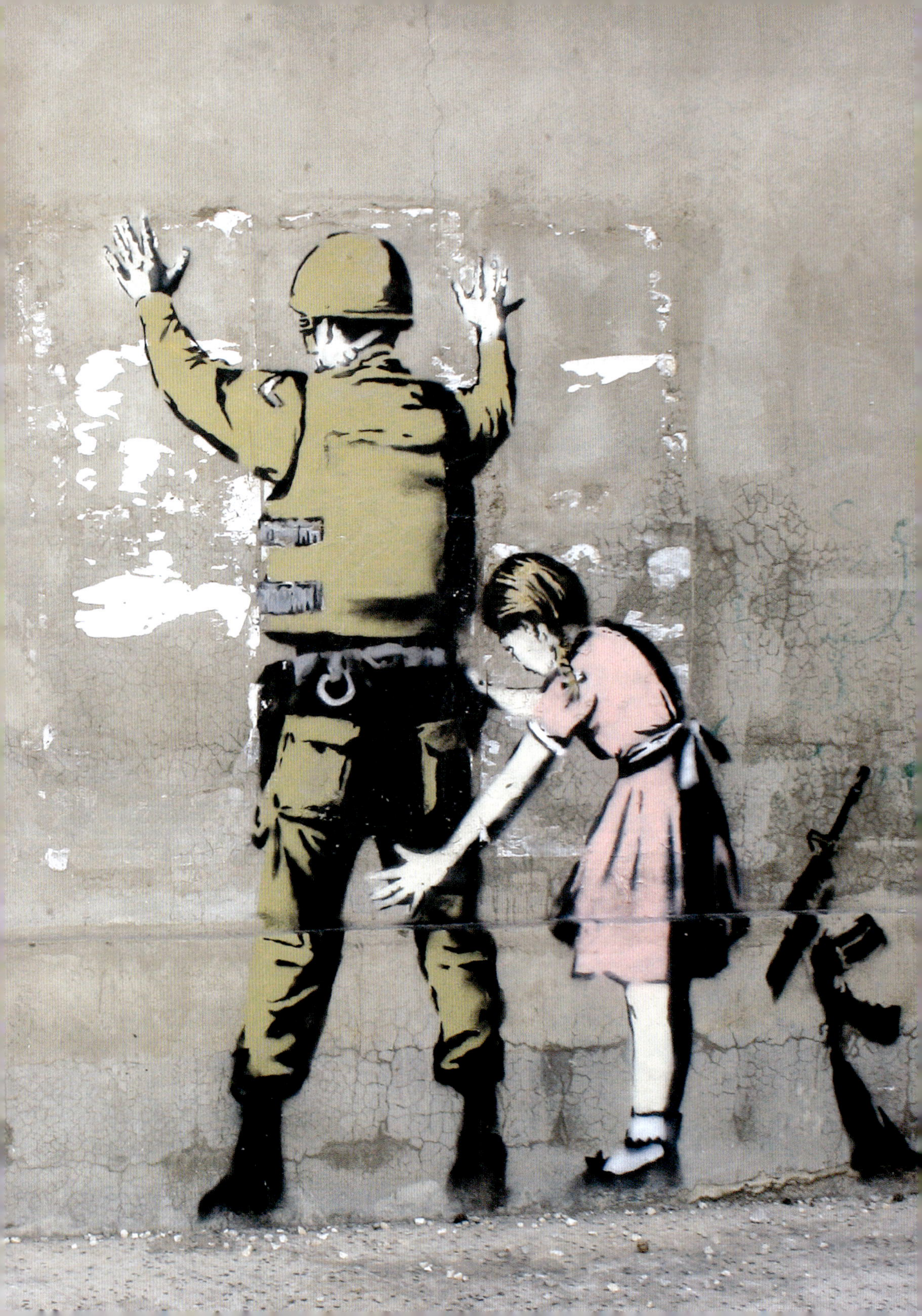

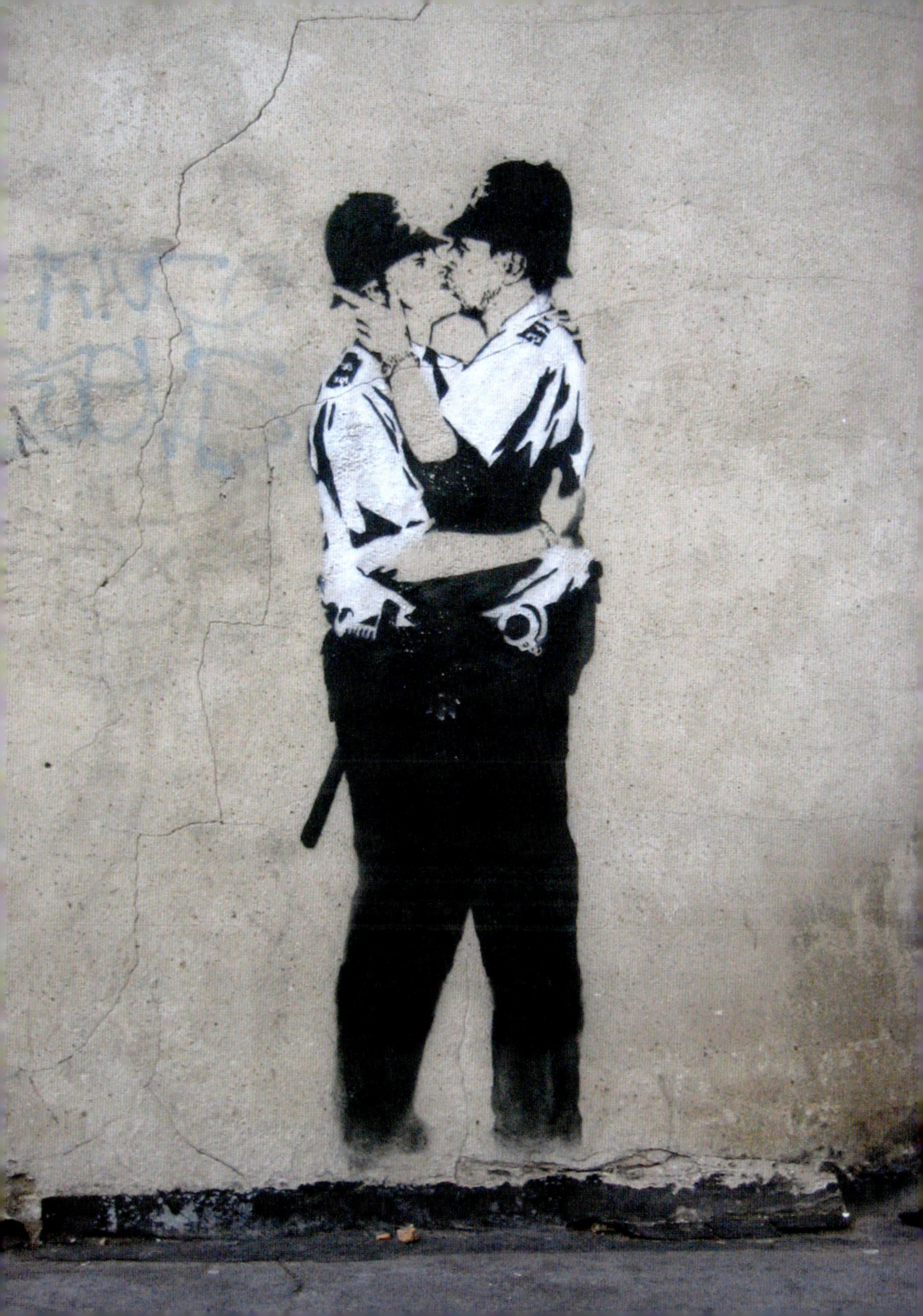

I WANT TO SHOW THAT MONEY HASN'T CRUSHED THE HUMANITY OUT OF EVERYTHING.

BANKSY

Banksy: Off the Wall

The Telegraph, 2008

This is an early quote and it strikes a hopeful note, perhaps a slightly naïve one. The whole debate around money has shifted so far from 1990's countercultural thinking, you don't hear this kind of opposition to thinking about money anymore. It was common to call people 'materialistic' and it was considered noble to 'follow your passions' instead of following the money back then.

These days the two ideas are not considered seperate. Following your passions is about becoming a media channel in your own right and monetizing your platform. Entrepreneurialism is the new bohemianism. The internet has allowed for the colonisation of all spaces that were once outside of the reach of money. Any group of enthusiasts is now a niche market waiting to be tapped. It's hard to imagine Banksy saying something this optimistic in 2020.

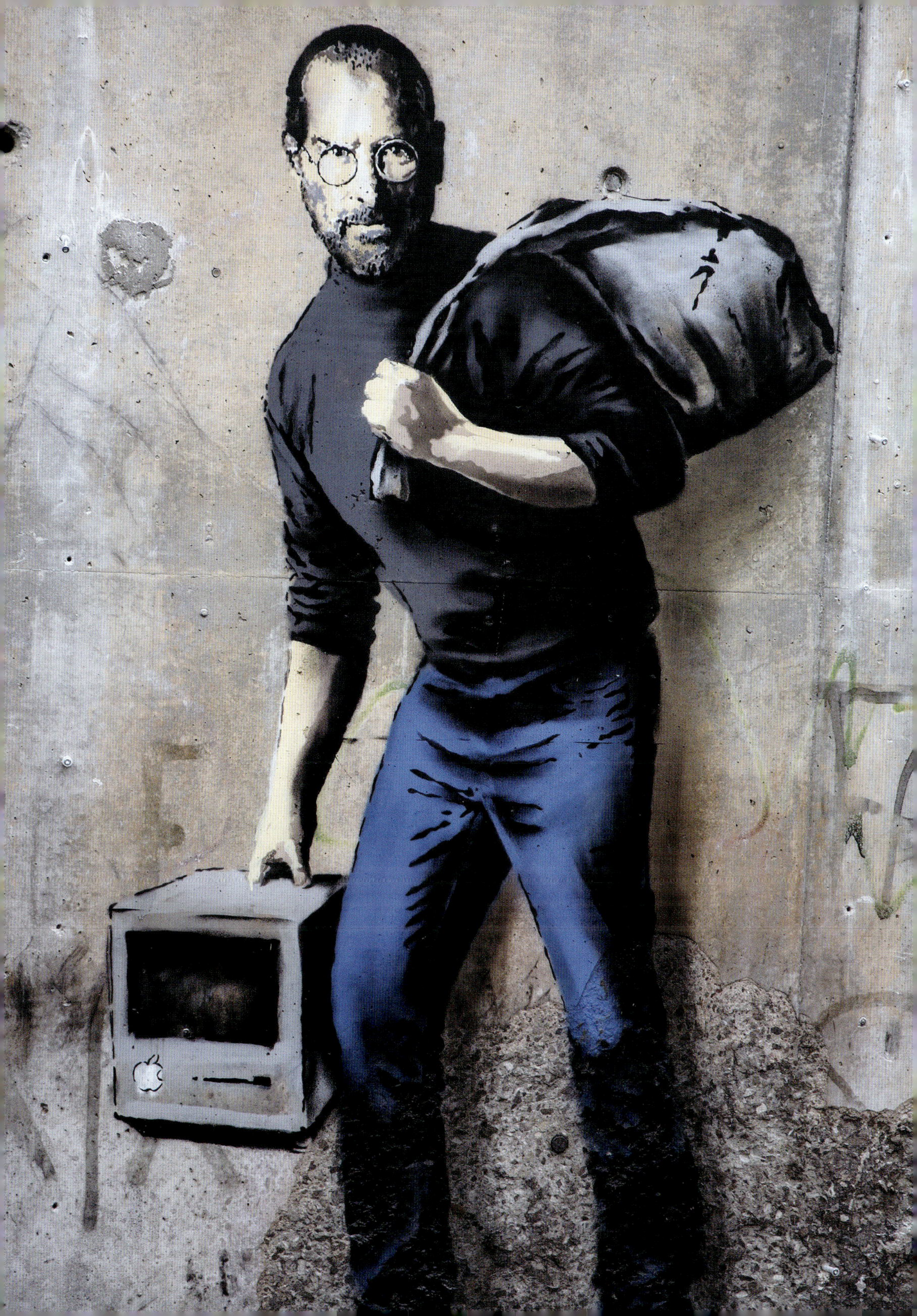

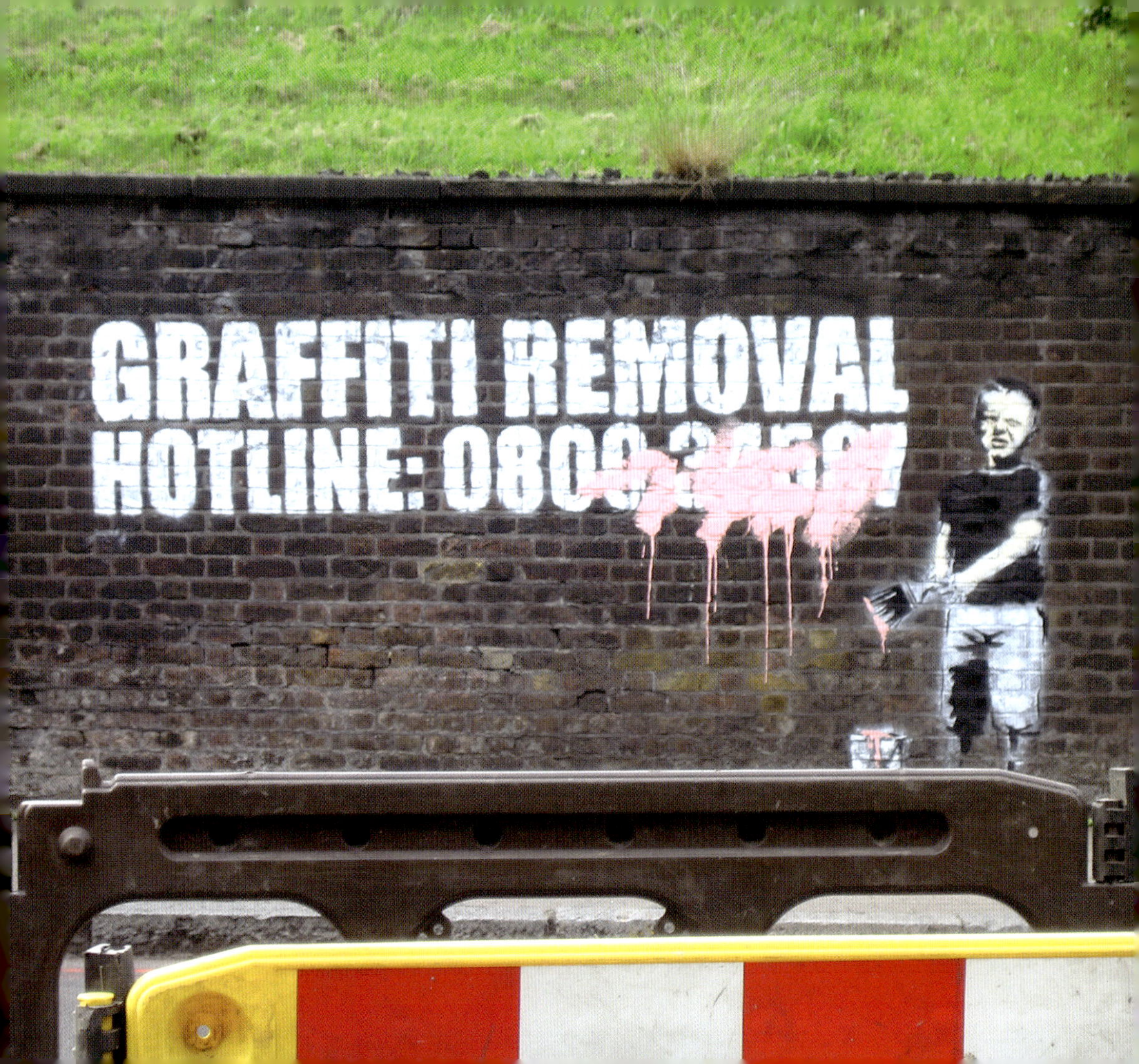

GRAFFITI REMOVAL
HOTLINE: 0800

I'M NOT SO INTERESTED IN CONVINCING PEOPLE IN THE ART WORLD THAT WHAT I DO IS 'ART,' I'M MORE BOTHERED ABOUT CONVINCING PEOPLE IN THE GRAFFITI COMMUNITY THAT WHAT I DO IS REALLY VANDALISM.

BANKSY

"Banksy revealed?"

Banksy interviewed by Shelley Leopold for the LA Weekly, 2010

These days it's a losing battle to convince people who run
the risk of arrest, heavy fines and jail time that Banksy, who
runs the risk of none of these things, that they are painting
on the same page.

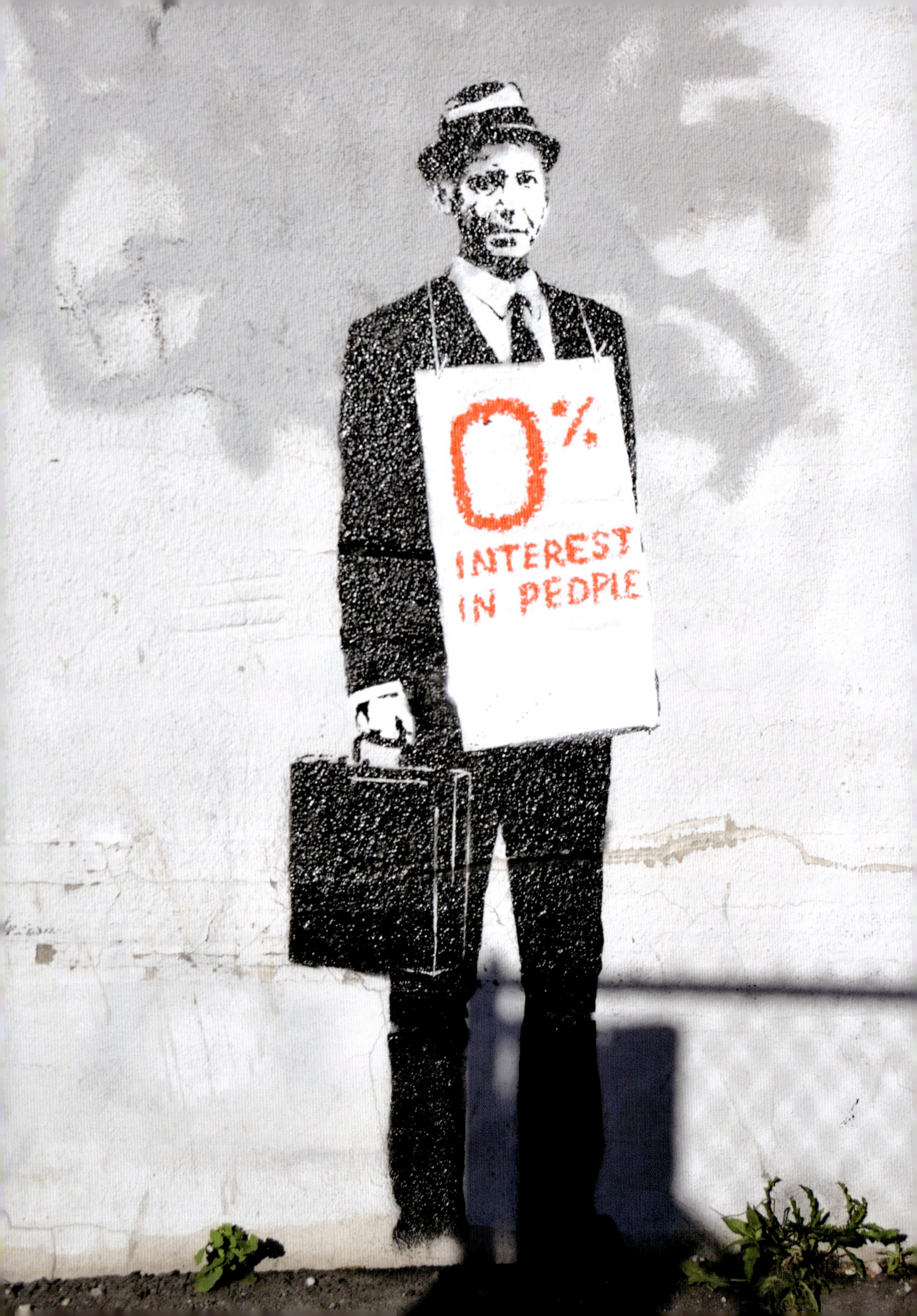

0%
INTEREST
IN PEOPLE

I LOVE THE WAY CAPITALISM FINDS A PLACE - EVEN FOR ITS ENEMIES.

BANKSY

"Banksy Was Here" Lauren Collins

The New Yorker 2007

Capitalism absorbs all forms of resistance and spits them back out as lifestyle choices. If you have any ideas for breaking out of this futile waltz then answers on a postcard please...

FIGHT THE FIGHTERS, NOT THEIR WARS.

BANKSY

"Cut it Out" Banksy

Weapons of Mass Distraction 2004

War is peace. Peace is war. We are all in Kafka's castle. Geo politics is so weird and absurd that we literally just don't even try and understand it anymore. The killer clowns have taken over the circus. And their strategy for maintaining the status quo is just pure chaos, great drifting swarms of misinformation pumped out by computerised lying factories. Anyway, it's a lovely day - shall we go for a coffee?

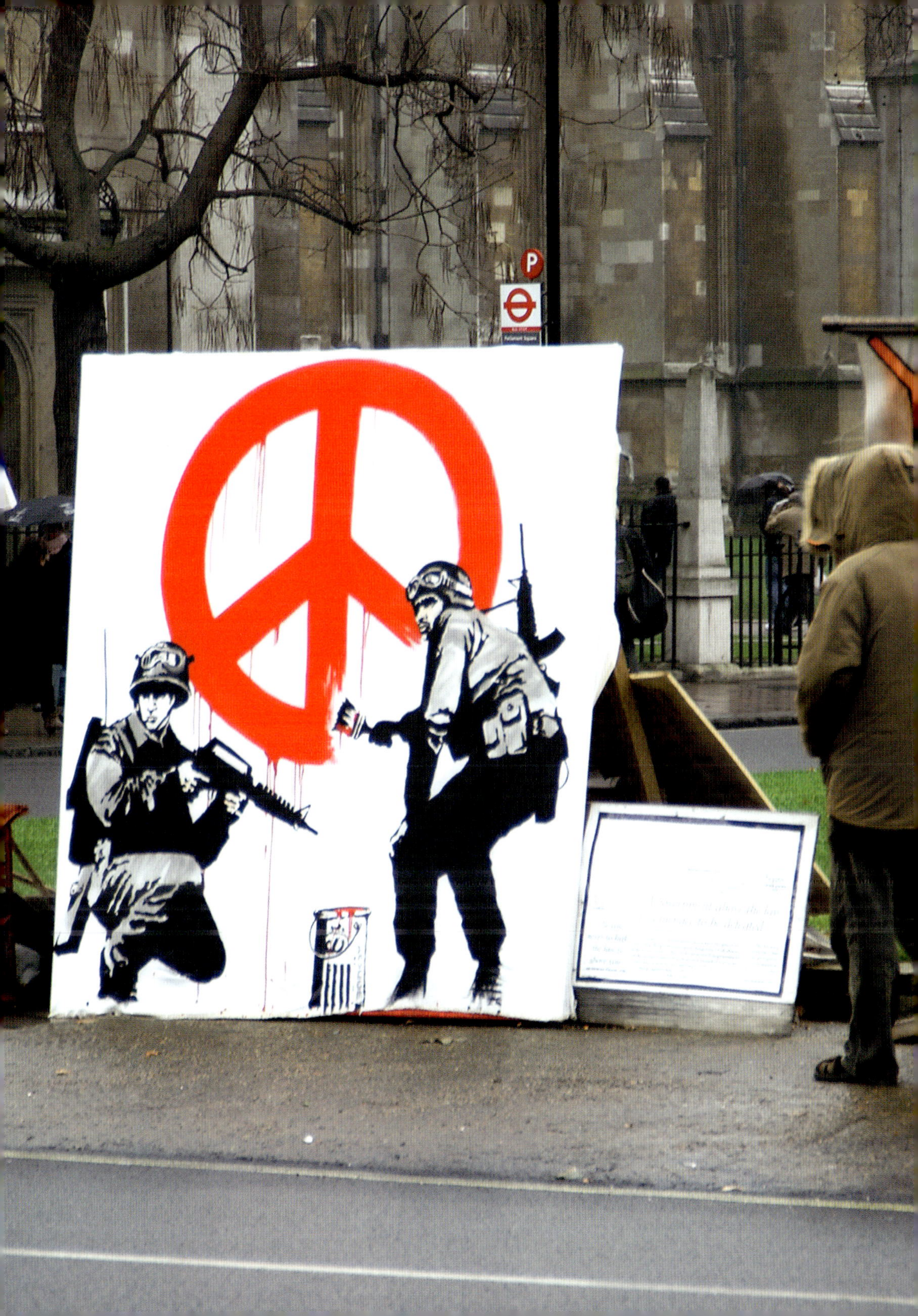

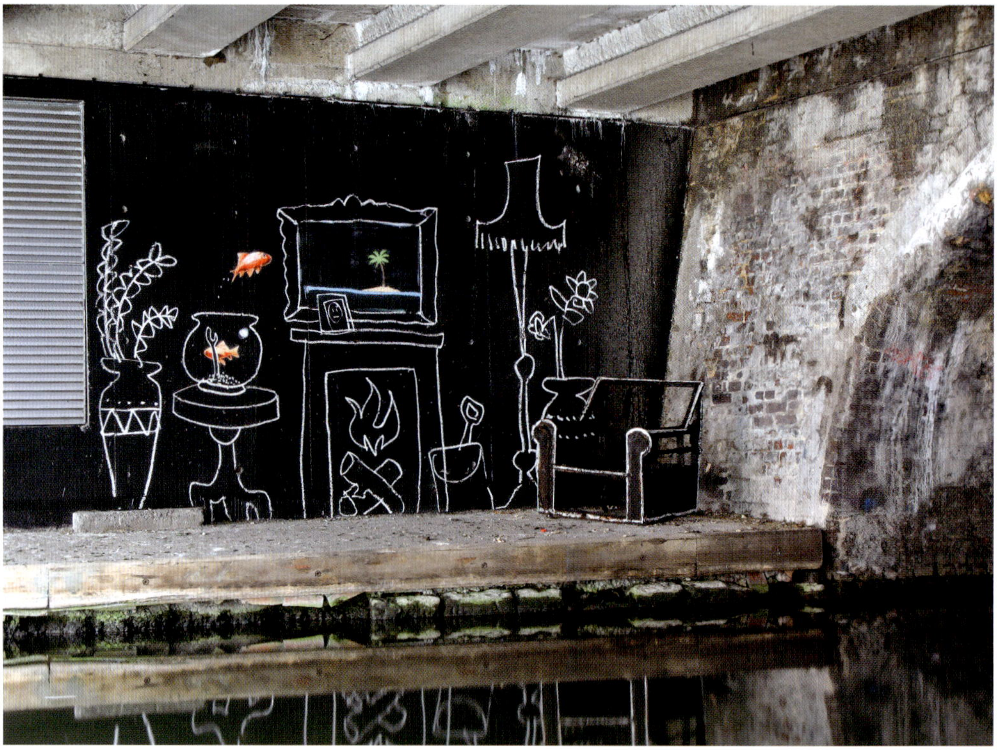

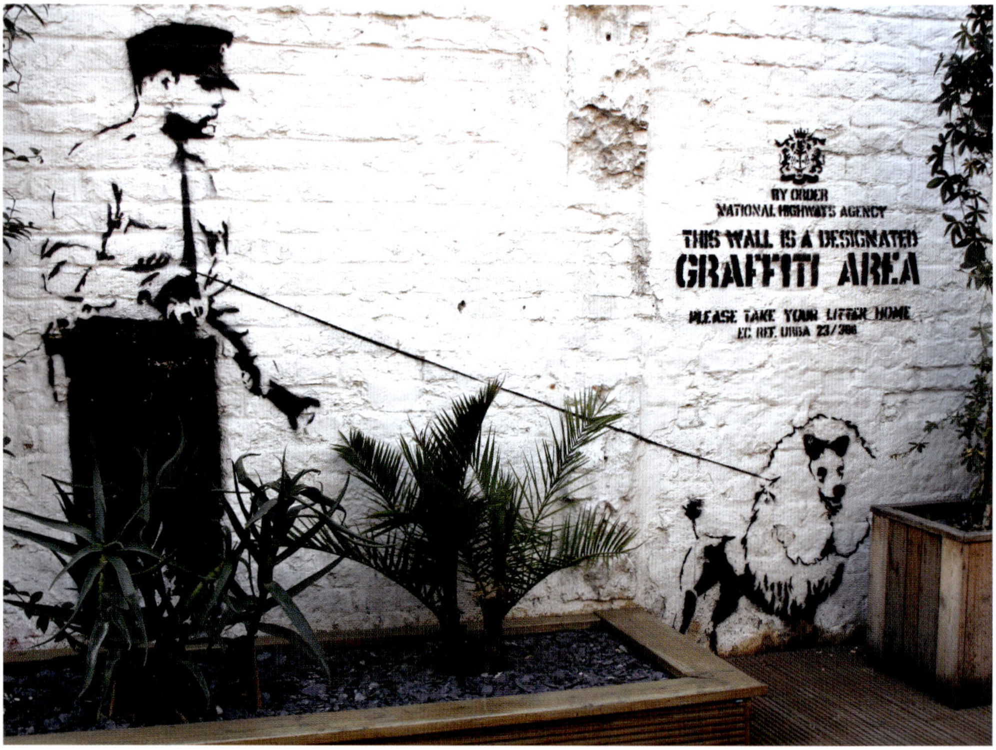

BY ORDER
NATIONAL HIGHWAYS AGENCY
THIS WALL IS A DESIGNATED
GRAFFITI AREA
PLEASE TAKE YOUR LITTER HOME
EC REF. URBA 23/366

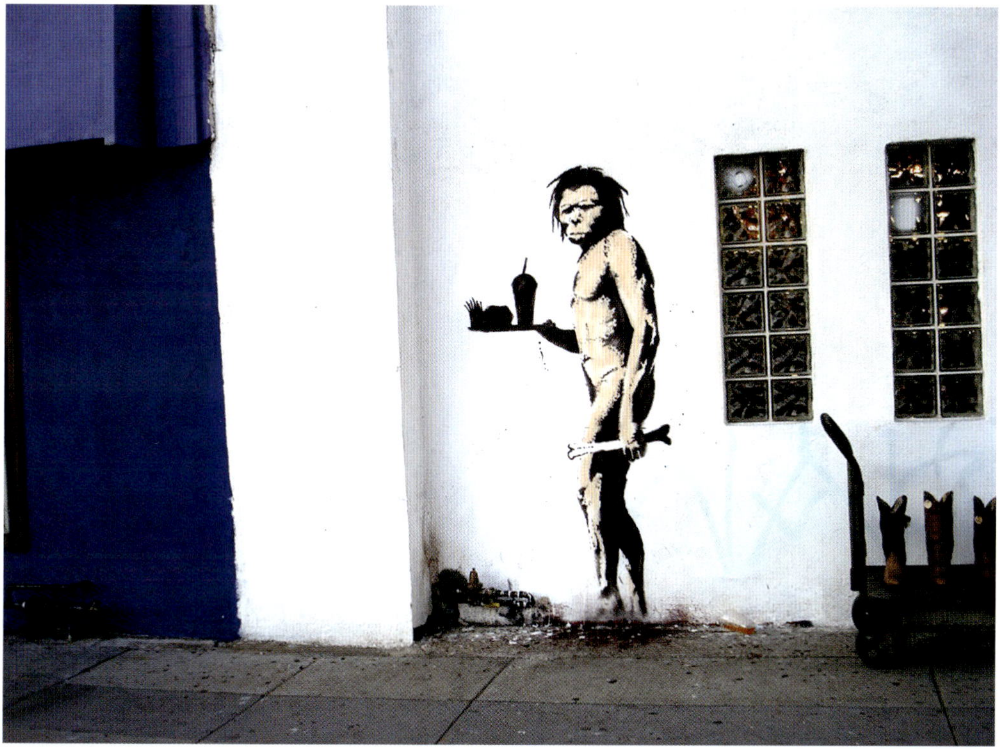

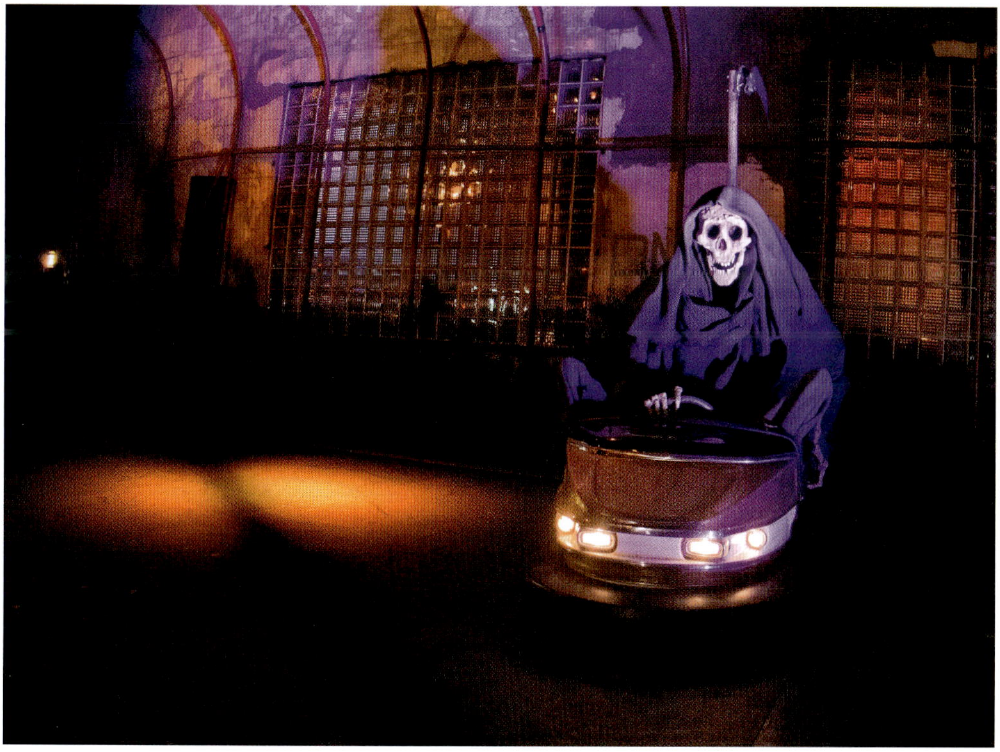

LIVE AS
A VILLAIN,
DIE AS
A HERO.

BANKSY

"Wall & Piece" Banksy

Vintage Publishing 2006

Nobody remembers well behaved people. True story.

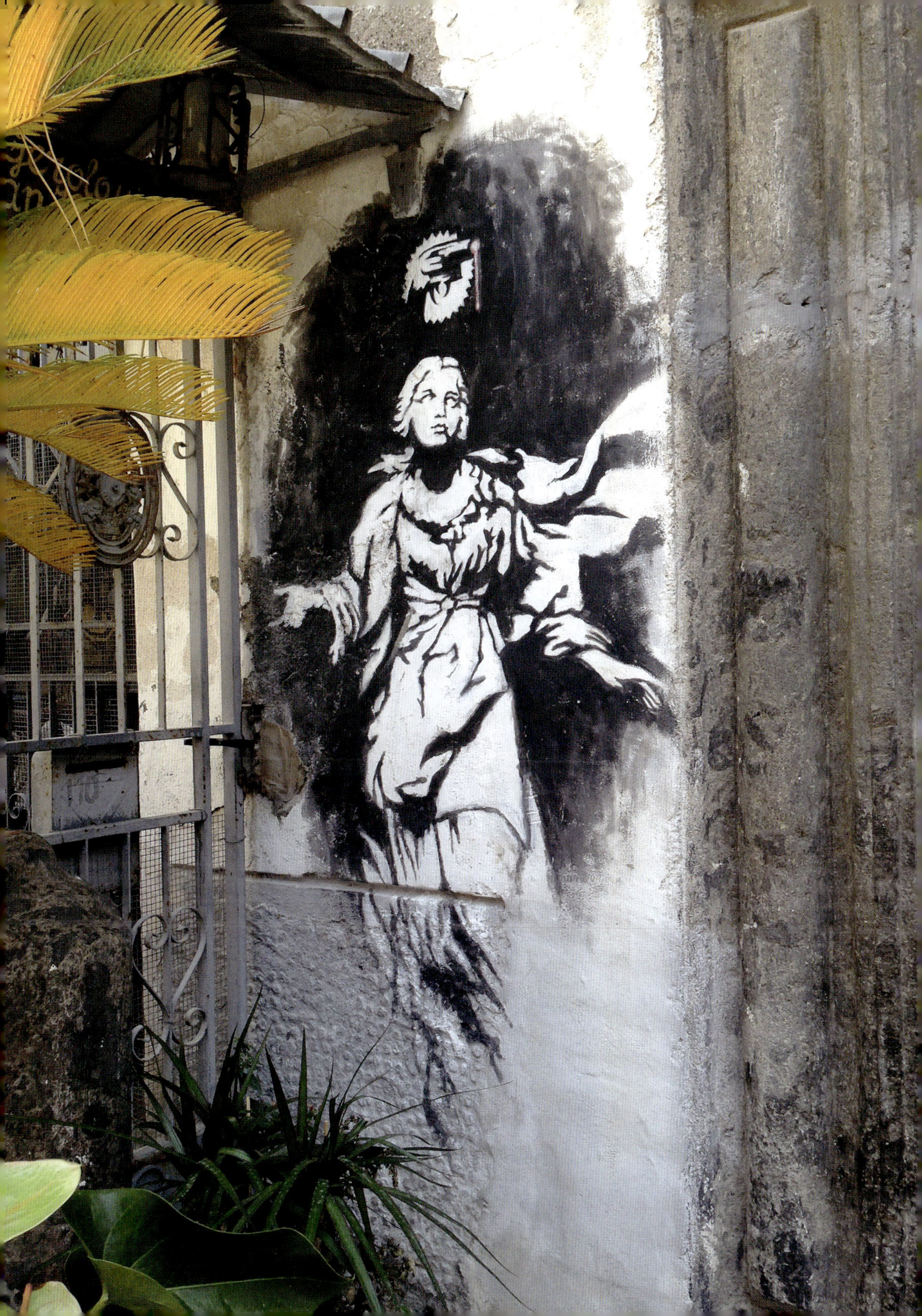

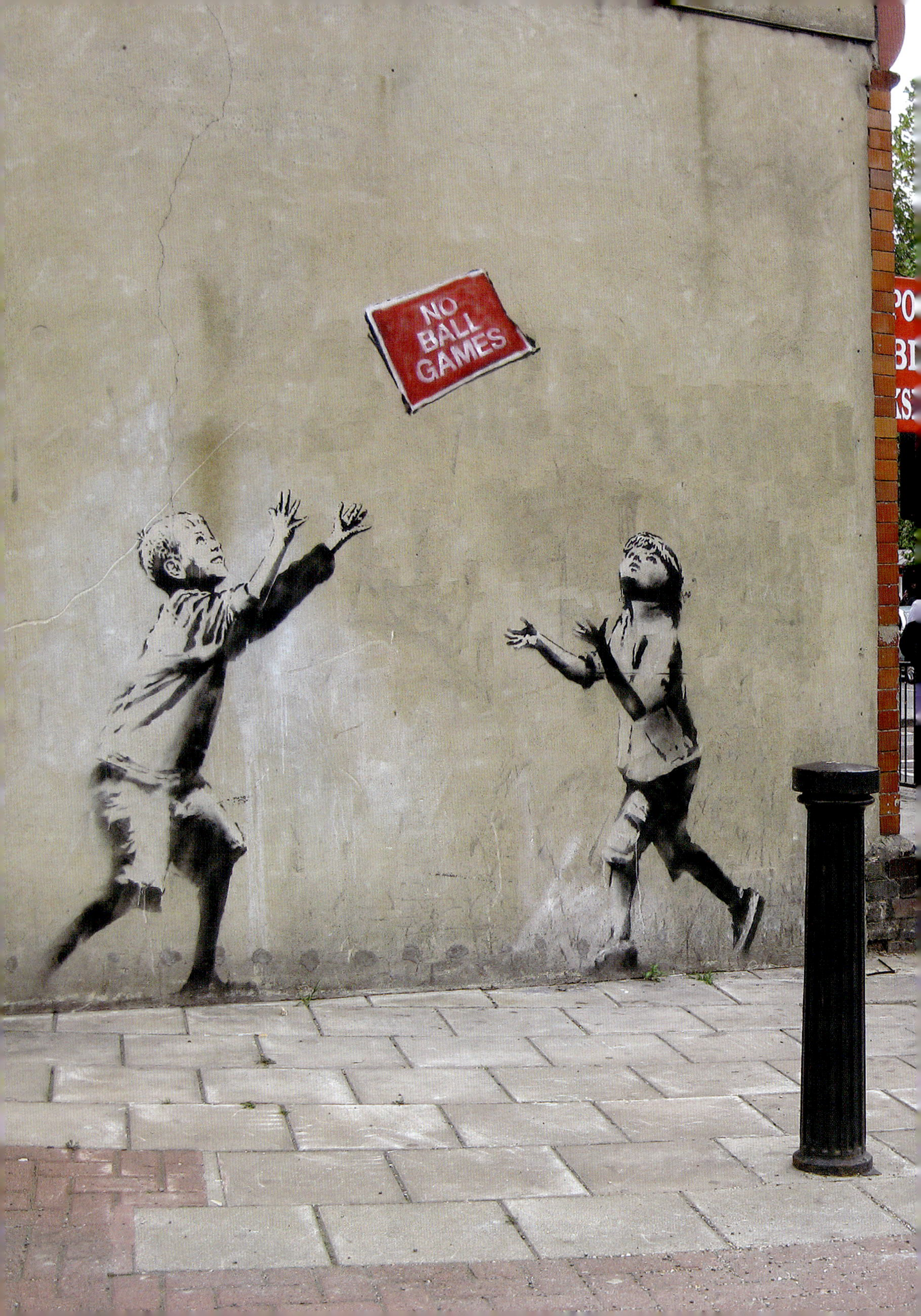

NO
BALL
GAMES

A LOT OF MOTHERS WILL DO ANYTHING FOR THEIR CHILDREN, EXCEPT LET THEM BE THEMSELVES.

BANKSY

"Banksy interview" Ossian Ward

Time Out London 2010

This is the only Banksy quote about family life. Alongside a handful of relentlessly bleak comments about sexual love - one suspects that maybe Banksy has not been lucky in that aspect of love. Is Banksyism compatible with being a dad?

THE
WALLED OFF
HOTEL

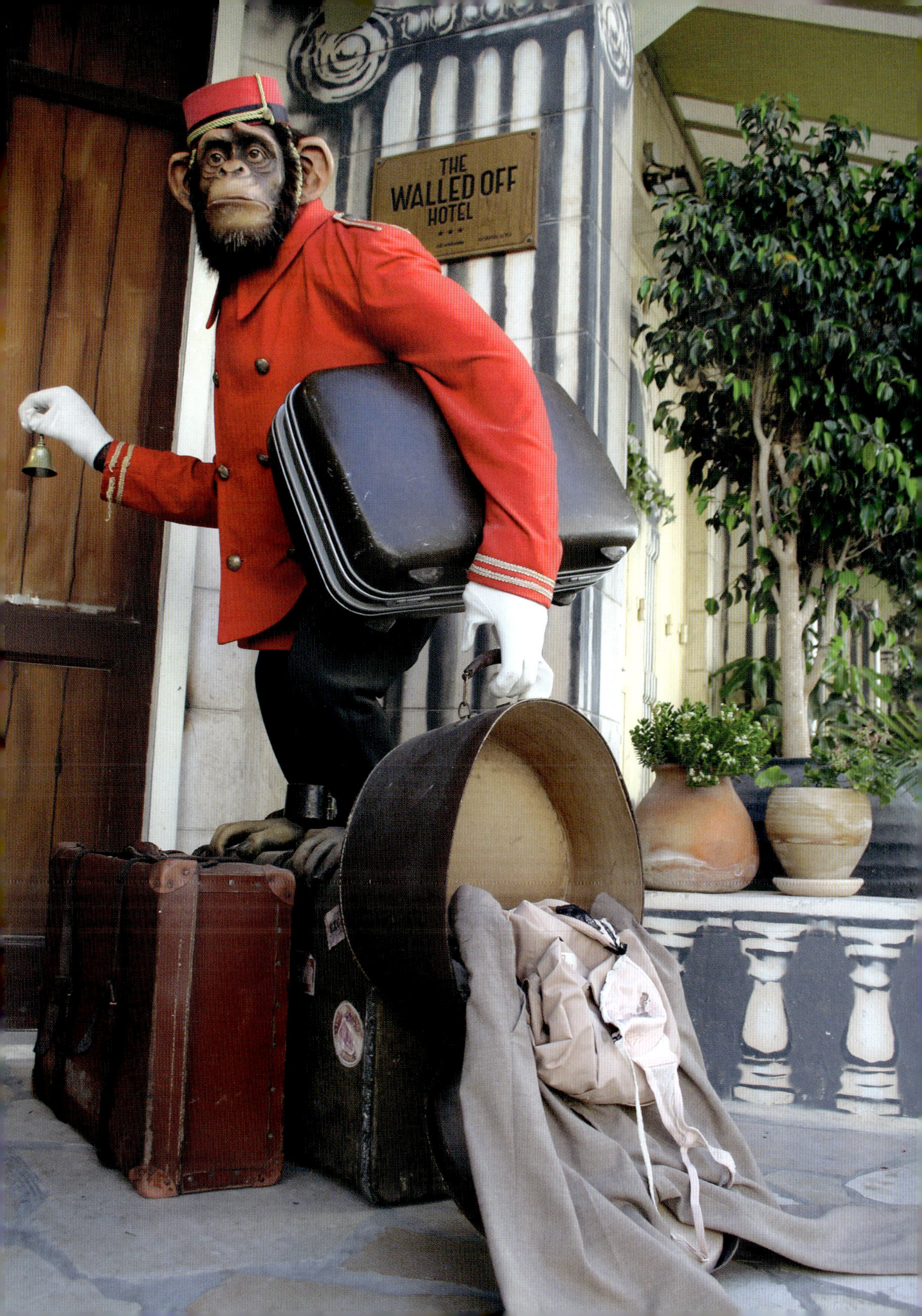
THE
WALLED OFF
HOTEL
★ ★ ★

There is a bloody great military wall dividing Israel and Palestine and some of it runs it's windy way through Bethlehem. This is where Banksy opened his hotel, yes an actual real working hotel, with extensive views of the infamous wall.

"The worst view of any hotel in the world."

Banksy Interview, VICE Magazine, March 2017

The British created the state of Israel after World War I. It was done in a clumsy and imperious way, laying the foundation for a century of conflict in the region. Most British people don't know, because it isn't taught in secondary schools that we had anything to do with the Israel Palestine conflict. So Banksy has done a great job in reminding people of that.

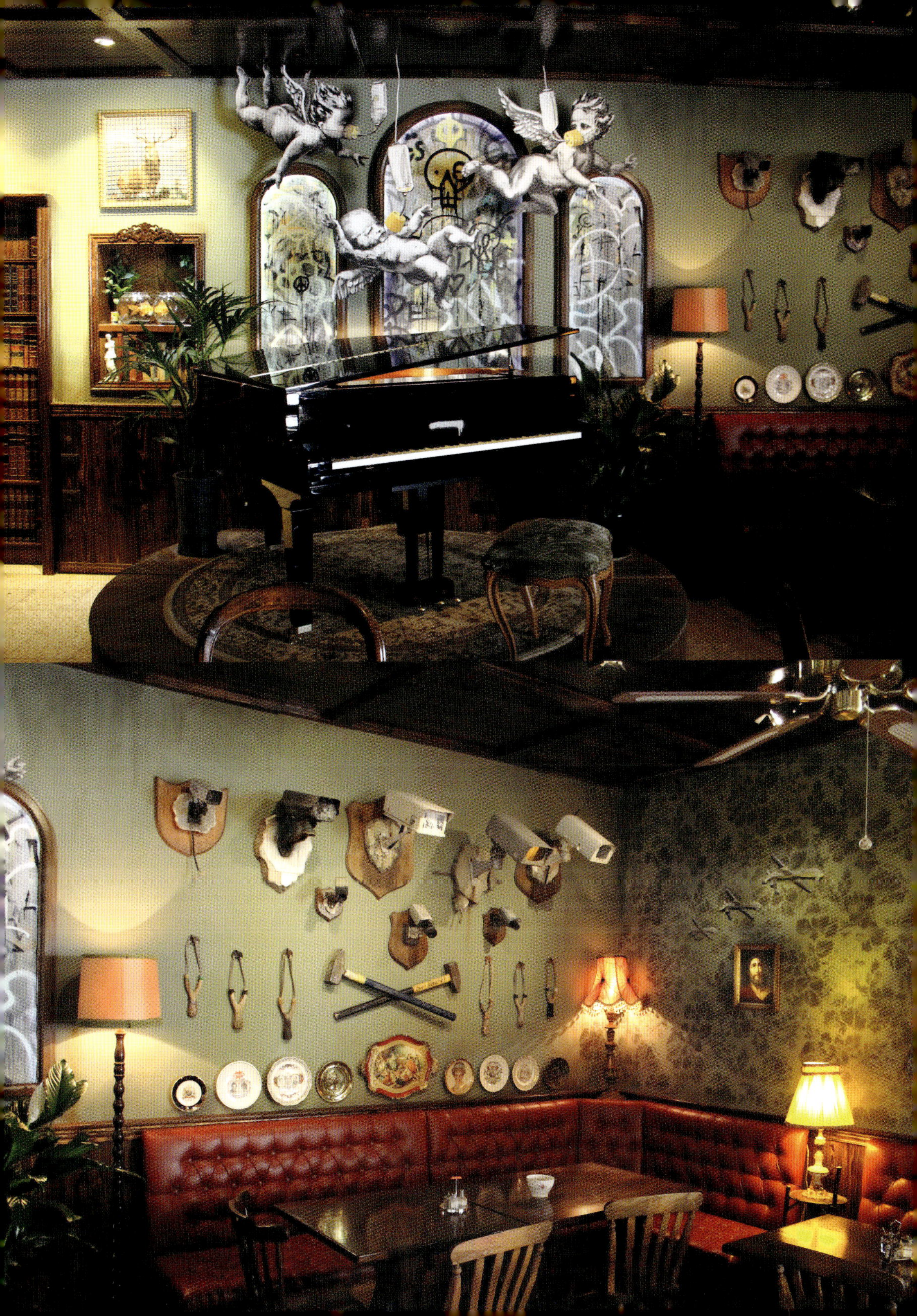

"It's exactly one hundred years
since Britain took control of
Palestine and started
re-arranging the furniture
- with chaotic results, I don't
know why, but it felt like a good
time to reflect on what happens
when the United Kingdom
makes a huge political decision
without fully comprehending the
consequences."

Banksy Interview, VICE Magazine, March 2017

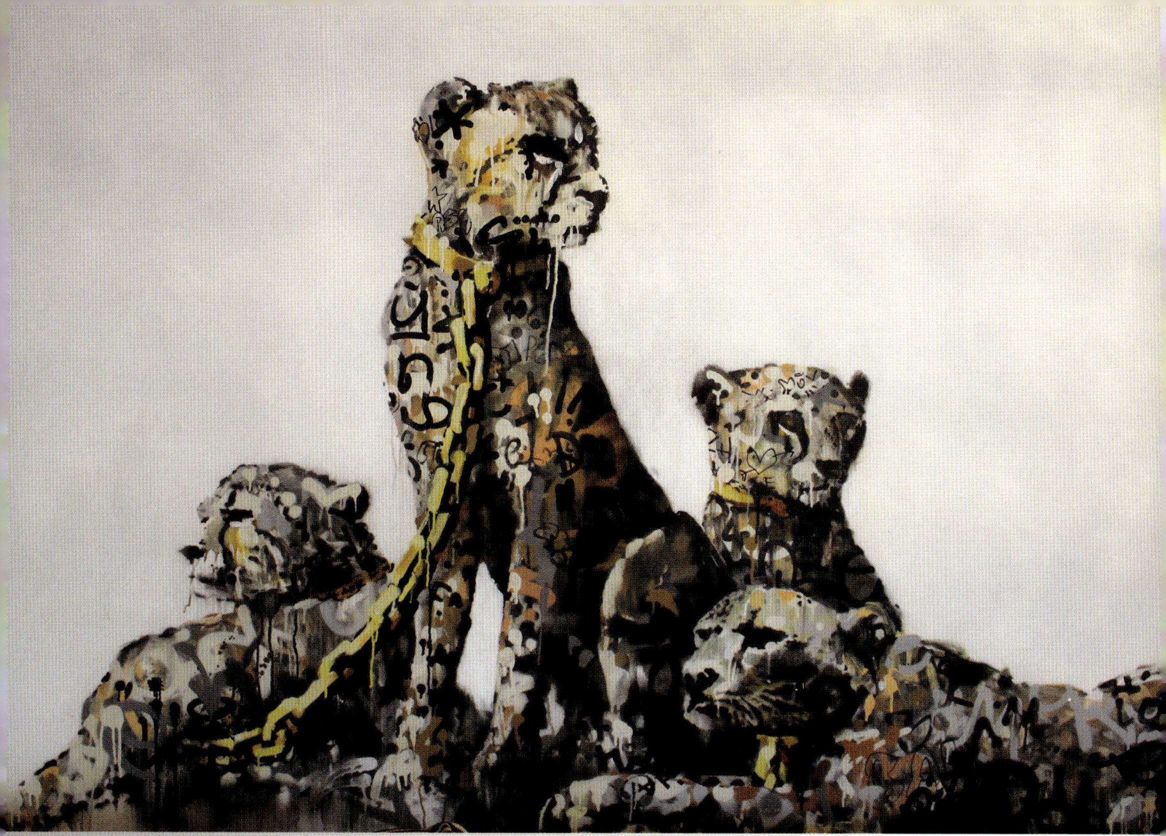

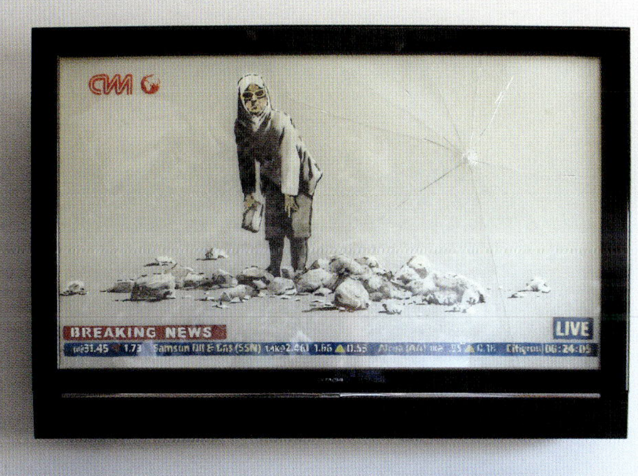

CNN
BREAKING NEWS
LIVE

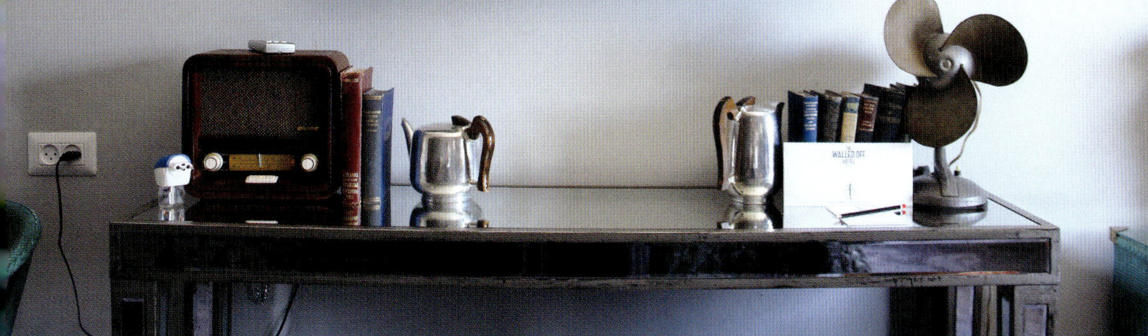

Banksy's work in Palestine is extensive and considered. It has fans and haters in Palestine and Israel. But most journalists report a generally positive regard amongst the locals.

"There aren't many situations where a street artist is much use," he says. "Most of my politics is for display purposes only.

But in Palestine there's a slim chance the art could have something useful to add - anything that appeals to young people, specifically young Israelis, can only help."

Banksy Interview, FT, December 2017

The hotel proudly declares itself a safe space for people from both sides of the conflict to meet and talk.

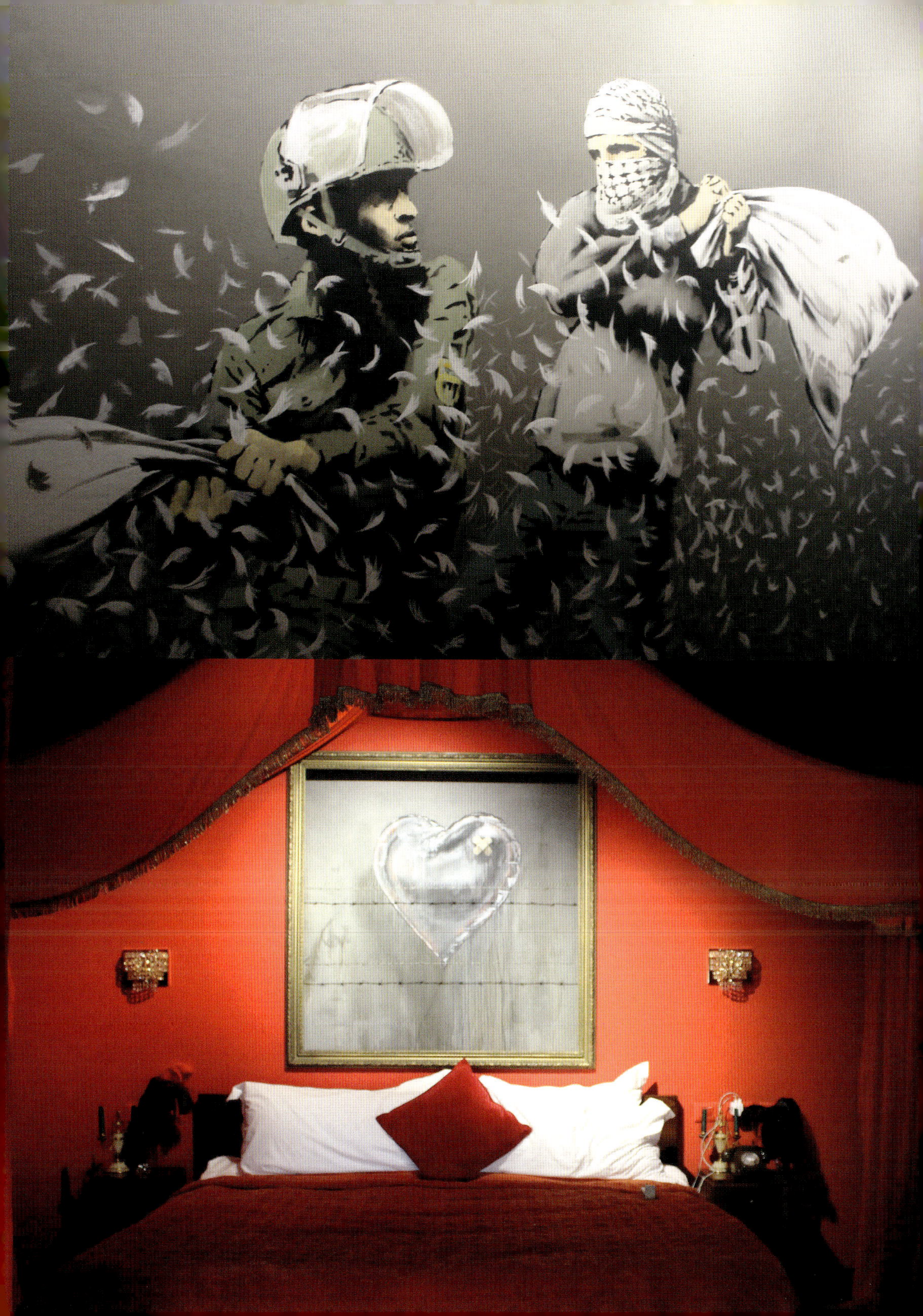

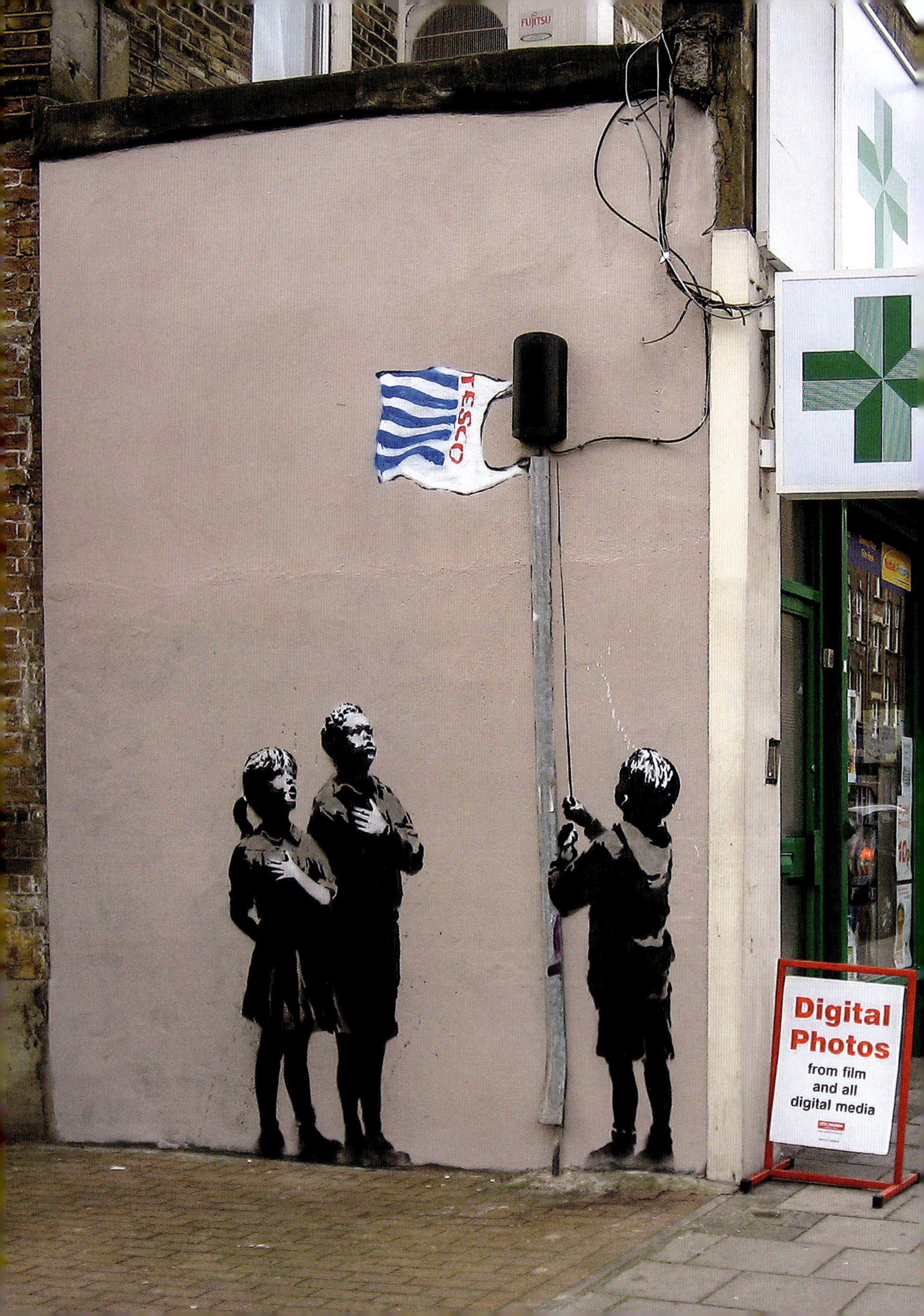

TESCO
Digital Photos
from film
and all
digital media

THE QUICKEST WAY TO THE TOP OF YOUR BUSINESS IS TO TURN IT UPSIDE DOWN.

"Banging Your Head Against a Brick Wall"

Banksy, Weapons of Mass Distraction 2001

If you're young and hungry and looking for a way into something - you've got to flip the script. Banksy made a clear statement in 1998 when he painted a mural of classic wildstyle graffiti dying on on hospital bed, for the Bristol 'Walls on Fire' festival. His stencil approach flipped the graffiti world on it's head, making a new category called street art, of which he was then the leading figure, largely because of the media grabbing strategy of his incredibly ballsy placements, coupled with the carpet bombing effect of just being EVERYWHERE, made possible by the speed of stencil work. If you want to win a game quick, change the rules.

SPEAK SOFTLY, BUT CARRY A BIG CAN OF PAINT.

BANKSY

"Wall & Piece" Banksy

Vintage Publishing 2006

Theodore Roosevelt, 26th President of the USA said he got the original proverb from South Africa 'Speak softly and carry a big stick'. 'Big Stick Diplomacy' presumably inspired Banksy's 'Big Can of Paint' diplomacy.

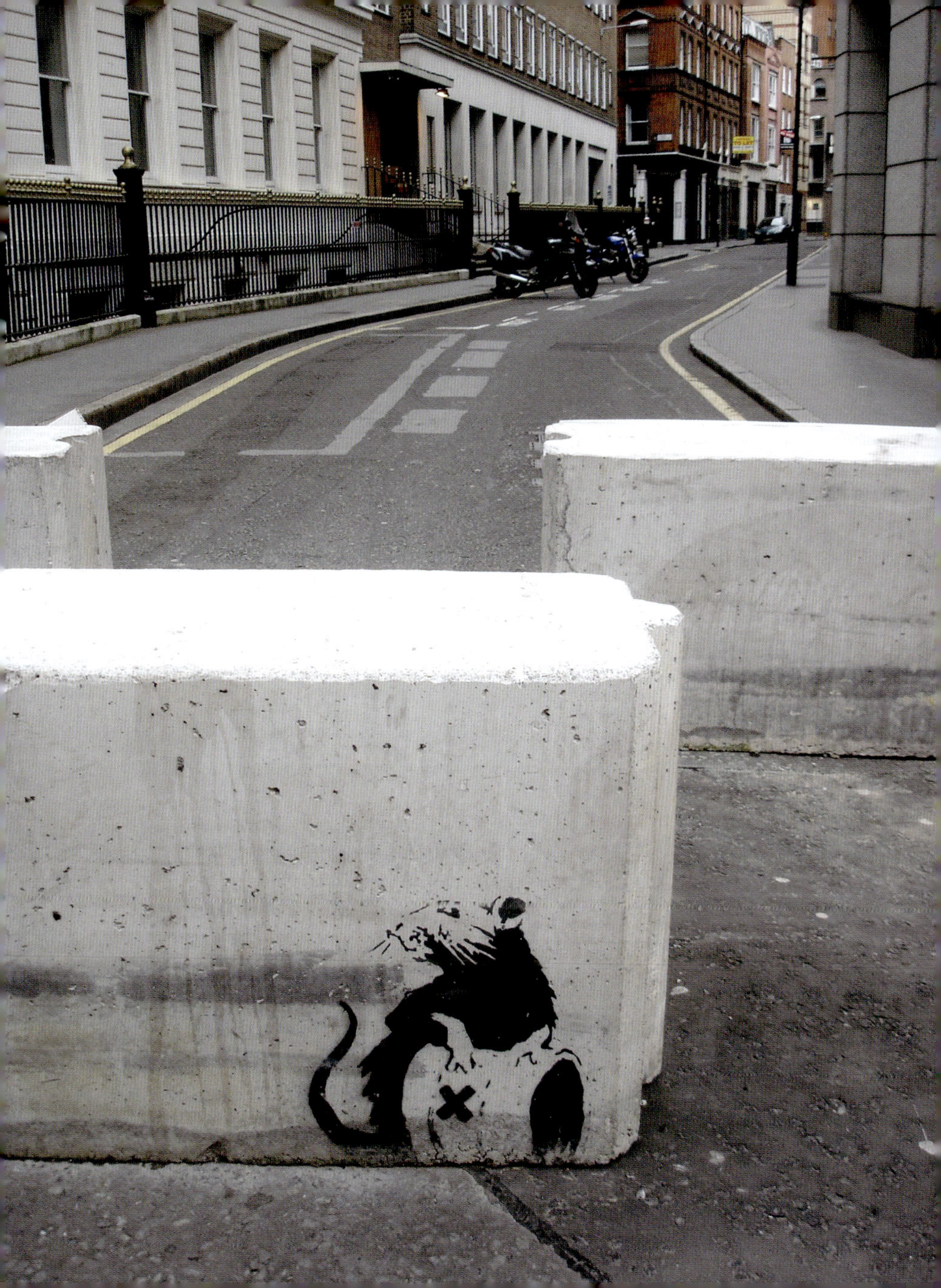

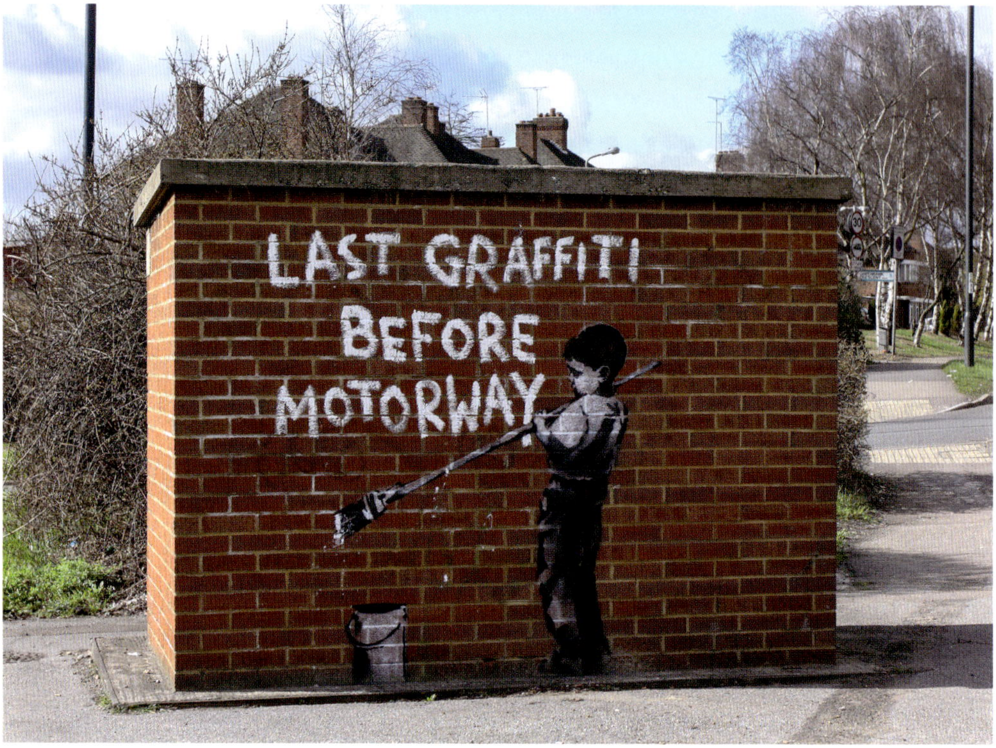

LAST GRAFFITI
BEFORE
MOTORWAY

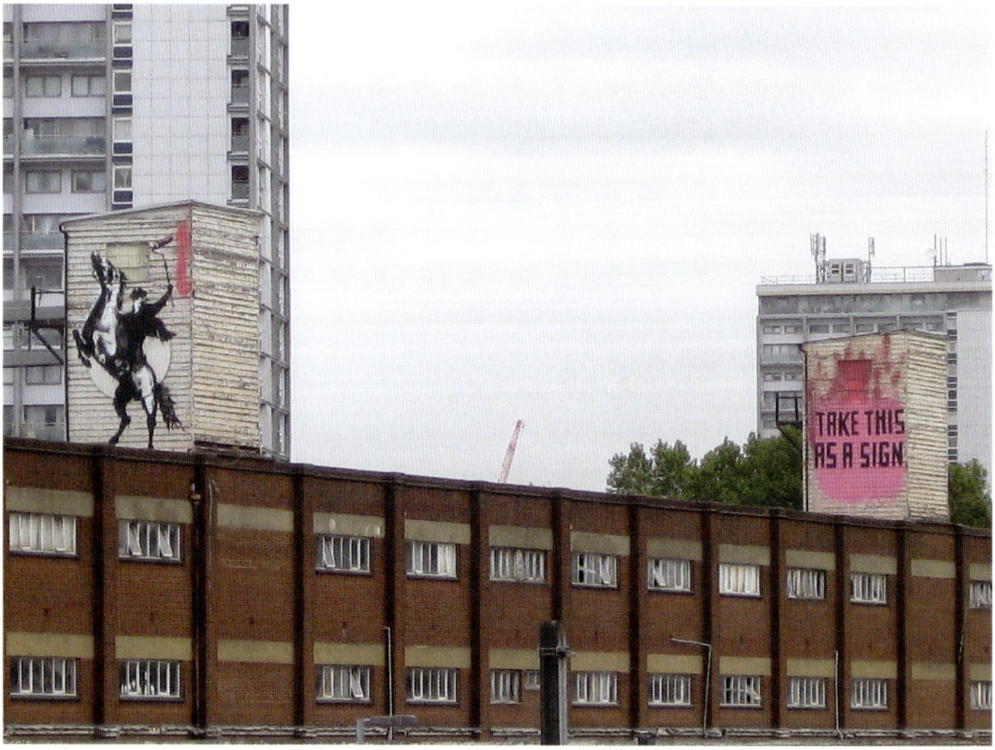

TAKE THIS
AS A SIGN

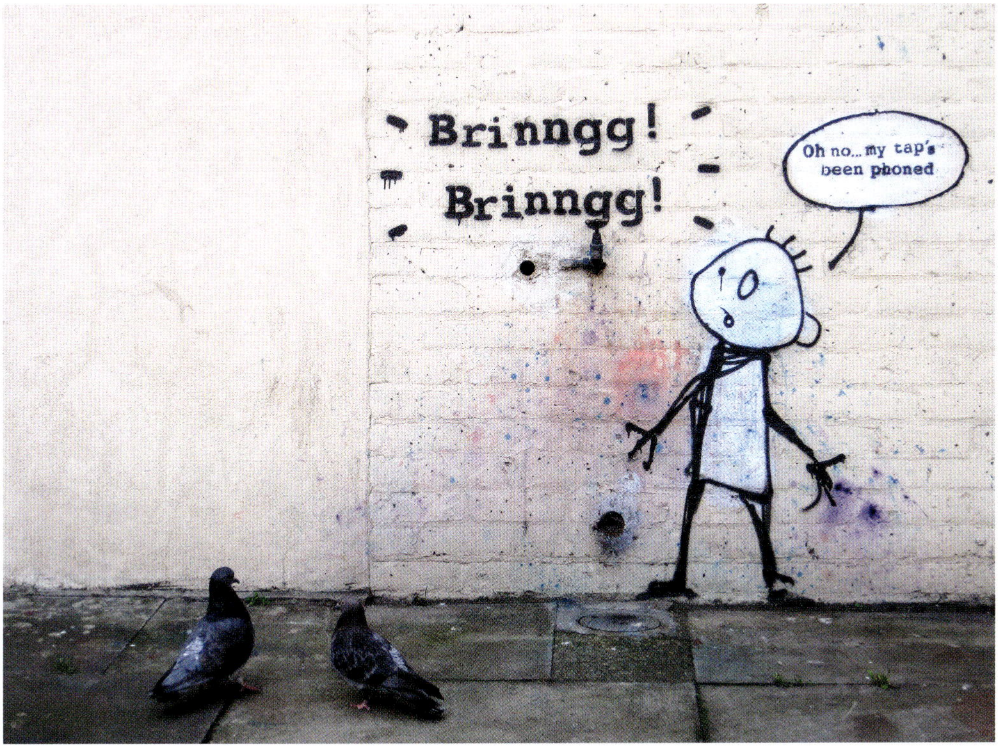

Brinngg!
Brinngg!
Oh no... my tap's been phoned

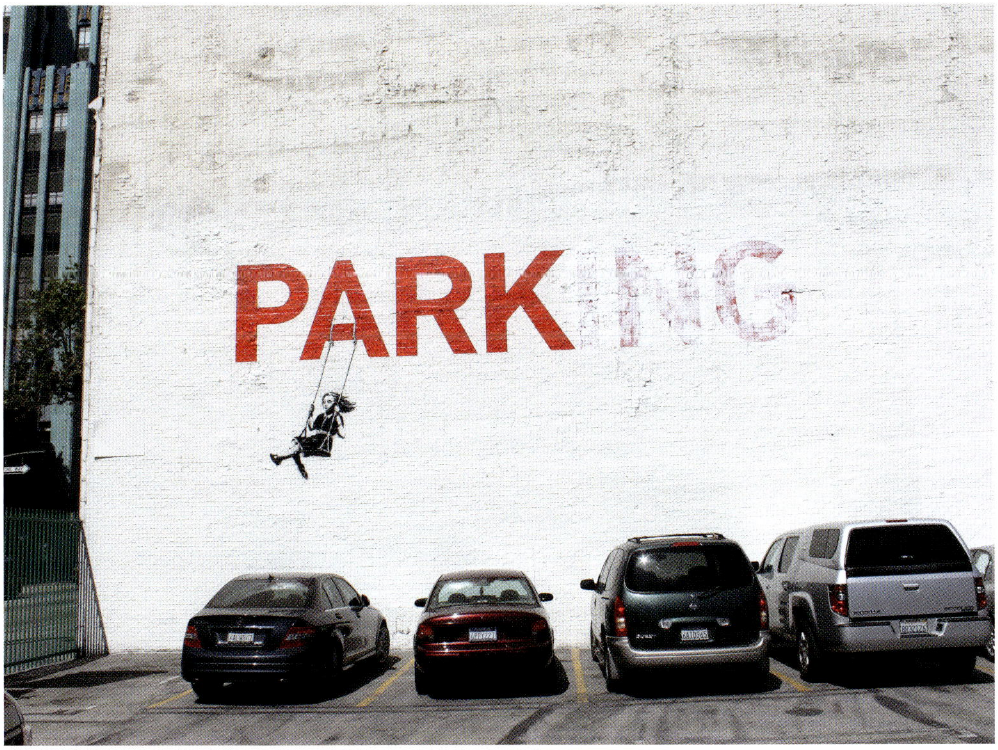

PARKING

SOME PEOPLE THINK
YOU SHOULD HAVE
BETTER THINGS
TO THINK ABOUT
THAN TRYING TO THINK
ABOUT BETTER THINGS.

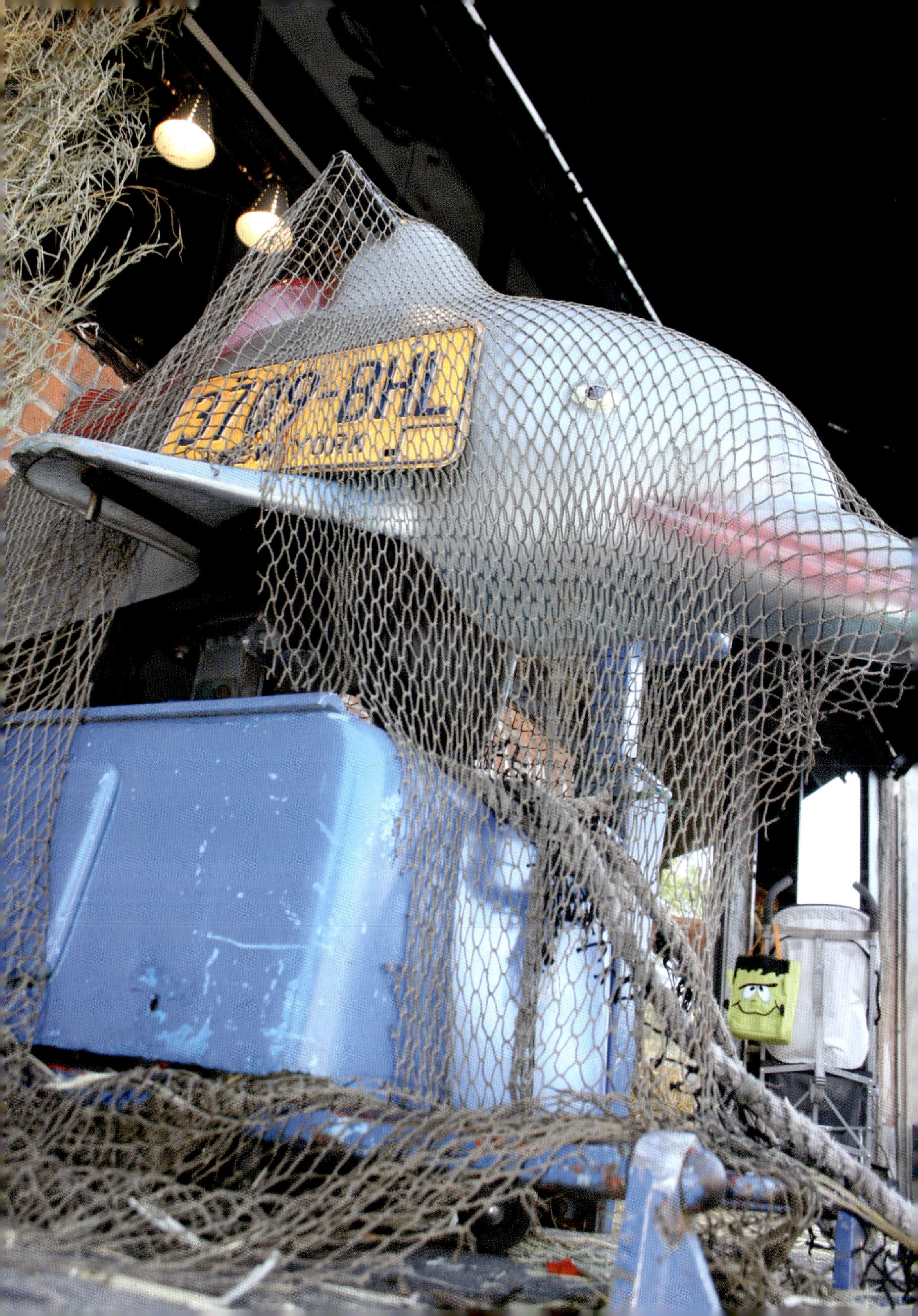

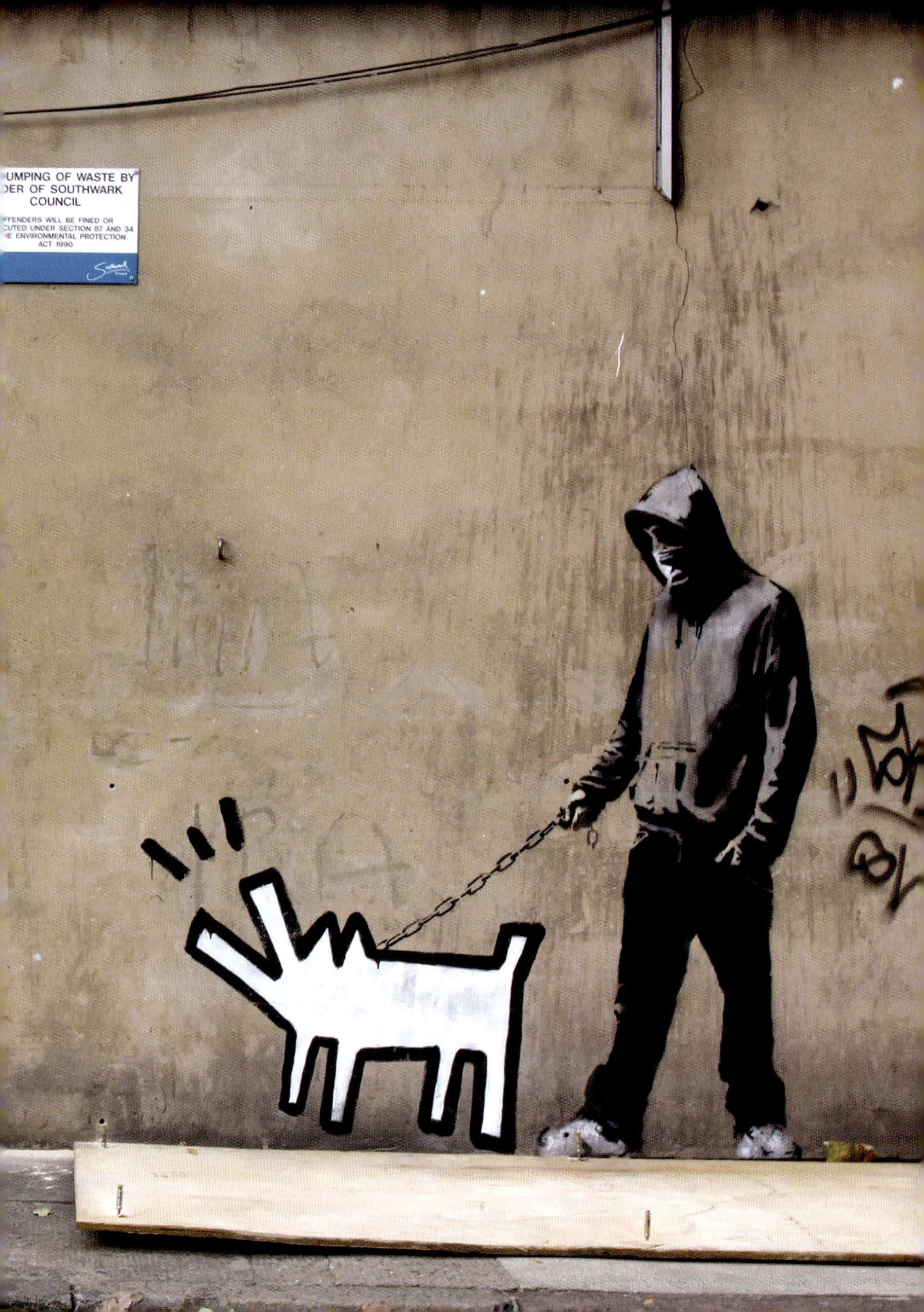
UMPING OF WASTE BY
DER OF SOUTHWARK
COUNCIL
FFENDERS WILL BE FINED OR
CUTED UNDER SECTION 87 AND 34
HE ENVIRONMENTAL PROTECTION
ACT 1990
Southwark

IF YOU WANT TO SAY SOMETHING AND HAVE PEOPLE LISTEN YOU HAVE TO WEAR A MASK.

BANKSY

"Existencilism" Banksy

Weapons of Mass Distraction 2002

This is the head bending reality of our culture. People are messy, muddled and random collections of interests, ideas, moods and personalities. But the only way to get heard, is to pretend to be singular, consistent and simple – to make yourself into a brand, to turn yourself into an object. Not a real object. A symbolic object. It's a process that is now so familiar, that everyone is doing it. The mask is the brand. The brand masks the complexity of being human. When Banksy first complained about Brandalism he was criticising the war for mindshare waged by the big brands, but now the war has shifted to something more subtle, we have swallowed the idea of branding so deeply, it is now the whole logic of our culture, from our innermost thoughts outwards.

EVERY TIME I HEAR THE WORD CULTURE I RELEASE THE SAFETY CATCH ON MY 9MM.

BANKSY

"Banging Your Head Against a Brick Wall"

Banksy, Weapons of Mass Distraction 2001

A spectre is haunting Banksyism, it is the spectre of Guy Debord, through Malcolm McLaren and into the DNA of the British counterculture. Anti-Art, Anti-Culture, these things come into the Bristol scene through Punk. And they were introduced to Punk by McLaren and the Sex Pistols among a few other figures. McLaren was influenced by Guy Debord and the situationists who hated culture as much as they hated art. This Banksy quote could be lifted directly from a situationist zine. It's a gangsta hip-hop twist on a situ slogan. "Culture? Urgh! The one commodity that helps sell all the others, no wonder you want us to go for it."

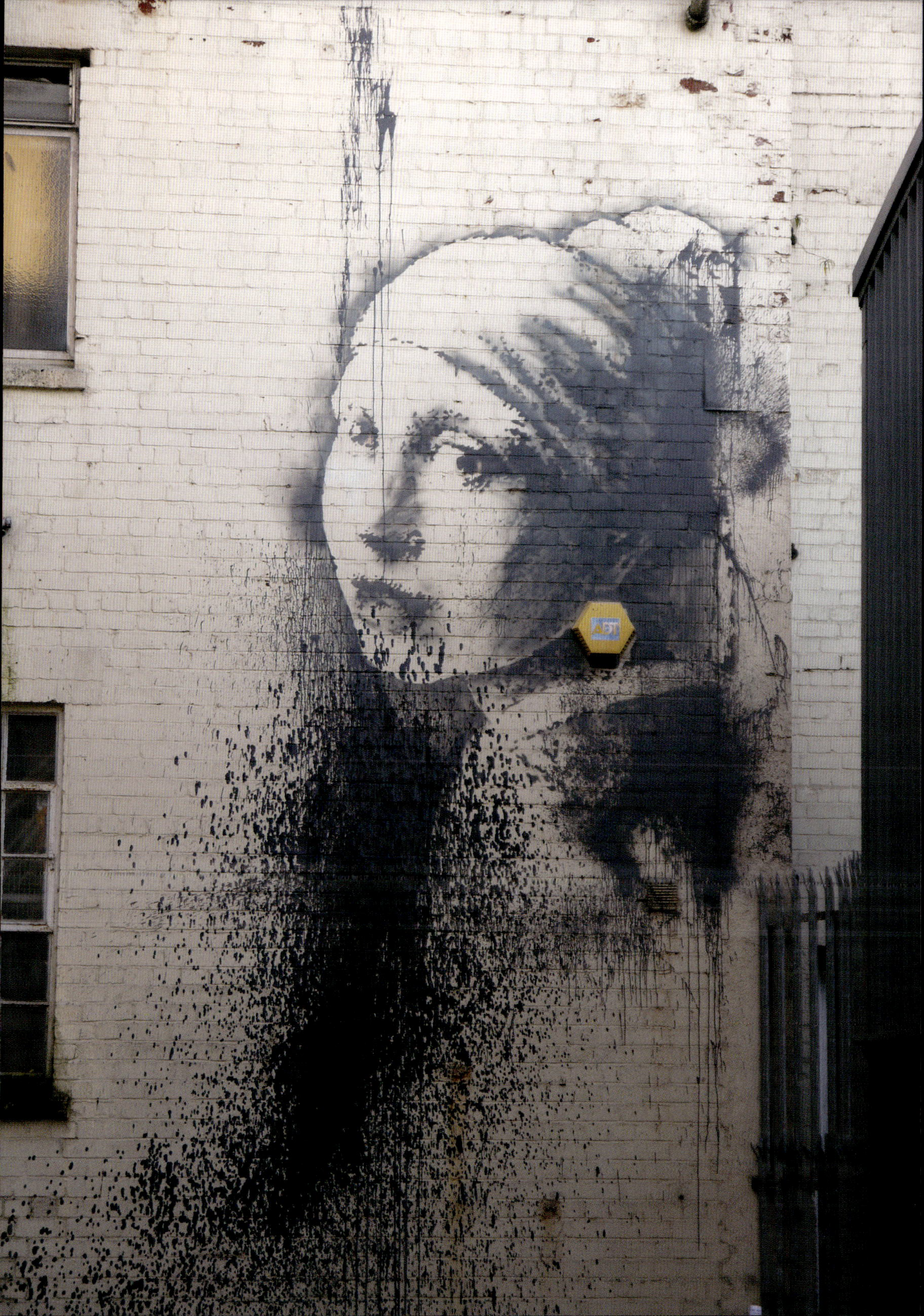

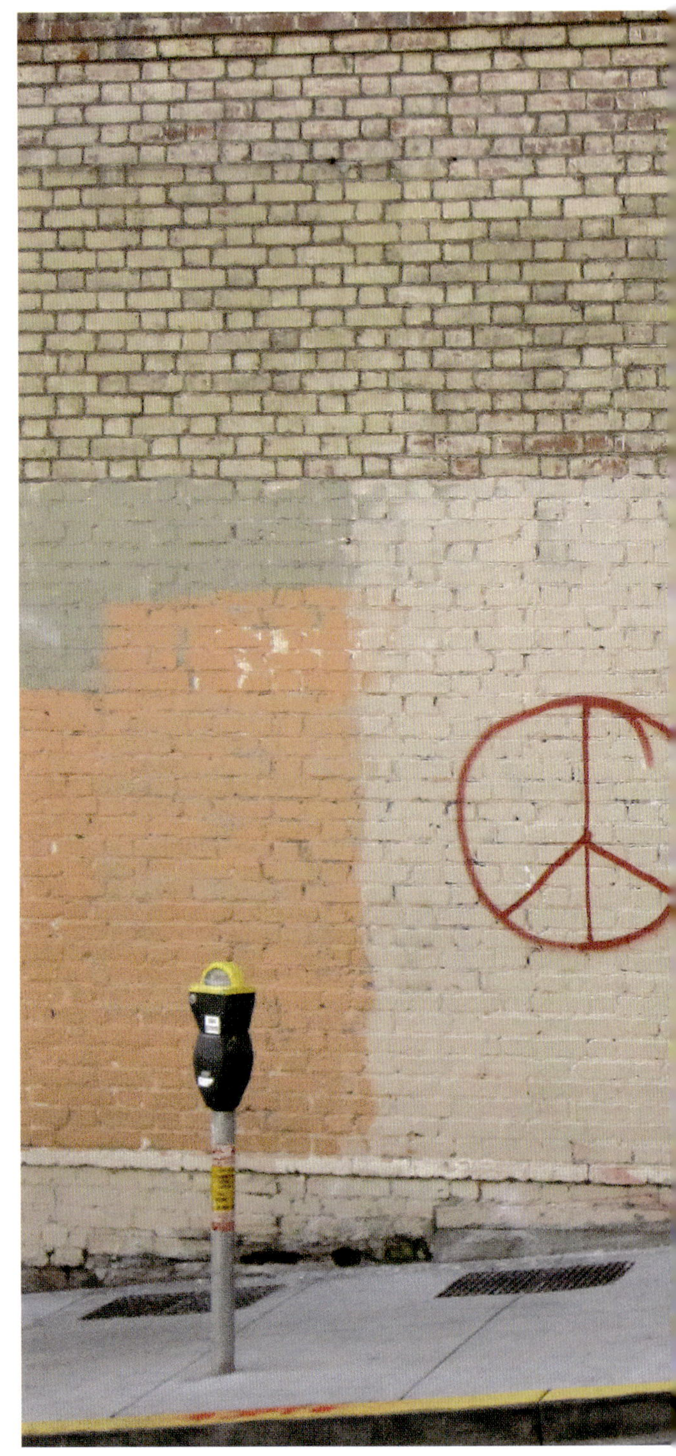

Banksy's San Francisco
sojourn, April 2010.

Three works are put up in the Mission,
as well as one each in Chinatown,
Soma and the Lower Haight.

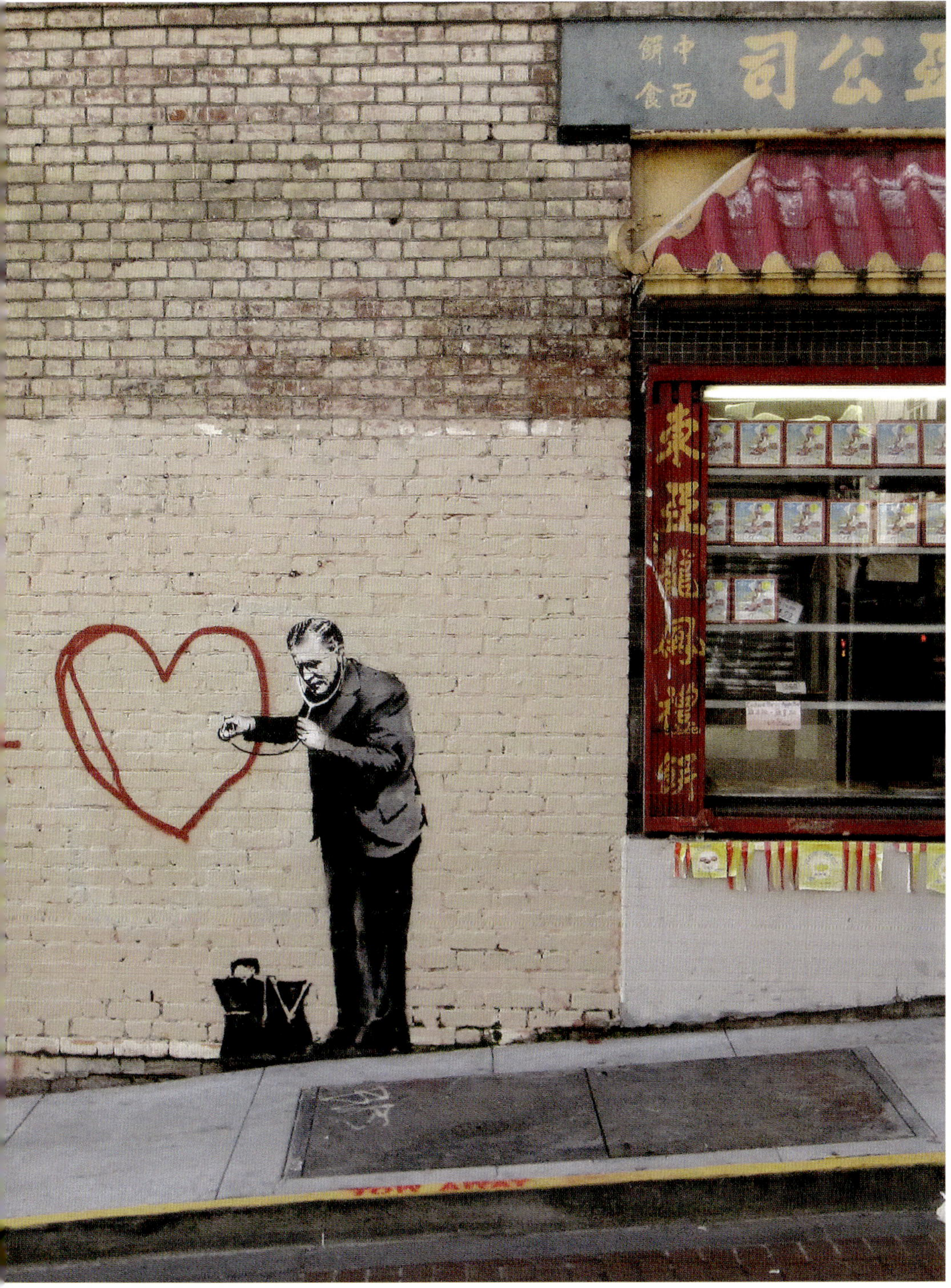

餅中
食西
司公亞
東亞糕餅
禮鳳
禮
餅

ART SHOULD COMFORT THE DISTURBED AND DISTURB THE COMFORTABLE

BANKSY

Cesar A Cruz, 1997

Another Banksy quote he probably didn't say. But it is a good one, because it's a very good yardstick for measuring the success of political art. Political art wants to provoke change, so it should provoke discomfort. The quote comes from the title of a 1997 poem by Cesar Cruz "To Comfort The Disturbed, and to Disturb the Comfortable: Onward children of the sun" which is a passionate anti-war poem.

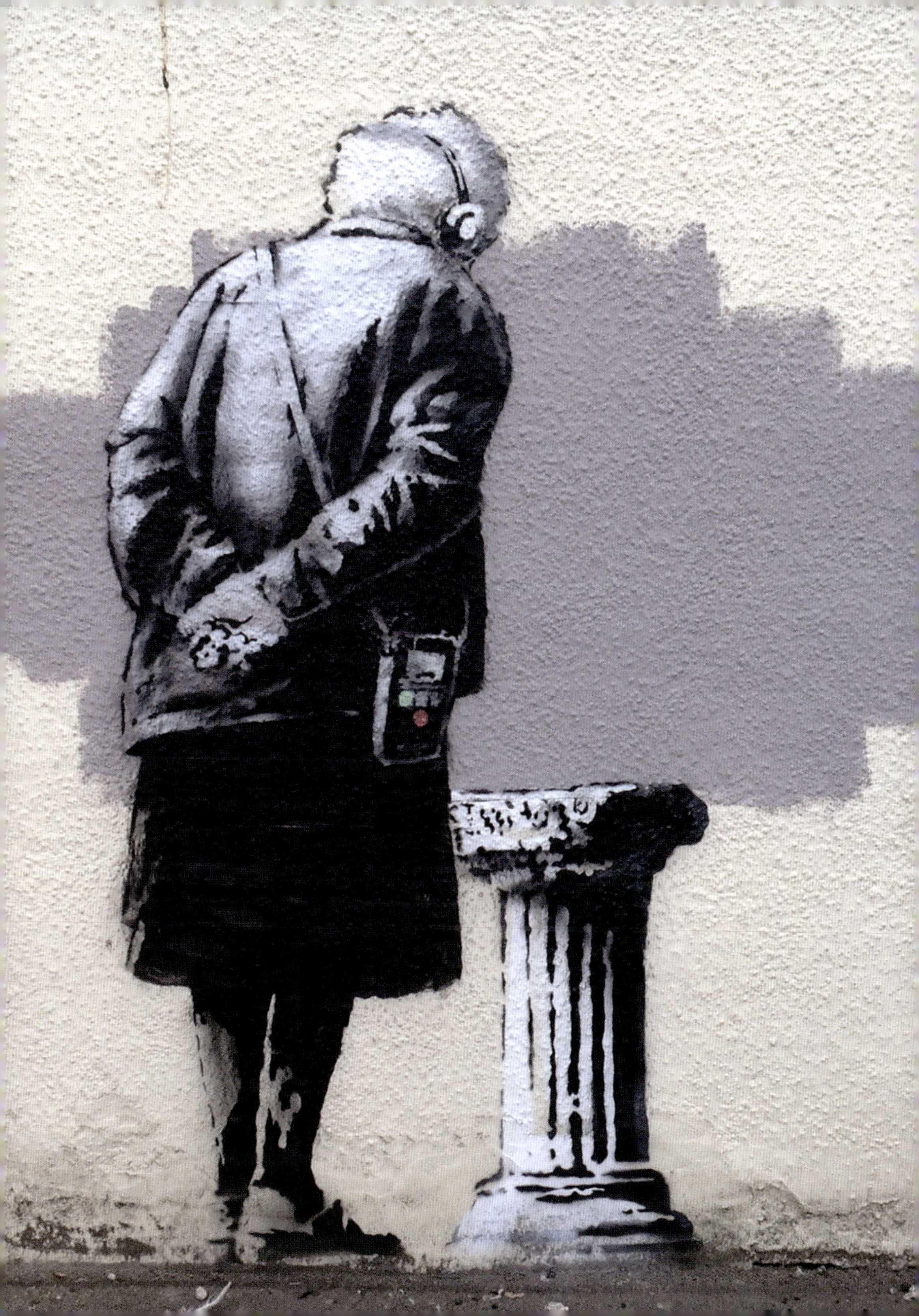

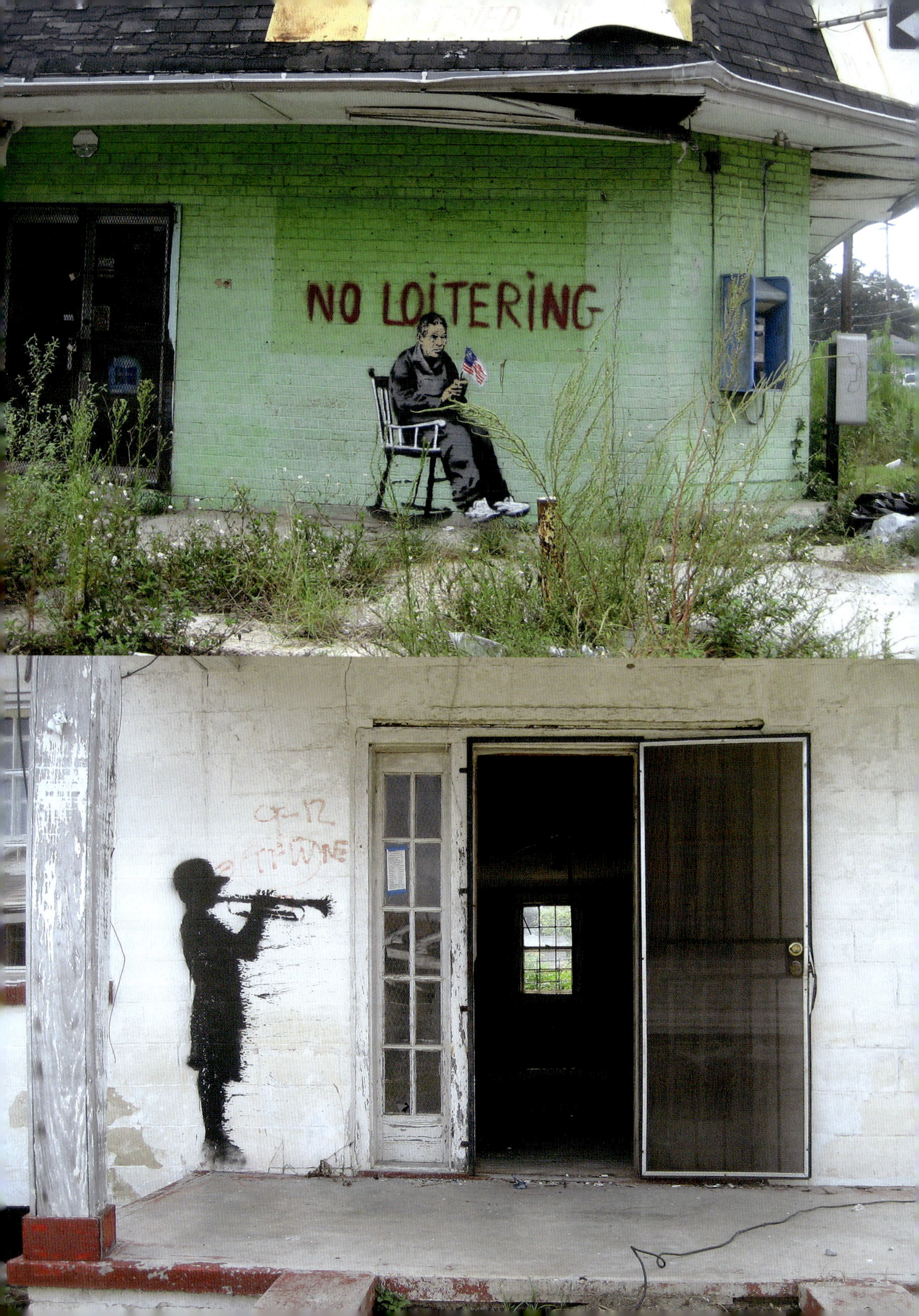
NO LOITERING

IF YOU GET TIRED LEARN TO REST, NOT TO QUIT.

BANKSY

"Wall & Piece" Banksy

Vintage Publishing 2006

Hey, you can't be a bad ass outlaw all the time. Self care
isn't selfish, yeah? Imagining Banksy in a spa retreat

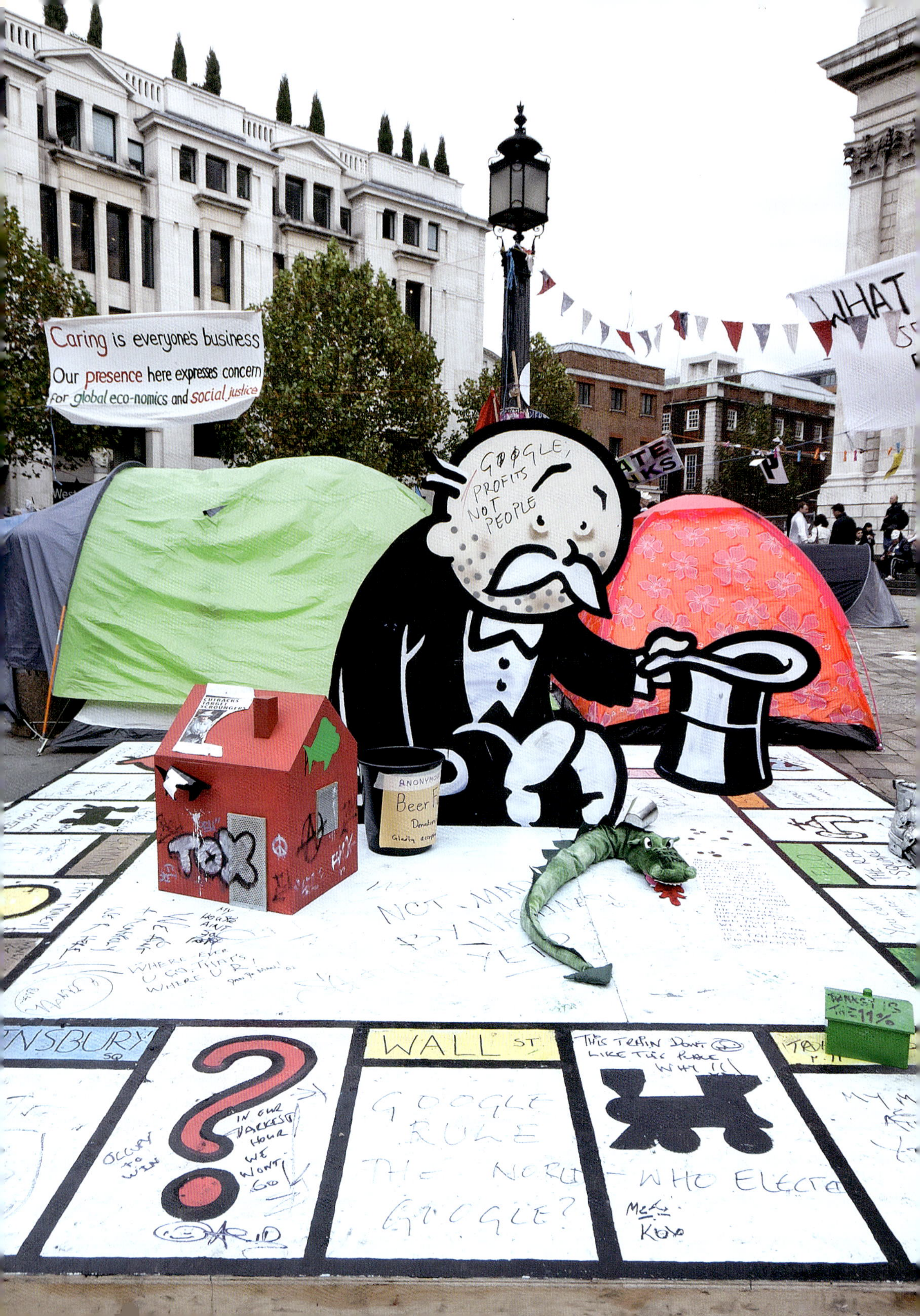
Caring is everyone's business
Our presence here expresses concern
for global eco-nomics and social justice
GOOGLE;
PROFITS
NOT PEOPLE
WHAT
ANONYMOUS
Beer Fund
Donations
Gladly accepted
WALL ST
THIS TRAIN DONT
LIKE THIS PLACE
WHY !!
GOOGLE
RULE
THE WORLD
GOOGLE?
WHO ELECTE
IN OUR
DARKEST
HOUR
WE
WONT
GO
OCCUPY TO
WIN
TANK ST IS
THE 11%

WHEN IT ALL KICKED OFF

In 2011, it all kicked off. From the London Riots to the Arab Spring, from Occupy Wall Street to the mass occupations of Plaza del Sol in Madrid, it looked for a moment like the opposition to capitalism had woken up violently after a long and intoxicated sleep. Riots spread to city centres all over the UK that August, including Banksy's hometown of Bristol. Where was Banksy in all this furore?

Well he was doing his bit, again showing his true colours as an old Bristolian anarchist, he released a limited edition print of a petrol bomb in a Tesco value bottle, in support of the Stokes Croft rioters legal fund. This was a reference both to a local dispute with Tesco and a classic and very popular Banksy mural from 1999 called the Mild Mild West, where a fluffy teddy throws a molotov cocktail at riot police.

Again in 2012, Banksy got involved in Occupy London, leaving a large sculpture of a Monopoly Board featuring a broke ass Uncle Penny Bags and a house with a Tox tag.

I ORIGINALLY SET OUT TO SAVE THE WORLD BUT NOW I'M NOT SURE I LIKE IT ENOUGH.

BANKSY

"Artist Scholar: Reflections on Writing and Research"

James Daichendt, 2011

This was apparently in an email to the New Yorker in 2008.

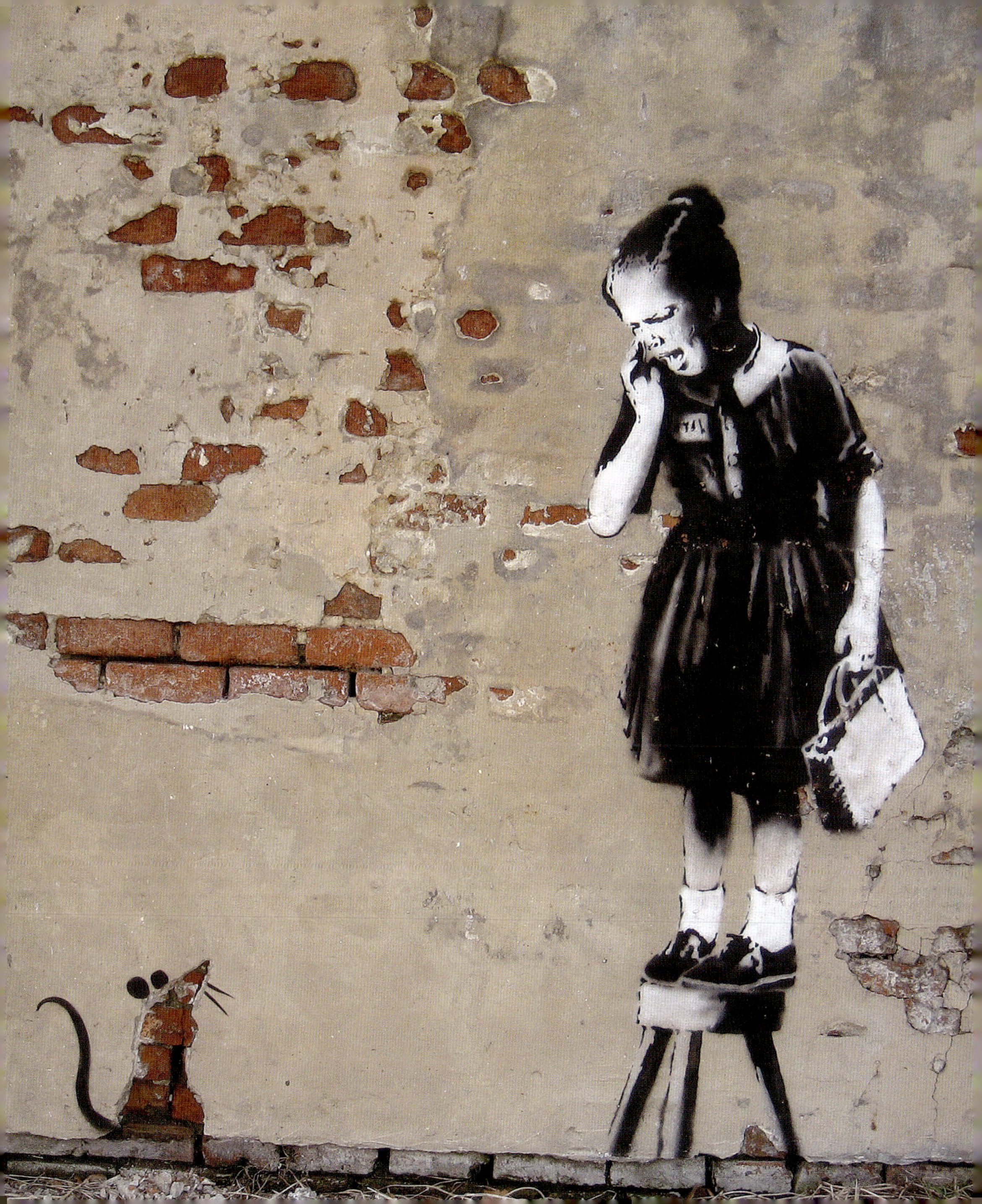

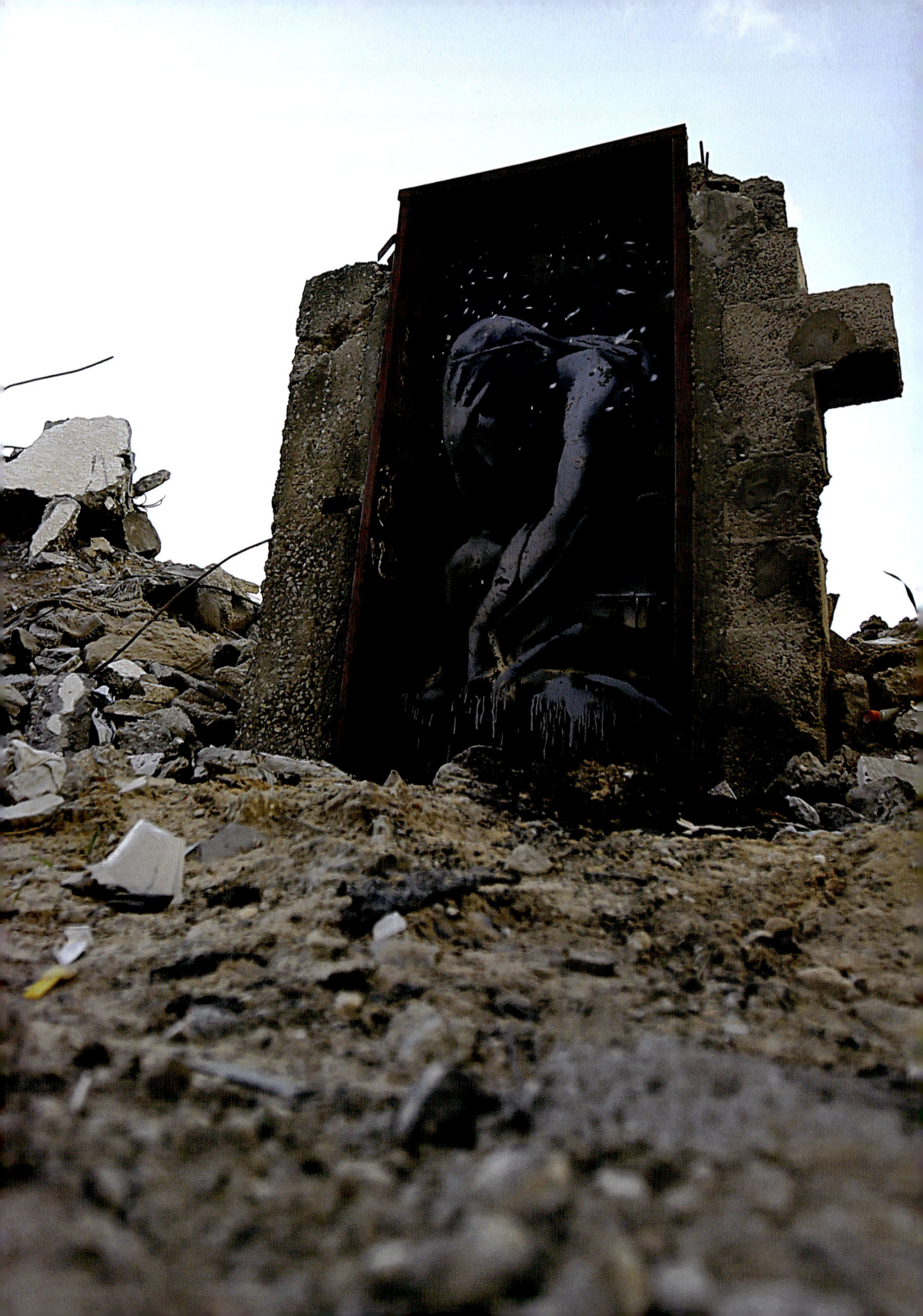

I LIKE TO THINK I HAVE THE GUTS TO
STAND UP ANONYMOUSLY
IN A WESTERN DEMOCRACY
AND CALL FOR THINGS
NO-ONE ELSE BELIEVES IN
- LIKE PEACE AND JUSTICE
AND FREEDOM.

BANKSY

"Wall & Piece" Banksy

Vintage Publishing 2006

This is one of those classic Banksy double ironies, where the irony had been folded so far back on itself that it's formed a kind of mobius strip of infinite reflected ironies. At this point one cannot be sure if there is any meaning intended by any of these words, or if it is all some kind of wordy sudoku? Is he taking the piss out of himself, or western democracy or peace, justice and freedom? Does he even know? Are we overthinking this? Well, it'll look nice on instagram.

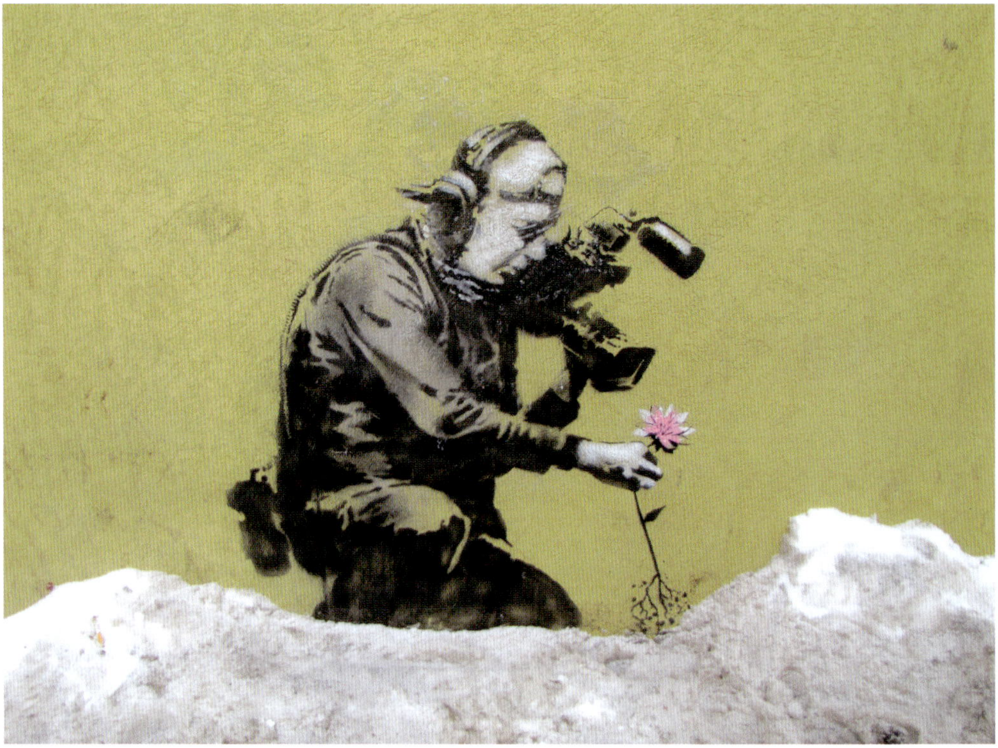

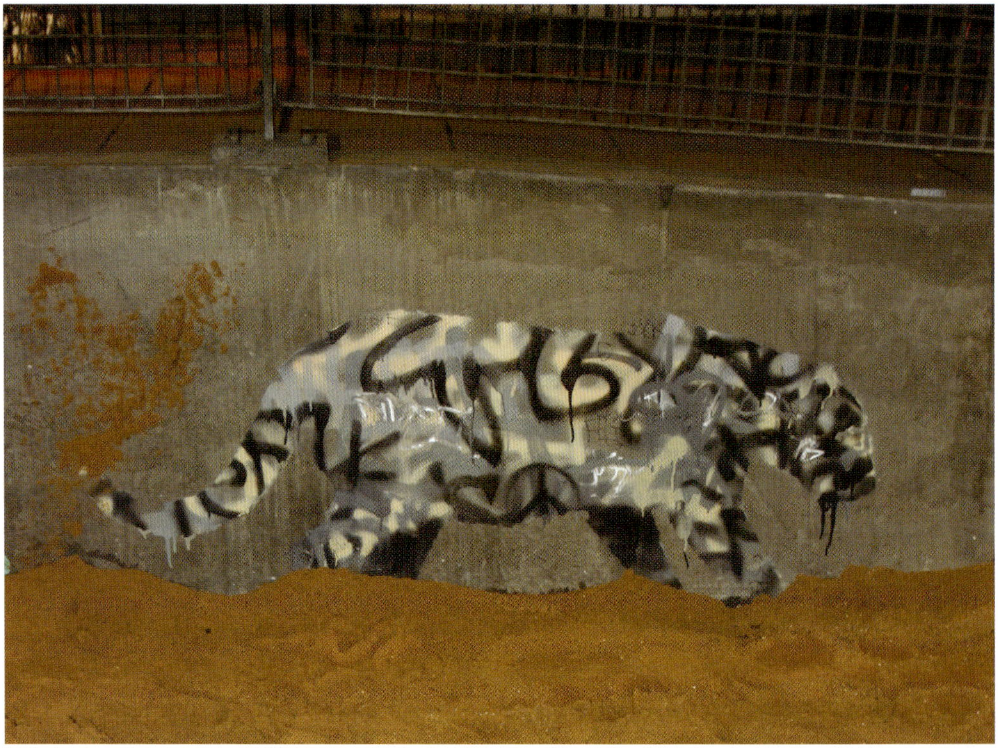

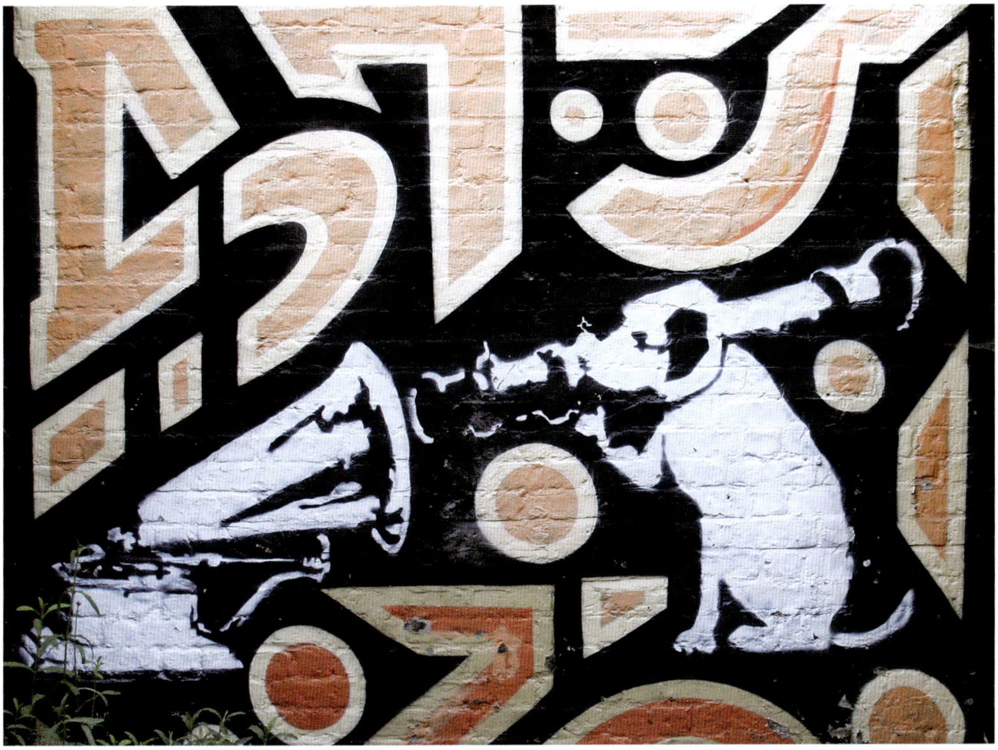

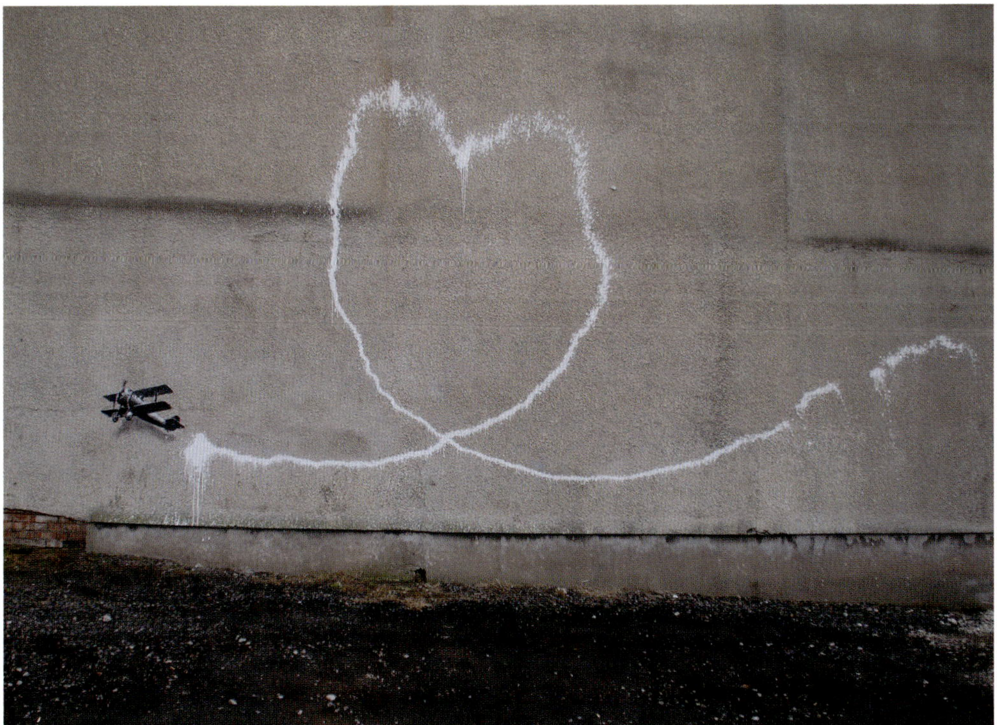

LET'S GO OUTSIDE

Never in history has going outside been a more loaded act than it is right now, in the heart of 2020's global pandemic moment. But it brings into stark relief an essential fact of Banksyism. Banksy is the last champion of going outside, in a world growing ever more intent on staying in, virus or otherwise...

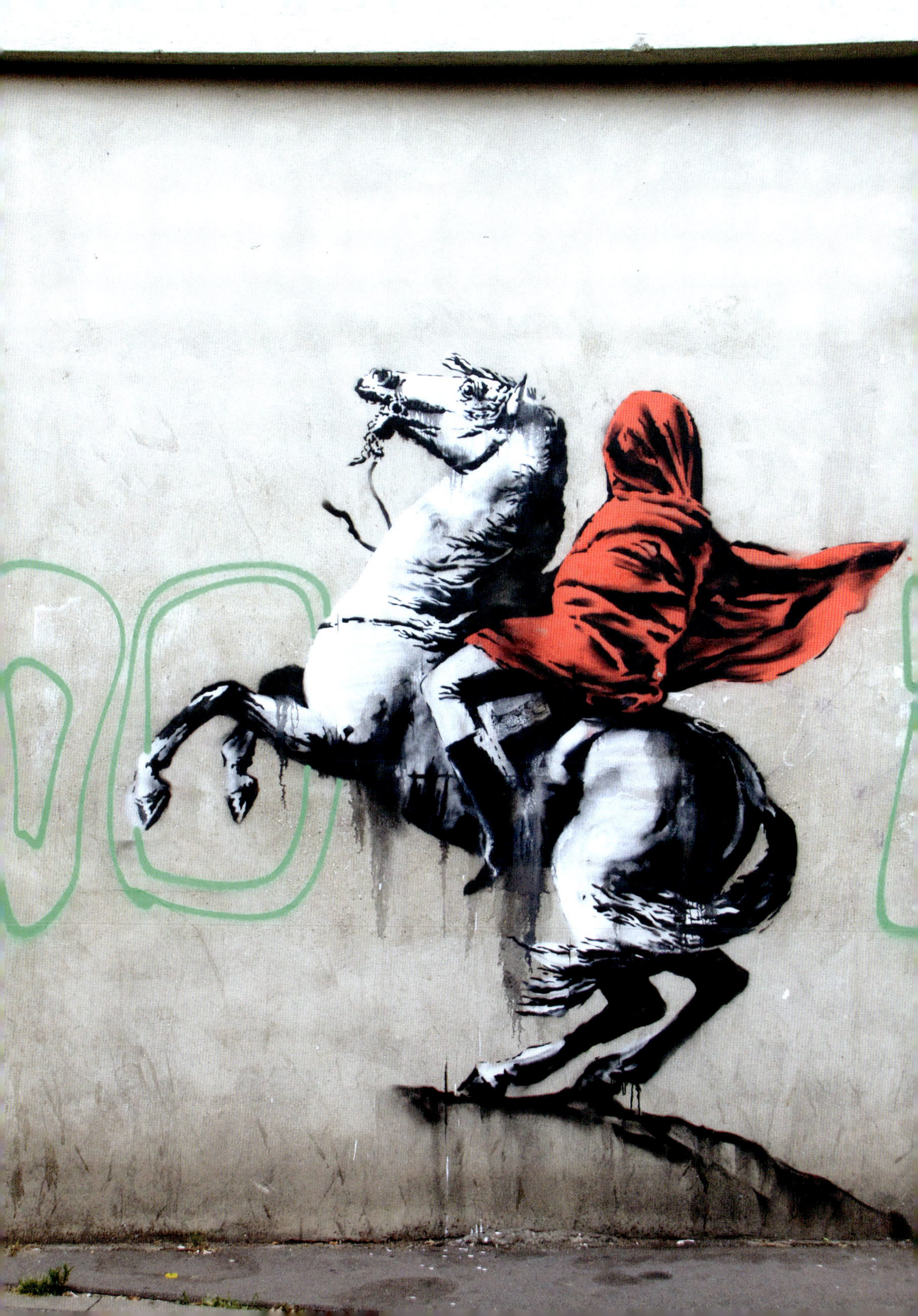

What makes Banksy relevant? Maybe it is this insistence on questioning our relationship to public space. As the world grows ever more urbanised, and urban space is widely regarded to be the best hope for a sustainable future - cities, in spite of how much the hippies despise them, are a more ecological solution than a spread out population, we find ourselves urbanites all. There is nowhere to tune in and drop out. Nowhere to escape the rat race and the city.

But everything in the city is owned, and it's privately owned. So our public spaces, the spaces which make society possible - are not social spaces, nor are they even strictly 'public' spaces because they ain't ours and we have no right to do as we please in them.

The city itself is designed to manipulate us. Our urban spaces are designed to bombard us with the right kind of messaging, the messages that turn us into good little consumers, and obedient subjects of the crown. They are designed to channel us through a series of spending opportunities.

Banksy continues to challenge that, reminding us that the flow of messages doesn't have to be one way. Not all communication is marketing. Not all social interaction is shopping. Not all culture is a spectator sport. And for that alone, Banksy remains relevant, because nobody else ever mentions that you can, and really maybe should, go into the city and act as if it were really yours.

Banksy is the last of us who actually goes outside.

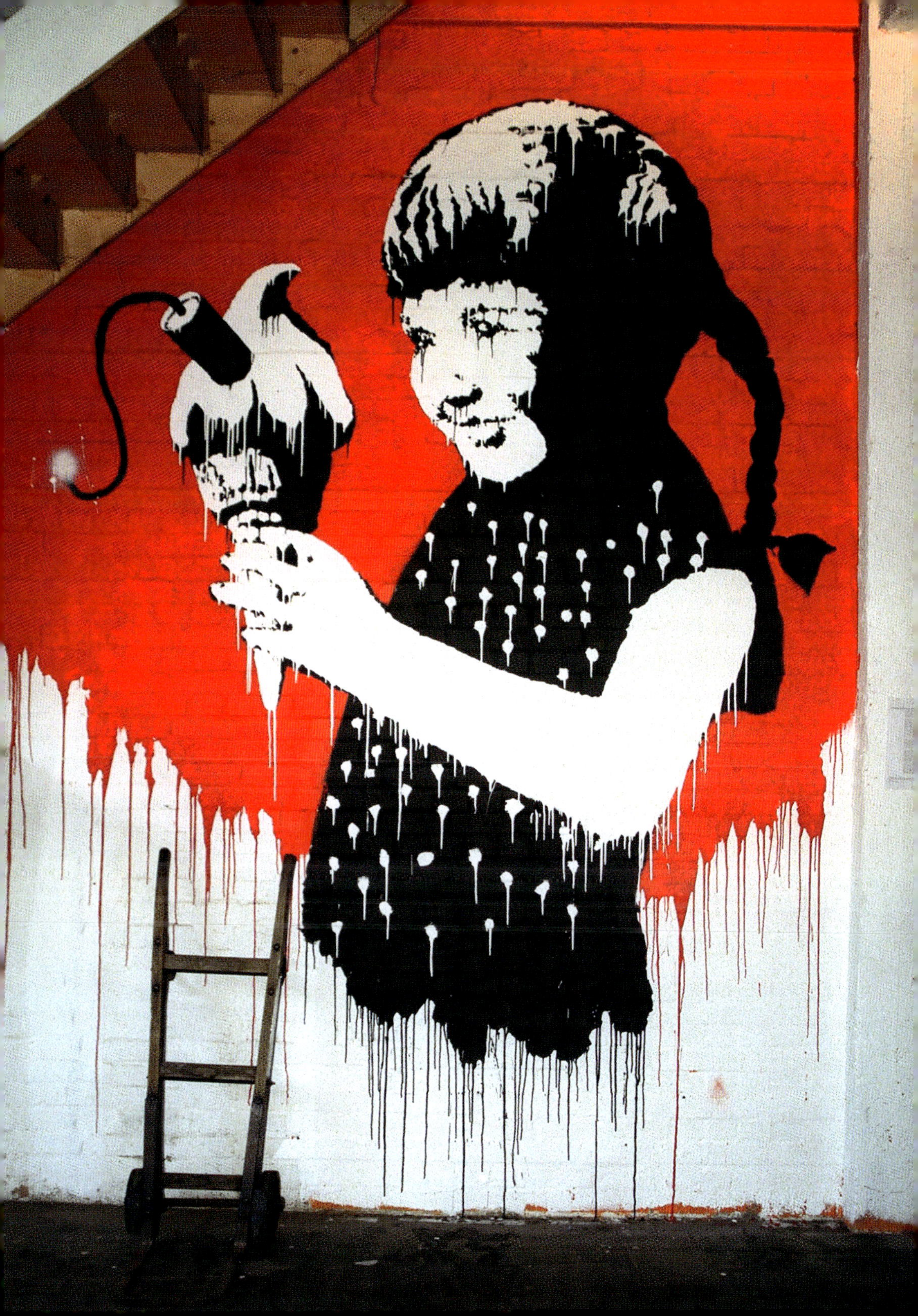

LOCATIONS & CREDITS

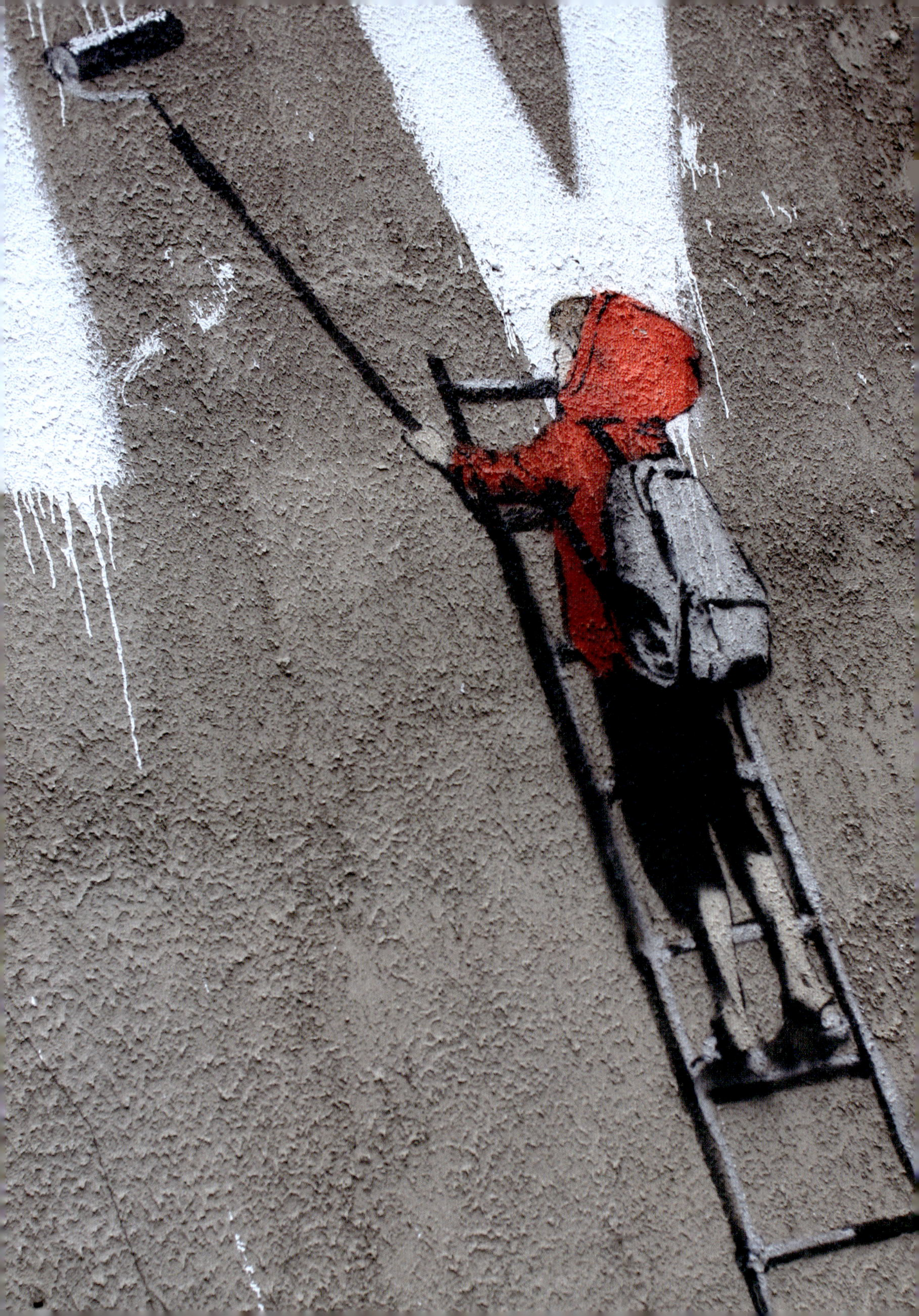